Advance Praise for

RADICAL SIMPLICITY

Jim Merkel offers a special mix of practicality and idealism: a workable mix. I defy you to read this book and not come away thinking of ways your life might change for the better.

— Bill McKibben, author of *The End of Nature*

The delight of this book is that it is written so clearly from the author's heart. Merkel's passion for creating a more humane world shines through on every page. A real inspiration!

— Janet Luhrs, author of *The Simple Living Guide*, and *Simple Loving*, and editor of *Simple Living* newsletter

Jim Merkel has written the most persuasive argument I have yet seen for all of us to radically change the way we live day-to-day. As a former engineer working on weapons who went through a dramatic change in consciousness, his words have a special power. *Radical Simplicity* joins the evidence of science to a fertile imagination. At a certain point in his life, Merkel became, as he puts it, "free and on fire" and he conveys that excitement to his readers, in an engaging style. Furthermore, he has carried out his ideas in his personal life and as a social activist, illustrating the practicality of his proposals. This is a profoundly important book.

— Howard Zinn, author of *A People's History of the United States*

Square two simplicity at its best! Jim Merkel takes us beyond extended vacations and cleaning closets to hardcore simplicity that aims to save the planet. Radical Simplicity gets to the root of our sustainability dilemma and proposes practical ideas for boosting our quality of life, caring for Mother Earth, and practising right livelihood based on justice and love. A wonderful contribution to the voluntary simplicity literature.

— Mark A. Burch, author of *Simplicity: Notes, Stories and Exercises for Developing Unimaginable Wealth*, and *Stepping Lightly: Simplicity for People and the Planet*

Jim Merkel wants to do nothing less than save our planet and our very lives. *Radical Simplicity* is an empassioned blueprint for the practice of sustainable, accountable living that can't fail to give joy to old hands. As for newcomers — watch out! Jim has started a revolution, and this book just might change your life.

— Laura Waterman, author of *Wilderness Ethics*

Radical Simplicity is the best thing since sliced bread — but with a much smaller Ecological Footprint! It gives you the tools you need to make this planet the world of your dreams; a world that provides vitality to all people and all species. And, even better, you can start living this dream today! This book shows you how.

— Mathis Wackernagel, Ecological Footprint Network and Redefining Progress

The wisdom of experience that Jim Merkel brings to this book allows him to speak with authority, concrete practicality, humility, and inspiration, inviting us into a world of serious simplicity achieved joyfully. *Radical Simplicity* is about the discovery of abundant choices, the adventure of reclaiming a meaningful life, and the fulfilment of connecting social values to life practises. This is a powerful and convincing case for living consciously and lightly on the Earth, for beyond gentle persuasion it provides the tools for both assessing the impact of life choices and asserting the real possibility for change. We need this book now more than ever.

— John Saltmarsh, author of *Scott Nearing: The Making of a Homesteader.*

In the tradition of the Nearings and Donella Meadows, Jim Merkel's *Radical Simplicity* is a compassionate, hands-on, compelling argument for ecological and spiritual living. Merkel provides brilliantly conceived ethical arguments for the necessity of simple, but deep living. The book is filled with wonderful anecdotal examples, superb workbook-like assessment tools, and just plain common sense. This is must reading for anyone who is concerned with environmental quality, global equity, and social justice. I would like to see this book in every high school and/or college classroom in North America. There is no better hands-on, learn-by-doing curriculum guide for ecological citizenship.

— Mitchell Thomashow, Chair, Department of Environmental Studies, Antioch New England Graduate School, and author of *Bringing the Biosphere Home: Learning to Perceive Global Environmental Change*

In our work, we have the unusual opportunity to meet people who have both extraordinary wealth and a heartfelt concern about sustainable consumption. We are excited to be able to show them this book. Never before have we seen the ecological footprinting model framed so concretely and within a motivating, long-term map for achieving sustainability. Beyond the solid thinking of his book, Jim's warmth, positive outlook, and the integrity he models in his way of life all inspire us into greater awareness and action.

— Christopher Mogil and Anne Slepian, Co-founders of
More Than Money journal

The average American creates an ecological footprint several times larger than what the Earth can sustain, but this book shows us how we can all do much better. Even those of us who've been involved with the Voluntary Simplicity movement for a long time have been awed by how lightly Jim Merkel has learned to live on the earth. *Radical Simplicity* explains in concrete and engaging language exactly why and how he does it. Read it and don't weep — simplify your life, save the planet and have more fun besides.

— John de Graaf, co-producer of the Affluenza television series
and co-author of *Affluenza: The All-Consuming Epidemic*

Most Americans want the life that Jim Merkel knows is possible: one that expresses what we really love, what inspires us, what matters most. *Radical Simplicity* offers a clear vision for what we can restore to our lives and how we might imagine our lives differently. It asks questions of mythic proportions: How do we want to be? Do we surrender to a culture defined by self-interest and apathy toward community, or do we choose, instead, to be defined by our self-restraint and a sense of service? To embrace this vision is to accept another story for ourselves: that humans are not the only measure of things, that humans can be defined more by our fairness and compassion and our desire to belong.

Jim Merkel is an important teacher and practitioner. In helping us to bring radical simplicity into our lives, he is helping each of us to renew our sense of service, tolerance, humility, and joy. He is helping all of us to re-define what it means to be human in this century.

— Peter Forbes, a leader in the American conservation movement,
and author of *The Great Remembering*

RADICAL simplicity

small footprints on a
finite Earth

JIM MERKEL

FOREWORD BY
VICKI ROBIN

NEW SOCIETY PUBLISHERS

Cataloguing in Publication Data:

A catalog record for this publication is available from the National Library of Canada.

Cover design by Diane McIntosh. Image: Photodisc RF. (Digital Retouching: Diane McIntosh).

Illustrations by Phil Testemale.

Printed in Canada by Transcontinental.

New Society Publishers acknowledges the support of the Government of Canada through the Book Publishing Industry Development Program (BPIDP) for our publishing activities.

Paperback ISBN: 0-86571-473-8

Inquiries regarding requests to reprint all or part of *Radical Simplicity: Small Footprints on a Finite Earth* should be addressed to New Society Publishers at the address below.

To order directly from the publishers, please add $4.50 shipping to the price of the first copy, and $1.00 for each additional copy (plus GST in Canada). Send check or money order to:

New Society Publishers

P.O. Box 189, Gabriola Island, BC V0R 1X0, Canada

1-800-567-6772

New Society Publishers' mission is to publish books that contribute in fundamental ways to building an ecologically sustainable and just society, and to do so with the least possible impact on the environment, in a manner that models this vision. We are committed to doing this not just through education, but through action. We are acting on our commitment to the world's remaining ancient forests by phasing out our paper supply from ancient forests worldwide. This book is one step towards ending global deforestation and climate change. It is printed on acid-free paper that is 100% old growth forest-free (100% post-consumer recycled), processed chlorine free, and printed with vegetable based, low VOC inks. For further information, or to browse our full list of books and purchase securely, visit our website at: www.newsociety.com

NEW SOCIETY PUBLISHERS   www.newsociety.com

TABLE OF CONTENTS

FOREWORD
BY VICKI ROBIN

Open to page 136 of *Material World* (the book of photos by Peter Menzel showing people and their possessions from around the world). Don't have a copy? No problem — I'll tell you what the picture is. It's the Skeen Family from Pearland, Texas, selected because they are "deep in the heart" of the American experience. Their income approximates the average US level. They have two children — Michael, age 7 and Julie, age 10. Like all of the 30 families representing 30 countries that were selected for this coffee table book, they stand in front of their home with all their furniture and appliances arranged in the cul de sac behind them. It's a nice but modest array, nothing compared to the stage set of many sitcoms. Every family from around the world was asked what their most valued possession was — for the Skeens, as for many Americans, it's the family Bible.

Now turn to page 14. Mali, in Africa. The Natoma family of eleven (two wives, eight children, one father) sits on the roof of their mud and straw adobe home, surrounded by cooking pots, baskets and various kitchen and farming implements. Perhaps half of these everyday items were made by the family themselves. In the background is a bicycle, which is Papa's most prized possession. The clothes on their bodies and on a makeshift drying rack (a pole balanced between the house and the mud wall) are colorful. Their faces sport big smiles. They have a radio but no TV, no telephone, no VCRs and no automobiles.

These two families are separated by many thousands of miles, many years of development and many layers of creature comforts. If you are like me, you can appreciate the simplicity of the Mali household and even wonder at their apparent delight in circumstances that would send most any American into helplessness and despair. Almost everything arrayed behind the Skeens would have to be plucked out of the picture to put them on a par with the Natomas. Best to close the book.

But we can't close the book. You, I, the Natomas and the Skeens, along with perhaps 6.1 billion other humans and hundreds of billions of other creatures, live together on one planet. The "have-nots" can be out of sight and even out of mind, but they breathe the same air, drink from the same scant supply of fresh water, and birth children who will grow up to work with our children to finish the job we've barely started; they will have to find a way for *all* of us to live well within the Earth's means.

Jim Merkel, a former weapons engineer, accepted this challenge 14 years ago. He whittled away at his stock of possessions and reduced the sheer volume, complexity and toxicity of the stuff that flowed through his life. He did it with gusto and good spirit, guided by passion and curiosity. His engineering background gave him the mentality and the tools to assess which of the changes he was making actually lowered his impact on the Earth. He lobbied his city council for bike paths so everyone who wanted to could choose to do without a car. He organized Earth Day celebrations that attracted hundreds of volunteers and thousands of people. His high spirits, humble integrity and winning ways were dished up along with his facts and figures about the devastating impact on the Earth of the American lifestyle.

He learned everything he could and experimented with every method he could find. In the process he met Mathis Wackernagel and Bill Rees who taught Jim about the Ecological Footprint, a relatively accurate way to actually measure how much of the planet's resources it takes to support us in the style to which we have become accustomed. He also sought out Joe Dominguez and me after reading *Your Money or Your Life.* Our method for lowering consumption while increasing quality of life was another key piece in the puzzle he was pondering: how do we get people to live within the means of nature and not feel deprived? Jim also jumped at the chance to go on a study trip to Kerala, India, to learn from the people in that state who have a quality of life almost as high as ours in North America — but do it on just over $550 a year per person.

From these building blocks he dreamed a big dream — starting a research and education center to teach people the skills of living lightly and the ways to know how much of everything it takes to support their lives. But from here on, how about I let Jim tell you his own story? What I really want you to know is that Jim makes living on less seem like so much fun that you'll want to try it yourself. He shares compelling facts through telling vivid stories about his own successive awakenings to both the peril and the promise of living on this Earth.

People, animals, plants, soil and the all the rest of the critters together make up this precious mantle of life on our exquisite planet. We *all* live here together — now, and now, and now. So now what? Jim has some answers. Listen to him and you'll see how plausible sustainability is — and how necessary. You'll want to do your part, because by then, Jim will be your friend and his plans will seem like the greatest adventure on Earth.

Vicki Robin is coauthor, with Joe Dominguez, of
Your Money or Your Life.

ACKNOWLEDGMENTS

When I arrived at mom and dad's house after 17 years out west, a room awaited me with a desk, bookshelves and a door with an "office" sign on it. The nearby Pleasant River of downeast Maine with its coyotes, salmon, moose, bears and porcupines kept me focused, while my nation waged war.

Until about the first two months of writing *Radical Simplicity*, I was under the illusion that I would simply sit down and write this book ... Wrong. Community radio, Weru and Amy Goodman of Democracy Now! kept me inspired with news of a worldwide peace movement. Had it not been for the support from friends, activists and family, I'd have given up.

First thanks go to my sister Marie Merkel who got me through the first few drafts. Janel Sterbentz and the folks at Redefining Progress; Chad Monfreda, Diana Deumling, and Mathis Wackernagel, and my partner Rowan Sherwood offered generous research assistance. Hank Colletto, Lily Fessenden, Monica Wood, Mathis Wackernagel, and Matt Chingos reviewed early drafts. When a manuscript was assembled, Ivan Ussach, Rowan, and my sister Michele Sorensen skillfully edited it.

When seclusion was necessary, a home was offered by Hawk and Lisa Henries, and then by Colleen O'Connell at Ravenwood, where organic vegetables nourished my body and soul. Throughout the entire project, Chris and Judith Plant and Ingrid Witvoet at New Society Publishers were there to encourage.

Most of all, I thank Rowan, who worked on this project from beginning to end, and whose steady love and support makes life more wonderful. I couldn't have done it without her.

Jim Merkel
June 2003

INTRODUCTION

A mongst the five-star shuffle of executives at the Royal Viking Hotel in Stockholm, Sweden, I nursed a dark Belgian beer. It was March of 1989. Planted at the broad, varnished bar, it felt good to catch my breath. I had just helped design a military computer that could work under water or on the deck of a battle ship. It was ruggedized to withstand a drop kick. It contained cryptographic algorithms, fit in the palm of your hand, could be held to the mouthpiece of any public telephone to transmit secrets, and could survive a nuclear blast. Casually, I surveyed the room. Confident I was not being watched, I opened a small notebook and refreshed my memory on foreign military sales procedures.

Tomorrow I would meet with some top brass of the Swedish Military. I would demonstrate for them that clever little top-secret beauty of mine. Perhaps I'd make a sale. More likely they'd peruse my design and remain loyal to our European competitor, a scenario my employer, TRW, and our consultants briefed me on at length. The TV roared out a beer commercial, reminding me to drink up. Suddenly, a special news bulletin flashed on the screen — into the room spilled a massive black oil slick, with an ocean of crude-soaked cormorants and crying seals floundering as they slowly bobbed toward a pristine shore. In the background loomed the wild mountains of Alaska — wolf-haunted forests, salmon-filled rivers, grizzly bears — Alaska, a place of how many boy-hood dreams!

As the reporters on-screen combed the Exxon Valdez crew for the guilty, I looked across the polished bar into the mirror and knew it was me. I drive. I fly. Four intercontinental and three cross-continental flights in just this last year. How could I plea bargain with a jury of 12 gasping whales? I knew the truth: fossil fuels are part of every item I consume. Of course, the entire industrialized world stood indicted beside me — our "need" for ever-more mobility, ever-more progress, ever-more growth had led us straight to this disaster. But in that moment, all I knew was that I, personally, needed to step forward and own up to the damage.

A day later, mission accomplished, I flew back to California. The bounce of touchdown woke me out of an odd dream where my van had disappeared from the airport parking lot and I was walking the sweltering San Luis Obispo streets toward home like an over-burdened burro. No, there it was — dusty, but still very much a part of my life. I drove straight to work, secured the crypto-gear in a top-secret locker, drove home and parked the rig with determination. There was nothing to rush inside for, only bare bachelor-pad cupboards, so I mounted pannier bags on the bike and took off to shop. I felt like I was still in that weird dream world. The supermarket aisles oozed petroleum: from the fertilizer, to the trucking, to the processing, to the packaging, to the little plastic toy prizes in all those cereal boxes. Suddenly, I saw a crude-covered cormorant come flopping out of the Cheerios and into America's cereal bowl.

I left empty-handed and cycled across town to the Cuesta Co-op. The veggies were not oil free, but they were local and 100% organic. I biked home with four full panniers and not a single new package. Next morning, I left for work ten minutes early and pedaled the quiet streets in a wakeful mist, breathing in the rolling green hills.

My evenings began to fill with info-tainment and meetings. A friend asked if I'd throw my name in the hat for the Sierra Club's Executive Committee; soon I was the vice chair of the Santa Lucia chapter. With a group of college students and a radical attorney, we founded the Alternative Transportation Task Force (ATTF) and drafted a proposal for an interconnected bike lane system — the visionary state-of-the-art transportation plan of our wildest dreams. We boldly called for a twenty-fold increase in bike funds at the annual city budget hearing. With our pinstripes, power-ties and colored pie charts on overheads, we made our case to a packed hearing chamber. That evening, dozens of bike activists crowded the corner bar to celebrate our first victory: a ten-fold expansion of the bike-lane coffers, from $20K to $200K per year! *Viva la Velorution!* And this time, the dark beer I enjoyed was from a local microbrewery.

If Lily Tomlin and Steve Martin in *All of Me* thought it was awkward to share one body, there I was: a jet-set military salesman who voted for Reagan by day, and a bleeding-heart pacifist, eco-veggie-head-hooligan by night. In July of 1989, the two minds could no longer share one body. We locked ourselves in the house, closed the blinds and broke open the engineering economics textbooks. Eco-Jim asked, "How much do I need?" while Jet-set Jim asked, "How much can I get?" We ran monthly cash flows for short- and long-range options. The inner engineer buzzed from the design challenge. Mr. Eco wanted a life so lean and free it would fit in the palm of Earth's hand. Free to fight for bike lanes and old-growth trees. Free to someday cycle to Alaska. Mr. Jet-set wanted a ruggedized personal economic package that could withstand a stock market free-fall and wouldn't run aground because of born-again, starry-eyed, shortsighted passion.

After working in the shadowy dens of military sales, both Jims made non-violence a critical constraint. The acceptable design had to wash our hands of funds to hired guns. More importantly, it had to systematically enhance peace — peace among families, among nations, and in the thick of yipping coyotes.

We stared at these last design constraints. The calculator lay idle upon the mess of additions and subtractions scattered across the bed, and a design grew like an aster from ashes. It seemed too easy. Set income below taxable level. Then not a single cent of mine would rain bombs and bullets onto peasants who live near coveted resources. But, how could I foster peace? I held the Earth up to my ear and listened.

What I heard was, "To foster peace, you must live equitably." Then I remembered a factoid from my new piles of eco-peace propaganda books. The average income of all the world's people was US$4,500. The uncanny coincidence hit home — I could live on a par with the human family and not fund guns. I jumped for the calculator. Like the wife in the film *The Bicycle Thief*, who sold her bed sheets in ravaged post-war Italy, I laid every single asset on the table. Then with a sharpened pencil I slashed away all possible liabilities: Boat — gone. Restaurants — gone. Beer — four a month. Van — off the road. Subscriptions — gone. Housing — rent the three spare rooms and reduce monthly bills from $1,100 to $200. Remove perks and privilege, plain and simple waste, come up with a column of numbers ... total these, propose amendments, run a new cash flow series ... total, amend, iterate ... on and on for hours. My brain needed a break. I picked up my bass and ran a steady blues line. A budget of 5,000 clams a year was where I was at. It started to feel alright.

Here was the plan: I'd quit workin' for the man and live off savings for four years while workin' for the mama. Meanwhile, boost the income from my four-plex through a refinance and sell off every bit of excess. Then, in four years, I'd sell the four-plex and my home and play banker. This way, I'd have years of mortgage income to cover my monthly expenses. With the down payments, I'd buy an inexpensive cabin on some land. Free from paid employment at age thirty? This was too good to be true. I ran worst-case and best-case scenarios. Worst case: I'd fritter my life away in fear, while I contributed to hell on Earth. The second to worst case: twenty years down the road, I'd need to get a part-time job. I gave notice on Monday, took the van off the road, rented out three of the four rooms in my house, and planted a garden. I was free, but more importantly, I was on fire.

. . . . .

Radical Simplicity is a practical guide and toolkit to help you begin your customized journey to simplicity. Along the way, you might be astounded by how big an impact or footprint you actually leave every day, and even more amazed by how small you truly would like it to be. Being fourteen years along in my search, what I've found to share are three very specific tools. With the tools from the book *Our Ecological*

Footprint, by Mathis Wackernagel and William Rees, you will find the equivalent of a monthly Earth checkbook balance statement, a method to measure just how much nature was needed to supply all you consume and absorb your effluent. Then, building on the steps from the book *Your Money or Your Life* by Vicki Robin and Joe Dominguez, you can start to design your own personal economics. It will be one that is ruggedized for the hardball of global markets, and yet allows you to save money, get free of debt and align your work with your values. And by holding the Earth to your ear and listening for its secrets, you just may feel inspired to walk the path to a wild Earth shared by all people and all species. The mystery and magic of this world will unfold and reveal your niche in a sustainable backyard ecology.

When these tools are combined, a self-reinforcing cycle takes on a life of its own — suddenly, you have more time and more savings. Who would have thought it? You have more security and more skills, more responsibility, integrity, and a completely new perspective on freedom. The possibilities are limitless, and new dreams can begin. There are infinite dreams to be lived that would restore the earth, infinite dreams that neither heal nor hurt, and infinite that would harm and are best left in the ethereal world of fantasy. We have evolved and socialized into beings that are both complex and Pavlovian, magnificent and ugly, enlightened and dysfunctional, kind and greedy. With all these seeming complications and contradictions, is there a way to cut through it all — now — and create a dream world for all beings?

. . . . .

We have everything to lose and nothing to lose — everything to gain and nothing to gain. And we have our life as the greatest expression of our commitment to the ones we love, to the voiceless, to the land, and to unborn generations.

PART I

JOURNEY TO SIMPLICITY

ONE

BUILDING THE CASE FOR GLOBAL LIVING

Every creature is better alive than dead, men and moose and pine trees, and he who understands it alright will rather preserve its life than destroy it.

— Henry David Thoreau

Imagine you are at a potluck buffet and see that you are the first in line. How do you know how much to take? Imagine that this potluck spread includes not just food and water, but also the materials needed for shelter, clothing, healthcare and education. It all looks and smells so good and you are hungry. What will you heap on your plate? How much is enough to leave for your neighbors behind you in the line? Now extend this cornucopia to today's global economy, where the necessities for life come from around the world. Six billion people, shoulder to shoulder, form a line that circles around the globe to Cairo, onto Hawaii over ocean bridges, then back, and around the globe again, 180 times more. With plates in hand, they too wait in line, hearty appetites in place. And along with them are giraffes and klipspringers, manatees and spiders, untold millions of species, millions of billions of unique beings, all with the same lusty appetites. And behind them, the soon-to-be-born children, cubs, and larvae.

A harmonious feast just might be possible. But it requires a bit of restraint, or shall we say, a tamed appetite, as our plate becomes a shopping cart, becomes a pickup truck — filling our home, attic, basement, garage, and maybe even a rented storage unit with nature transformed into things. As we sit down for a good hearty meal with new friends and creatures from around the world, what is the level of equity that we would feel great about? At what level of inequity would we say, "Wait a minute, that's not fair?"

The Global Living Project was founded back in 1995 with a mission to discover how to live sustainably in North America. "Global living" was defined as an equitable and harmonious lifestyle among not only the entire human population, but also among the estimated 7-25 million other species[1], and the countless unborn generations. When one practices global living, each of our daily actions improves the health of the whole — locally and globally. The ecological, social, political, and spiritual systems at all levels are then able to regenerate and flourish.

· · · · ·

So there you are, plate in hand, first in that mega-line. You are determined to be fair as you look over the wonderful buffet, which looks limitless. You glance over your shoulder at the line — its length is too hard for you to fathom. If you had landed on an island paradise with three friends, the answer of how much to take would be intuitive enough, similar to sitting around a large pizza on Friday night — a no-brainer. But the scale of the buffet is too big to wrap your mind around. As you contemplate your real-world life, a soft voice whispers one or more of the following in your ear:

- There is abundance in the universe, plenty for everyone, isn't there?
- If I don't take it, someone else will.

- It's the corporate elite who take too much.
- We all do the best we can.
- Everything is this way for a reason.
- I've really worked hard for my money.
- When I get my next raise, I know I'll do some good with it.
- If I didn't do my part as a consumer, everyone would be out of work.
- Until everyone else takes less, it's futile.
- You could almost say we are biologically programmed to consume — survival of the fittest.
- Come to think of it, in some ways, I'm an exception. I need my (fill in the blank) because (fill in the blank).
- Who knows? It might even be my karma to have so much — otherwise there would be no have-nots.
- What's with all this guilt tripping? Dig in and eat!

You see a burger sizzling on the barbecue that smells really good. "That will get me started." Just as you are ready to put it on your bun, you remember reading *Diet for a New America*.[2] Eating high on the food chain uses much more land, up to fifty times more than a vegetarian diet. The line is long. You remember staring at corn stalks for days on end on a cross-country trip – corn grown only to feed to cattle. You remember the cleared forests and prairies, the manure and soil running off into streams, lakes, and coastal waters, and that 43 percent of the US is grazed or grows feed for livestock. Meat's impact on the environment is second only to automobiles.[3]

"All, right, all right," you say as you look for a tofu burger. Both burgers will require processing facilities, packaging and shipping. Each will leave a trail of waste and pollution. You've heard that soybeans are lower on the food chain — they produce an equal amount of protein on one-sixteenth the land needed for beef. The tofu burger is not perfect. The thought of genetically modified beans grown on monoculture fields sprayed with pesticides leaves you a bit queasy. But it's a substantial reduction in cost to the Earth. And it's tasty.

With appetite abated, your mind wanders to dream getaways. This grand buffet has it all. Two tickets to Bali and in just 22 hours you could be released from the icy grip of the coming winter. "I can taste those mangos, feel the hot sand. The plane is going anyway ..." You think it through further. Well ... not exactly. You do a quick calculation and discover you'd need four acres of forests working year round to absorb the jet emissions for your seat on this once-a-year 44-hour roundtrip flight.[4] You realize that the non-renewable jet fuel once burned will push atmospheric CO_2 levels higher. A second consciousness-raising thought enters: the $1,280 tab for this flight is equal to the annual wages of five typical Balinese.[5] "I'll stay home then," you conclude. Then you think, "To pass those long cold days, I could use a faster computer. With the latest information, I could do some great activism." But wait. You remember reading that a computer uses 1,000 substances, including 350 different hazardous chemicals in its manufacturing processes.[6] Computers' designed obsolescence earned 20 million machines an early retirement in 1998. You also remember reading about the rural rice-growing town of Guiyu, China, which has become an electronic waste (e-waste) processing center. Women and children earn $1.50 per day to strip computers down to components. Soil and water tests there have revealed lead levels 2,400 times greater than those allowed by the World Health Organization's guidelines. Several other heavy metals tested far exceeded the Environmental Protection Agency standards: barium by 10 times; tin by 152 times; and chromium by 1,338 times. A year after the operation started, the village had to truck in water. Many of the substances are known carcinogens or cause birth defects and skin and lung irritation.[7]

Let's face it: in North America it can be challenging to find products that don't have a large, negative environmental impact. And just as challenging is to say no to what is so easy for us to have ... to say no to what just seems *normal* to have. As we look more deeply into the products and services we use, one question we can ask ourselves is: "Am I in control of what I choose to put on my plate?" If not, then who is? Why do we feel such a knee-jerk resistance to taming our appetites? This is a spiritual, social, psychological, and emotional question. Does it come from internal fears of not having enough? Or is it the product of pathological pressures generated externally?

INSIDE OURSELVES

More desperate whispering in the ear: "If I decided to attempt radical simplicity, might I wind up without adequate food and shelter? Will I be able to pay for new clothes and healthcare? How will I finish my education, or pay for my children's? Who will hire me? How can I afford to just kick back and have a good time now and then? Will I lose status, respect, and friends? How will I ever get to travel, and do all those other things I've dreamed of? My children will hate me, my partner will never understand. Mom and Dad might not ever say it, but somehow, I just know they'll be disappointed. And then, someday I'll be old, and who will take care of me? Who will pay the bills?"

Global living: A nice concept, but pretty scary.

OUTSIDE OURSELVES

Have you ever wondered where the pressure to consume comes from? Does the rush of modern culture keep you plunging forward on the same unquestioned path day after day? Have you become resigned to the realization that there is no longer enough clean water available, no longer a way to avoid the catastrophic consequences of global warming? All of society — our government (we elected them), our employers (we went to work for them), and the church and schools we have chosen to attend, all seem to support economic growth and unsustainable behavior from A to Z. Mainstream media and corporate advertisers seem to control the bulk of information, and influence who gets elected, so much so that millions of people don't even vote. With the corporate dream machine cranking away, it's easy to see why. In the US:

+ 99.5 percent of households have televisions.
+ 95 percent of the population watches TV every day.
+ The average home has a TV on for eight hours a day. The average adult watches for five hours; children between ages two and five watch for three and a half hours; and adults over 55 for nearly six hours.
+ Aside from sleep and work, watching TV is America's primary activity.[8]

If you grew up like other North Americans, you have watched 40,000 TV commercials a year.[9] Add to that the bombardment of sales pitches from radio, print media, billboards, and signs and logos, and your internal landscape may very well be etched with a lust and desire for things. Once we are able to satisfy the hunger for this or that, we are still tempted into more exotic vacations, more trips to the hair salon or meditation center, and more gas-guzzling experiences skiing or snow-mobiling. Advertisers know how to get to the money in your pockets. They are trained to have you seek fulfillment outside yourself, for your dreams to include their products, their view of life — for their dream to become your dream.

If you received 12, 16, or 20 years of institutional education, you'll have other influences to overcome. In *Dumbing Us Down*,[10] John T. Gatto, a New York State Teacher of the Year, shows how public schools have mostly taught young people to follow orders. Some schools might be excellent, but often our intrinsic creativity, spark, curiosity, and ability to self-motivate are dampened during our most dynamic and open years. All this time spent indoors, sitting in rows, with someone else calling the shots while the natural world beckons, is a sad injustice. To initiate a lifestyle of our own design, in alignment with our personal values, is a skill we just haven't been taught unless we were lucky enough to have family, adult friends, or an inspiring teacher who modeled the behaviors that make dreams come true.

Most cities and towns have been redesigned for cars, while bus systems and bike lanes are few and far between. Neighborhoods with services accessible by foot, the corner store where you chat with neighbors and carry home some provisions, are mostly things of the past. Our homes may be ten to eighty miles from work, with groceries in a strip mall in the opposite direction. Our favorite park might be clear across town; our best friend, across the state; and our family spread across the continent. Many towns have laws that make it illegal to have a home business, a composting toilet, or a greywater system. Building codes often make a simply-built home illegal. Making a small outside fire at night to sing around is often illegal, even on your own property.

Yes, at the start, reinventing our own slice of life can look pretty much impossible. The more deeply we search for the causes of our world's drastic imbalances, the more we realize the full extent of the violence we have unknowingly supported. Who would have thought that children in China would get sick from our e-waste? Or that a meat-based diet destroys habitats in Brazil? That the sea level could rise and aquatic habitats in Polynesia become contaminated with toxins because of our fossil fuel dependence? And that, with the flick of a light switch, we may contribute to the genocide of indigenous peoples in Arizona?

By participating in the economics of globalization and the politics of corporate-government rule, backed up by the military-industrial complex, we are actively involved, day to day, in the greatest exploitation of people and nature that the Earth has ever witnessed. Consider these statistics:

- Currently the world's wealthiest one billion people alone consume the equivalent of the Earth's entire sustainable yield. All six billion people are consuming at a level that is 20 percent over sustainable yield.[11]
- Human numbers are predicted to reach nine billion by the year 2050 and peak at 11 billion.[12]
- Private consumption in high-income countries rose from $4,752 billion in 1980 to $14,054 billion in 1998.[13]
- Scientists estimate that between 1,000 and 100,000 species of life become extinct every 24 hours, a rate 100 to 1,000 times faster than the natural rate.[14]
- More than half of all accessible surface fresh water is used by humanity.[15]
- The concentration of atmospheric CO_2 has increased from 280 parts per million (ppm) before the Industrial Revolution to 360 ppm today, and is predicted to reach 560 ppm by 2050. A panel of 1,500 scientists warned that average global temperatures might rise between 3.6 and 6.3 degrees Fahrenheit by 2100.[16]
- Over 70 percent of remaining oil reserves lie under the soil of Islamic nations of Asia, from the Red Sea to Indonesia.[17] The US imports $19 billion in oil annually and spends another $55 billion annually safeguarding these oil supplies. The Gulf War

of the 1990s killed between 160,000 and 220,000 Iraqi people while 19 Americans died.[18]

• Over the last century, wars have claimed 175 million lives. Worldwide, $780 billion is spent annually on military, $380 billion by the US.[19]

With all these forces, inside and out, conspiring against us, it is understandable that we might ask whether global living is simply impossible.

WE HAVE NO OTHER CHOICE

We must know first that our acts are useless, and yet we must proceed as if we didn't know it. That is a sorcerer's controlled folly.

— Don Juan[20]

If we want a sustainable future, sharing Earth with all is humanity's only compassionate, long-term choice. Our intellect, backed by the best of science, concludes that economic growth on a finite planet is suicide. The intuitive self knows this, and might even have the solution. Our ethical and spiritual selves yearn to secure the future for all life. To avert the ecological catastrophe already in full swing, we have no choice but to radically reduce consumption, immediately stabilize population growth, and rapidly make better use of technology. If we make these changes now, the damage can be minimized. If we delay, a crash is inevitable, with the holders of the most weapons dominating until the bitter end. We have no choice but to stop damaging the Earth's life support systems.

The Dalai Lama, when talking about how to solve world problems, said, "But first we must change within ourselves .... If there were another method that was easier and more practical, it would be better, but there is none."[21] As long as we ourselves contribute to the crisis, happiness will be elusive — in the shape of a melancholic surrender, or a party-till-the-cows-come-home abandon. If we live like there is no tomorrow, we will create just that — no tomorrow. It comes down to,

"If not me, then who? If not now, then when?" At some point, we will have no other choice but to make our stand.

Global living is a modern-day journey to reclaim our connections to the Earth, however ancient, and to fall in love with the land again, wherever we decide to call home.

TWO

A CULTURE
OF GLOBAL LIVING

We might all agree that the challenge of global living is a difficult one, maybe even scary. But don't trust the findings presented here — do your own research and tune into your own intuition. Hopefully, we will agree that it is desirable, even necessary.

For societal solutions to succeed, individuals must have first-hand experience in sustainable living. Then, when groups of individuals join together and share their practical global living experiences, they will know that change is possible, and believe it can be done. After having worked through many of the practical difficulties, they will be ready to demonstrate a working example, and be taken seriously by others.

In essence, the serious practice of global living discontinues payments to the oppressors, to polluting corporations, to the military industrial complex, and to all their subsidiary brand names. Our day-to-day purchases, our hard-earned dollars, as it turns out, are our strongest votes for the world of our dreams. We can create change with each dollar we spend — or better yet, don't spend. A tamed appetite is the core of global living.

And our personal choices do add up. An individual's ecological footprint is a measure of the land and sea space needed to supply what they consume and to absorb their wastes. If 10 percent of North Americans reduced their ecological footprint by one-third, 270 million acres of land, or 422,000 square miles — an area larger than California, Oregon, Washington, and Idaho combined — would be liberated. Put more humbly, if only *one person* reduces their footprint from the average American 24-acre level down to 4 acres, there will be 20 more free and wild acres. That's an area over 96,800 square yards, or 968 paces by 100 paces — we're talking 18 football fields. A lot of nature can take place in a forest this size. With habitat in short supply, this accomplishment deserves a celebration!

To better frame what we are calling "global living," let's take a moment to examine some of its elements. These elements are intertwined, but for the time being, we will separate them into the material and non-material realms.

MATERIAL

The material realm encompasses the full cornucopia of nature, from the most primary elements to their transformation into products, the thousand-and-one items you and I use — for survival, for comfort, for luxury. Materials feed and transport us, shelter and clothe us, entertain and inspire us. Think about your use of material objects and ask yourself:

- Can ecosystems keep pace with my use of nature?
- How does my income and consumption compare to the world community?
- Does my employment (which relies upon material flows) restore the Earth, further damage the Earth, or is it neutral?
- Am I inspired by my material surroundings? Do they appeal to my eyes, ears, nose, intuition, or spiritual sense?

NON-MATERIAL

As you contemplate the non-material aspects of your life, some questions to ask are:

+ Do I take time for art, poetry, music, dance, or other creative expressions?
+ Am I fair in my relations with other species and other people?
+ Is my life free enough so that I feel chronically *un*stressed?
+ Am I able to make my own choices about my life?
+ Do I take full responsibility for the implications of my actions?
+ Is there laughter and fun in my life?
+ Do I take time to care about others? Do I feel cared for?
+ Is there a spark of adventure in my life?
+ Do I take time to explore whatever unseen, spiritual realms call to me?

Global living seeks to integrate the material and non-material into a healthy lifestyle. By getting the material aspects of life pared down, prioritized, and in good order, we free up time to explore the non-material realms. And, through attention to the non-material, you might find that many of your perceived material "needs" were actually not needs at all. Many who experiment in simplicity speak of an increased freedom, once they strike the right balance. How do you feel about the balance in your life?

As we begin the journey toward global living, many questions will be raised and assumptions challenged. As with any culture, along with the wonderful aspects, so worthy of being cherished, there's bound to exist a certain amount of excess baggage which weighs us down, including old ideas that are no longer appropriate.

THREE SACRED COWS

The sacredness of cows in India seemed absurd to my youthful practicality. But messing around with a culture's sacred cows is tricky business. It's the kind of business where you meet the incredible blindspots of your own perception and come face-to-face with the strength or weakness of your own will. My naiveté about their sacred cows was flattened when I became a vegetarian, baked in the sun when I became a vegan, and then thrown in the fire as fuel while I lived in a village in Kerala, India.

By not eating their cow, they get daily milk, manure, and fuel. Indigestible plants and green wastes are recycled back into food. And by bringing the fodder to the cow, instead of open pasture grazing, several thousand years of cows in India have not done the damage the American cattle industry has done in 300 years. But still, in India, the forests and wild animals have been displaced by each sacred cow. If the areas grew vegetables instead of cows, 30 to 100 times more food would result. It is not always obvious which cows should become chop-meat. It might serve the whole if certain cows were sterilized and given a good life.

But what about our own sacred cows?

1. Be fruitful and multiply.
2. More is better.
3. Technology will find solutions to our problems.

I've chosen these three because they lead the stampede toward unsustainable behavior. If we are to work toward a sustainable future, be it at the family, community, regional, national, or planetary level, humanity will have to have smaller families, consume less, and use safe, efficient technologies sparingly.

Ecologists use the equation:

Impact = Population x Affluence x Technology[1]
Or
I = P x A x T or IPAT
Where:
    I = the total impact of a given population
    P = the size of the population being studied.
    A = the total affluence or consumption per person in a population
        being studied; i.e., all the things we own and use, which
        includes two parts:

1. Capital stocks (each car, bike, book, house area, and paper-clip); and
2. The throughput or flow of resources needed to maintain each stock (electricity, gas, coffee, cat toys, water, soap, barley, and chop-meat).

T = our technologies. The energy efficiency of each technology multiplied by the environmental impact of the process used.

The smog we see on the hope horizon might have to do with the way the world's one billion high-impact individuals and many others treasure these sacred cows so dearly. In Donella Meadows' book, *Beyond the Limits*,[2] a sophisticated computer model predicted that substantial changes are needed in all three areas — population, affluence, and technology — for sustainability to be achieved. To see the dynamics of this IPAT equation, let's consider two families: an average family in India, (a husband, wife, and three children) and an average American family, (a husband, wife, and two children). According to the World Bank's 1998 statistics, the people of India had an annual per capita GNP of US$440, while in the US it was $29,240.[3] Below is a comparison not including technology (I = P X A).

The family in India:

I = 5 people x $440 = $2,200

The family in the US:

I = 4 people x $29,240 = $116,960

The American family has an impact 53 times higher than the Indian family, even with fewer children. Let's say each family decided to have one less child. The Indian family would decrease their impact by $440, while the American family would decrease their impact by $29,240. Each average American has an impact equal to 66.5 people in India. This doesn't mean that India doesn't need to work toward smaller families; however, the contribution of affluence far overshadows population when we compare these two families.

If technology is the silver bullet, then shouldn't the American family, with its superior information and developments, have a smaller impact than the Indian family? Although technology could drastically reduce human impact, its applications in warfare, consumer goods and services, and for-profit medicine result in serious side effects. While its benefits are celebrated, its performance record is one of accelerated environmental impacts.

LOVABLE LIMITS

Geese limit themselves to one mate for life. We may never know exactly why, but in strictly practical terms, it works for them. Faced with migrations that span continents, short summers to hatch and feed a brood, and danger lurking wherever they zoom in to feed and water, they stand by each other through thick and thin. They protect each other, circle back to help a hurt friend, take turns breaking the wind, even honk and encourage those out front. They need each other. They simply don't have extra time and energy to exhibit flirt-plumage, or to become suave and slick for a new mate each season. They save time and energy by not worrying about chasing away other aggressive males or females. In some cases, limits are lovable.

Loving our limits can set the stage for our life. As we recognize that we only have one Earth — which has finite capacity to support life — becoming comfortable with limits will open our minds and hearts for the work of taming the appetite.

Global living doesn't attempt to impose limits on others. It doesn't necessarily advise one to escape to the country or move into compact urban cubicles. It seeks to inspire our creativity, our ability to see that there are infinite satisfying lifestyle packages compatible with living on a finite, equitable share of nature. Global living seeks to give you the tools to be the architect.

THREE

SUSTAINABILITY IN ACTION

When I first started out on my journey to simplicity, back in San Luis Obispo in 1989, the path I was to take was not clear. Sitting on that Stolkholm bar stool, I felt an internal readiness for big changes; I wanted my life's journey to contribute to a better world. But back at work, I was asked to market the cryptographic computer I'd designed to the arms dealers of Turkey, Pakistan, Israel, Iran and Iraq. I got my hands on an Amnesty International year-end report that listed in horrifying detail the tortures and human rights abuses these governments committed against their citizens. It was a relief to quit that job; still, my contribution toward a peaceful society was not clear.

I had become friends with Mike Zurate and his mom, Pilulaw Khus, from the Bear clan of the local Chumash tribe. They told me about the forced relocation of 10,000 Dineh (Navajo) people from the area known as Big Mountain, Arizona. They said the elders could use some help.

With nine truckloads of donated humanitarian aid, a newly formed Big Mountain Support Group convoy departed San Luis Obispo, California in November of 1990. For two days, ceremonies were held as we sorted tons of food for three hundred families under siege. I interviewed dozens of traditional elders who stated, in no uncertain terms, that they would rather die than be forced off the land. One elder said, "In our language, there is no word for relocation. To relocate is to disappear and never be seen again." The promise of tract-house assimilation to them meant a welfare-check spiral-down. Any native person in Arizona faces terrible racism — a jobless Indian on the dole; racism squared. The essence of what one elder told me was this: Here we have sheep, corn, medicine plants and the bones of our ancestors. If we move to those houses, how will we live? How will we pay the bills? We will be heartbroken. Unfortunately, their homeland contained an estimated 21 billion tons of coal, valued at $100 billion dollars. The "New Lands" offered to them were the site of a 1979 spill of 94 million gallons of radioactive waste by United Nuclear, a spill that contaminated 68 miles of the nearby river, Rio Puerco.

Our deliveries took several days. We drove hundreds of dusty miles, through sage and juniper hills, to the self-reliant family settlements scattered widely across a big-sky desert. At our last delivery, an elder woman, who spoke only her native tongue, waved us in. Her weathered, warm smile glowed in flickering candlelight. She handed me a bowl and gestured toward the bubbling kettle of mutton stew on the woodstove. Drying herbs hung from the rafters in the center of her earth-and-wood hogan. Our guide and interpreter, Tom, chatted and laughed with the elder as we settled on the hand-woven woolen blankets. Then she told us about the latest attempts to break her people. To the best of my memory, this is what she said:

> For seventeen years they slaughtered our sheep and put cement in our wells. If we fix our roof or fence, they drag us into court. Here, look at these papers they give us. Now they blast Mother Earth apart. Look at the crack in my home. They drop a bomb on Japanese people with uranium from our mountain. We are a peaceful people.

They pump the aquifer to slurry coal. Now the plants are
dying. Who is this Peabody Coal Company anyway?
Who are these people from Washington? Who gives
them the right? They make up stories about Hopi and
Navajo fighting when what they really want is the coal
beneath us. We are friends. They make some marks on a
piece of paper and come out here and push us around.
This is our altar — we will never leave.

As she finished speaking, the horror of a 1990s silent genocide
grabbed hold of my solar plexus and twisted. "What can I do to help?"
I asked. She said, "Go back to your people and tell them to live simply.
Then they wouldn't be out here digging up Mother Earth for coal and
uranium."

I realized that my people would not be open to being *told* to live
simply. Are we too addicted? Am I too addicted? But I knew that
somewhere, somehow, there must be a language to open our hearts
and minds. Out on that arid, yet alive landscape, I witnessed a time-
less way of life and of beauty. A vision whipped up like a hot wind
and said yes — there is a better way. We don't have to drive salmon
or cultures to extinction in order to electrify our homes. The elder
had so much respect for "all my relations" — every rock, plant, animal,
river and mountain — every inch of Mother Earth was sacred to her
and her people. A sustainable life, one that passes the land to the next
generation without degradation, was woven into the stories I heard in
the sweat lodge and around the fire at night. The rich Dineh culture,
contrasted with the "more is better" culture I was raised in, stirred a
second vision that said *yes* — *my people are hungry for that better way.*
But before I could open my mouth, I knew that I had to transform
myself.

Returning from Big Mountain, the elder's wisdom helped reset the
parameters of my design. Could what I do every day be repeated by
six billion people? I wanted my life to be in harmony with the entire
multitude of Earth's magnificent and nagging beings. I wanted to live
with them, learn from them, respect them and, without illusions, but
to the least degree possible, even consume them, while still having a

spiritually rich and meaningful life. And I wanted to do all this within these parameters:

> **Design Parameter 1:** There would be no losers; human, Earth or other species.
>
> **Design Parameter 2:** Each step could be taken by everyone, everywhere; not just by those with privilege.
>
> **Design Parameter 3:** The steps and solutions had to prove sustainable, indefinitely.

My engineer's gut sense said, "With all our technology, wealth, and information, global living right here in the city can't be that difficult." I was not under siege, and enjoyed considerable freedom. But what did I know? I had lived my entire life separate from indigenous ecological principles.

LEARNING FROM THE CHUMASH

I began to wonder what could be learned from the native people who inhabited the land around San Luis Obispo. Chumash people have lived here for over 9,000 years.[1] What did this place look like when it was a Chumash village? Might their place-based wisdom be essential to understanding how to meet the design parameters in this specific location? I wanted to know more, so I began spending time with Pilulaw and Michael, who openly shared their traditional culture.

I learned that the Chumash included 450 different plants in their diet. Their acorn harvest from the oak woodland matched the caloric equivalent per acre of a monoculture wheat field. Although they worked the groves to boost their yield, the ecosystem remained intact: there were still deer, bear, rabbit, herbs, tubers, fruits, pine nuts, mushrooms, and medicinal plants. Nearby salt and freshwater habitats pushed the harvestable bounty over the top. In the sand dunes lie deep middens where, for thousands of years, tools were sharpened and clams shucked, testifying to a long lost abundance. During the 9,000 years of continuous occupation of the same villages, the ecosystem evolved from pines to oaks as the glaciers receded. When the Spaniards arrived in the eighteenth century, an estimated 85 villages were home to 25,000 people. Top level predators such as grizzlies and mountain lions helped maintain balance. The Chumash had a sustainable lifestyle.

"To a traditional Indian, all things are related," Pilulaw said. She continued, "As a woman of the original people of this land, as a Chumash elder, I walk this land, and my ancestors and those who are still coming walk with me."

This concept directly guides our alignment with Design Parameter 1 — no losers. Sure, each carrot or deer loses its life. But over time, peoples, species, and ecological systems are offered the respect of a relative and are free from domination.

Design Parameter 2, that each action could be taken by all, was practically implemented among the Chumash by two behaviors:

1. Not amassing personal wealth. As one elder said, "The Chumash go fishing if they are hungry." When the land is fat, there is no need to hoard. Healthy ecology is security. Tribal culture is based upon sharing and cooperation.
2. Not over-populating the region. Many factors contributed to the stable population, including higher infant mortality, shorter life spans, use of herbs and practices that reduce fertility (including breastfeeding), lack of poverty, and high female status (matriarchal culture).

The Chumash's 9,000-year relationship with their homeland is testimony to the spirit of Design Parameter 3, long-term sustainability. To Pilulaw, "seven generations" meant that her actions should ensure that all relations persist seven generations into the future. From what we know about the Chumash, past and present, it would seem they have succeeded.

By contrast, in a little over 200 years, the Europeans decimated the Chumash. Hills and dales have been flattened and stripped of 90 percent of their forest cover. The entire biome has been replaced with alien grasses, grapes for wine, cats, dogs, and too many cows. A Forest Service employee told a Sierra Club group that if you went to bed before cows arrived on the scene and woke to 200 years of their impact, you'd think an atomic bomb had gone off.

When I first arrived in Chumash territory, not having an inter-generational memory of the region, I thought it was a pastoral paradise. As I learned more about the history of the region, I began to wonder what a fully intact ecosystem would look like — one where the full range of large predators was still intact. I wanted to know first hand if bears, wolves, cougars, coyotes, and wolverine were as problematic and dangerous as my culture, including men much stronger than me, had claimed. I theorized that getting along with these species would uncover more secrets to the three design parameters.

THE MUIR TRAIL

My buddy Dave telephoned one September day with an invite to join a 13-day walk on the Muir Trail, from Lake Edison to Mt. Whitney in California. I was after a non-linear approach to the three design parameters and a direct experience learning from nature; in Chumash country, I had learned of the vision quest, a solo time in the wilderness without food. On this trip, there would be four guys and lots of food, but also plenty of space to quiet the mind and be open to visions. In my own way, this journey was framed around the four phases of a vision quest:

1. To separate from one's daily routine and go into the wilderness.
2. To embark on an epic journey, either metaphorical or real.
3. To allow for a ceremonial death and rebirth — a death of ideas, actions, or beliefs no longer appropriate for one's new world.
4. To integrate one's reborn self back into the community.

For this quest, my intention was to relax the rational, linear mind and open myself up to visions of global living. This was the polar opposite to the linear design I'd learned as an engineer.

We slipped out of the city under Orion, with a choir of crickets. Out of the coast range, we added our CO_2 to the foggy bottom of the San Joaquin valley, John Muir's Serengeti, now fully under the tiller with rows upon rows of monocrops — no mistake why Edward Abbey said the plow has probably done more harm — in the long run — than the sword. We made Fresno by first light, then snaked our way up through oaks and manzanita into the Sierra foothills — Shaver Lake, Big Creek, and on to our trailhead.

In the morning chill, we hoisted backpacks and six-packs onto our backs and set off — separation. In ten minutes, I was sweaty. After a half-hour, my quads burned. After an hour my hips screamed. By hour three, I began to have second thoughts. Holy smokes, my epic journey had begun. Hour four, I almost couldn't walk — and stopped to rest. Dave looped back, "Let's ride this thing up higher," he said, seeing the belt around my hips. In the last hour, my legs felt better, but my hips were bruised. We arrived at the camp, dropped the packs and popped a beer.

A splendid afternoon drifted in filtered sun. Before nightfall, we secured our camp. I tied a rock to the end of a long rope and tossed it over a 20-foot high limb, then hoisted up 35 pounds of food, every toiletry, and anything scented. I watched shooting stars from my bivvy and promised after each, just one more, then I'd remove my glasses and go to sleep. A long, deep sleep ensued. In the morning, the scolding of a Douglas squirrel broke my slumber — a bear had gotten someone's food. I wrestled out of my bivy and, in a half-stupor, stumbled toward my hang. "Ah-man!" I said, "Oats a-la-bear-spit." I tracked the crumbs and packages through the forest to the chewed open stuff-sack. One hundred percent lost — well, at least I was saved from 13 days of agony! To my secret relief, there was clearly no way I could continue the trek now.

I cleaned up the mess and the guys fed me breakfast. The conversation centered on bears as we lingered around the fire. I got a well-deserved chewing-out — each "problem human" creates a "problem bear," soon to be shot. The guys showed me a proper hang — higher up, further out, on a live limb, no other adjacent limbs that mama bear or baby bear could swat from.

As the morning's gloom lifted, the towering trees elevated my spirit. I sat by the creek and opened John Muir's *The Mountains of California*. Relaxed, I fancied a scene from his account below the foot of Moraine Lake.

> There was a field of wild rye, growing in magnificent waving bunches six to eight feet high, bearing heads from six to twelve inches long. Rubbing out some grains, I found

them about five eighths of an inch long, dark-colored and sweet. Indian women were gathering it in baskets, bending down large handfuls, beating it out, and fanning it in the wind. They were quite picturesque, coming through the rye, as one caught glimpses of them here and there, in the winding lanes and openings, with splendid tufts arching above their heads, while their incessant chat and laughter showed their heedless joy.

I shut the book and could feel the presence of those women. My relief dissolved and suddenly I felt determined to do this trip — to understand the world as the Chumash or Dineh did. I hiked out and in eight hours returned with a full pack of food.

In the morning we were off. The body pains grew as the trail switched back and forth up through a welcoming open forest of massive proportion. Up and up — across clear creeks and thickets and back in amongst the trees. In the noontime sun we slogged up a dusty gully along a powerful river — icy tumbling cascades, pools, meanders and rapids. At a waterfall, we dropped our packs. In the roar, we remained silent and spread out on the flowing granite: ate, read, wrote in journals, or snoozed. Hot and sweaty, I submerged myself in a pool. After a nap, I hopped upstream barefoot, from boulder to boulder, among dragonflies, wildflowers, and trout. Rested and refueled, we continued our upward tramp as gradients of life unfolded — smaller, tightly spaced tamarack, pine, and spruce appearing as we neared the sub-alpine. Views expanded, air thinned. Peaks and ridges, chocolate brown to granite gray to bleached tan, rose up singing from ribbons of pine-clad avalanche chutes and richly forested valley bottoms. Higher still, we entered the alpine area, above the treeline, where stiff grasses met the lips of boulder-strewn dark blue lakes. We set camp for the night.

I had joined a well-oiled machine. Up at 5:30 a.m. Fire made, breakfast downed, packed and walking by 7:00 a.m. Day by day we marched along, fished the lakes, slept in the meadows, gazed awestruck at the alpine wonderland. A week in, I felt a shift. A calmness, an alertness, replaced my energetic being — as if the mountains inhabited me — or we merged — and I was now tuned to Earth's rhythms. That buzz of electrical energy, machines, people, and lawn mowers that had infused virtually every moment of my 31 years had gone quiet. Now I felt inexplicably different. It was my first taste of life in accord with natural law.

The bold California bears made several more attempts at our food. I was told to sleep near the hang with a pile of rocks, ready to defend it. If grizzlies were still here, aggression would be a death wish, but black bears can usually be chased off. On the ninth night, a bear was up in the tree after my chocolate bars — right above me. Broken branches fell as I hoped it would give up. It was midnight. I got up and shone the light into a pair of glowing eyes on the limb my rope straddled. I sent a few rocks sailing and it climbed higher up the tree and waited. For a half-hour, I sat silently with the light out. My heart pounded. The bear slowly began to descend the tree. When it was 20 feet above the ground, it suddenly dropped at near free-fall speed — and hit the ground running. On day 11, I quietly watched from twenty paces as a big dusty brown bear ambled through our camp. I felt a primal shiver, hairs on end — I was alive!

After twelve days of altitude acclimatization, we arrived at the base of Mt. Whitney, hung the last of the food, and headed for the summit. Fueled by adrenaline, we sailed up a steep route on the west flank. Near the summit, each step revealed another peak, until at 14,494 feet, a panorama encircled us. Muir's "range of light" glistened like a snake, from the south to the north. To the west, layers upon folded layers of mountains extended to the horizon — with the Kern gorge below — stunning, determined, and seaward bound. To the east, across the parched Saline Valley, rose the Panamint Mountains, surreal and inanimate, hiding Death Valley. After laying down a topographical map to identify peaks, I soaked up the sun in silence.

I reflected on how, for 31 years, I had lived in fear — fear of the wild, fear of the elements, fear of the bear, fear of not having enough. It was time for the ceremonial death of these fears. I visualized my fears as rose-hips. In the autumn sun they had shriveled — their essential goodness reabsorbed into the tree of life. As all of nature cycles from birth to death to rebirth, I felt a death wave come over me. I knew now that much of my life's fears stemmed from ignorance. Fear kept me separate from nature, but I knew now that in order to be fully me, I needed to be part of nature. Another fear faded, harder to describe, but it was the fear of my own death. Each rotted tree fed new life. I envisioned that I too could nourish life, even after physical death. My place in the big scheme of things was beginning to make more sense.

LEARNING FROM KERALA

Bombay — 2 a.m. I'm lying in bed with a man I met an hour ago. In the dark, we are talking about life. How did I get here? Well ... the young woman seated beside me on the plane invited me home to get six hours of sleep before continuing on to Kerala. After a word with her dad at the baggage claim, he put his arm around me as if I were his son and walked me to their car. As the reunion wound down, bed space was offered with her brother, a mechanical engineer my own age. India's hospitality was immediately revealed, but I had come to learn about sustainability.

Located on the southwestern tip of the Indian subcontinent, Kerala features lush mountains, lagoons, and sandy tropical beaches. Within an area the size of Vancouver Island, Kerala shoehorns in thirty million people, the entire population of Canada. The people are well-educated, live long lives, have healthy children, and small families. And their per-capita annual income is sixty times less than in North America.

Now here was a place one might find clues to Design Parameter 2, which specified that "each step could be taken by everyone, everywhere; not just by those with privilege."

I first learned about the "Kerala Phenomenon" from Dr. Will Alexander, professor emeritus at Cal-Poly in San Luis Obispo. Dr. Alexander retired from professorship in 1988 and founded a research effort through EarthWatch of Massachusetts to get to the bottom of this phenomenon. He led a unique inquiry. Teams of researchers would ask; what 21st century survival skills can be learned from one of the lowest income cultures on Earth?

Dr. Alexander realized Kerala's uniqueness; how it held lessons for not only the world's poor countries, hungry with needs, but also, for the world's wealthy, hungry with wants. A fellowship was offered for an activist to join Dr. Alexander for a month-long project in February of

1993 — all expenses paid. The activist was to bring back sustainability ideas that could be implemented in high-impact countries. I put in my application and was selected to go.

Dr. Alexander presented it this way: "Kerala's fertility rate and quality of life indicators are similar to those of the first world. At the same time, the indicator 'Gross National Product (GNP) per capita' equates with third world consumption." Social and political scientists and medical doctors had begun studying Kerala's riddle in earnest — how can they get so much from so little? Figure 3-1 gives a quick look at the quality of life indicators for Kerala, India and the US.

Figure 3.1: KERALA INDICATORS

	USA	Kerala	India
Population in Millions	292	31.8	1,069
Birth Rate per 1,000	16	17	29
Quality of Life Indicators			
Infant Mortality Rate	7	12	65
Life Expectancy, Male	74	68	63
Life Expectancy, Female	80	74	64
Adult Literacy Rate	96%	91%	44%
Resource Consumption Indicator: Gross Domestic Product (GDP) per capita	$34,260	$566	$460

We estimated the dollar figure for Kerala by multiplying the State Government's 2000 per capita stat domestic product figure of Rs 19,461 (GOK 2001:19) by 43, the approximate number of rupees per dollar during that year. We then added 25%, the highest estimated figure, to compensate for overseas remittances

The Kerala phenomenon can't be easily summed up. There are too many facets — historical, social, political, and biophysical — that have contributed to its success. For starters, Kerala demonstrated a way out of poverty other than increased incomes and industrialization. The "demographic transition" model of development holds that poor countries should move from "third world," "undeveloped," rural economies, to "first world," "developed," industrial economies. And the faster the better to avoid being caught in the "demographic trap;" a second world of garbage-filled streets, diesel smoke, and poverty. Often, proponents of industrial "development" have a resource exploitation agenda. The low-income nations become indebted to multinational corporations and the World Bank for "mega projects," then pay down the debt by selling minerals or timber and raising cash crops for export while poverty at home grows.

Kerala demonstrates an alternative to McWorld. It has remained rural while developing health and education to equal that of many "first world" nations.

Kerala's intellectuals are quick to point out the problems their state faces, such as 25 percent unemployment, little economic growth, and few in-state opportunities for their educated masses. A healthy debate continues over how skewed their per capita GNP data might be due to income from work abroad. Issues related to globalization are challenging Kerala's hard-won successes. But what I will share with you are first hand experiences with the citizens of Kerala, and practices we can learn from.

. . . . .

After landing in Kerala's capital, Trivandrum, I sputtered out of the city by auto-rickshaw between ox-carts, elephants, and fast, smoking buses. On the outskirts, rows of women sat before mounds of stones making road gravel with a hammer. Soon we entered a shady lane where fragrances of moist earth, forest, and blossom mixed with my driver's clean scent. As a lane opened to fields, a bare, muscled back worked alone in a sea of ribbed chocolate earth. A distant stick figure grew into a woman with a head-basket naturally balanced. Like a carnival ride, we raced through a small village of neat thatched-roof homes and gardens, one vehicle, hundreds of people and animals. Small shops were open to the streets: a tailor ready to stitch, snack stands with bananas and pineapples, and of course, tea shops. A boy smiled from a roadside bike shop as he pumped up a tire. Another boy trued a wheel — we exchanged waves.

After an hour the ride ended in the busy seaside town of Kovalam Beach. I had two days to rest before the research project began. I found a simple beachfront room, put on swim trunks, jogged across the sandy beach, and dove into the curling waves of the Arabian Sea.

I had just witnessed a stream of what appeared to be sustainable activities. This world was primarily human-powered. By contrast, the city of Trivandrum was, like most, a human-centered mess; the dirty fuels and garbage gave it that "second world" feel. Now in a village, light living dominated. A flock of friendly children approached and said, "Hi mister, one pen," or "One rupee" and held out an open palm. I searched through a Malayalam English phrase book, then said, "Ningal-day per enda." (What is your name)? They burst into laughter. I pointed to nose, waves, egrets, and houses and wrote names in my journal. An entourage took shape. We arrived at an outdoor mosque in this small fishing village and I said, "Moslem?" They nodded. Then I pointed to each of the eight boys and girls who remained. Two nodded and said, "Ondu" (Yes); the six others shook out a no. I'd read that Kerala was unique in religious diversity — 20 percent Moslem, 20 percent Christian, and 60 percent Hindu — now I was curious.

· · · · ·

The tour wiggled between thatched homes to another monument, again outdoors. This sacred place had an old shade tree and reeds delineated the area. We played the pointing game. Four nodded to "Hindu?" In a third direction, we came to an outdoor church, complete with a white cross. Two nodded to "Christian?" Close to the 20, 20, 60 split. Our project had floated in limbo two weeks earlier when violence between Hindus and Moslems broke out in northern India. I flipped through the phrase book ... there it was. I said "Kootakari?" (Friends?), and scribed an inclusive circle around the group with my finger. They all laughed, nodded and shouted "Kootakari," repeating it like a choir to correct my pronunciation. I held up fists as if to fight and they all laughed and shouted, "No! No! Kootakari!"

Here were boys and girls together, totally unsupervised, free, self-confident, and playful. Spontaneously, and without fear, they were skilled tour guides and teachers for several hours. They treated each other respectfully and never quarreled. The Dineh children at Big Mountain were like this too. "No TV?" I wondered. My concept of human nature turned upside-down. Could the peaceful nature of these children be a clue to Kerala's success?

The group whittled down to three boys who took me to a large wooden spinning wheel used to turn coconut-husk fibers into string. The strings are then woven into nets, ropes, and mats for export. They set the wooden, bicycle-esque technology smoothly into motion. Here was Gandhi's Khadi movement, symbolized by that glorious spinning wheel. A nationwide, mass-movement to boycott the brutal British imperialists by spinning their own cloth or "khadi" — like the great salt march to the sea, as political as it is practical. Village self-reliance, cottage industry, "swadeshi" — here it was, still alive, 50 years after India's independence and Gandhi's death. Hundreds of coconut husks were netted and submerged for ten months in the lagoon. The fibers then separated easily from the pulpy material and were dried in the sun to a golden fluff, ready to be spun. After the boys let me have a turn spinning, the call came for dinner and we parted with a, "Peen-nay-ca-num," (See you later).

· · · · ·

I slept lightly from the heat and excitement, but woke refreshed and went out for an exquisite vegan breakfast. To eat low on the food chain here is the norm. Most Indians are vegetarians, although fish and meat are eaten by some. Afterwards, I walked the village pathways, a tropical paradise with a crowded 20th century edge that lessened as I ventured into the hills. On a bluff, I looked down at the next beach away from the tourists. The children played naked in the water. Men loaded nets onto double-ender, oar-powered boats. Women filled urns from a fountain and carried them home on their heads. Three men gathered coconuts. The one in the tree sliced the nuts and green fronds free with a machete. On the ground, another gathered the nuts and fronds into piles. The third made sure no one got bonked.

Across the street, six women sat together in the shade and wove the dried fronds into panels, a sizable stack taking form. I didn't have to move to see the entire process. The raw material, green fronds, were pruned, gathered, and aged in the shade till brown, then exported across the street to be woven. The finished panels formed a roof here, home siding there, and a small bath hut around back. A few were exported to the beach to shade the nets, boats, or tourists, and to the village entrance to shade the women breaking rocks. Old decayed panels were used to mulch the ground, building the soil and reducing erosion.

Forward thinking Europeans have formulated a business policy which holds manufacturers responsible for their products, from cradle to grave. Here there is no grave — what designer William McDonough refers to as cradle to cradle, waste = food. There are no clearcuts, no factories, no fossil fuels, no insurance, and no marketing. These processes took only the fruits and pruned fronds. For six years, I was a process engineer in a high-tech factory in New York and designed manufacturing systems. Now, I was in a real-world sustainable-living factory. I linked yesterday's spun coconut fibers to today's freed nuts. I had seen husks go into the fire to heat a curry pot at the restaurant and tasted the coconut milk and meat in two meals. Fuel, food, shelter, fishing nets, ropes — all from one tree — and they never killed the tree!

I had heard that the coconut tree was not native to Kerala and that its introduction usurped a highly diverse and productive jungle that the indigenous peoples once inhabited. But even to me, a self-proclaimed deep ecologist, their bioregional economy surpassed anything I had ever seen in North America — by a long shot. Just think of what it takes to manufacture asphalt roof tiles, vinyl or wood siding, the metal and polyester for an umbrella, or a PVC tarp, all products this deep ecologist uses at home. The human-scaled local production I witnessed was village-based self-reliance in action.

· · · · ·

After years of mass movements toward independence, in 1939 Gandhi concluded, "You cannot build non-violence on a factory civilization, but it can be built on self-contained villages." In light of the massive protests against the World Trade Organization in 1999 in Seattle, and the US pre-emptive war agenda, Gandhi's clarity is still worthy of serious contemplation.

The bond between the rich and poor that develops from shared manual labor really hit home. In California, I'd never seen a white person in the fields, only Mexicans. At my engineering job at Vandenberg Air Force Base, near the factory farms of Guadalupe, I'd heard many racist statements toward Mexicans, yet few complaints about the cheap produce. Housework is looked down on, something for poor and middle-class women and servants. With an engineering degree, I too believed I was above manual work. But here, the scale was such that the work looked fun. I strolled on.

After lunch, I encountered eight men building a breakwater. A rope cradle was attached to two strong, eight-foot-long bamboo poles, one on either side of a waist-high boulder. From a squat, they rose together, levitating the boulder. They walked it out on the breakwater, slow and steady, and lowered it into place.

The elegant simplicity of cooperation and hard work was poetry in motion. This is what you do when you don't have a bulldozer, don't have cheap gas, and don't have a permanent wartime economy. These intelligent, creative solutions were outside of my box — a box that had begun to decompose.

. . . . .

The next day the research team assembled. A bus journey took us 15 miles inland to Vellanad. This small village is home to Mitraniketan, a center for rural self-reliance. We met with its founder, K. Viswanathan, a visionary who traveled widely, studying community movements. Viswanathan understood both the aberrations and the beauty of Kerala, and he inspired us to learn from what doesn't work as well as from what does. He urged us to not be afraid to experiment.

One night at his modest home, with the head of India's environmental programs present, we discussed the sad state of world affairs. As the conversation spiraled into negativity, I saw his irritation building. Finally, he trembled and said, "Wait a minute! We already have enough darkness! Adding more has no effect. Ahhh … to light a candle … let this be your life." His words struck a chord of truth. I wanted my time in Kerala to focus on solutions — how can high-income countries reduce their impact *and* recapture the joy of living?

I met my host family, as well as my full-time bilingual cultural associate. My research task was to glean sustainability skills applicable in the US by becoming part of the family, asking questions and participating in daily life.

Theories

Over the following weeks we met with leading doctors, social scientists, revolutionaries, tribal peoples, women's activists, historians and environmentalists — all from Kerala. Most offered sharp critiques of public policy and each had a pet theory to explain Kerala's successes and failures. Here are a few of the theories to explain their successes:

1. **High female status** in Kerala has contributed to a positive feedback loop. With women active in the allocation of the necessities for life, few have unmet needs; thus, life-quality measures improve. Once out of poverty, and in free control of their own fertility, women often choose to have fewer children. And with small families, each child receives the love and care they need. "Fatal Daughter Syndrome" is a systematic deprivation of food, health care, and education to girls. This syndrome plagues patriarchal, low-income countries, while Kerala families tend to be matrilineal and matrilocal, and value girls and boys equally.

   In a healthy society, there will be about 104 girls to 100 boys, as is the case in Kerala. In India, there are 93 girls to 100 boys, Pakistan 92 girls, and China 94 girls.[2] Dr. Alexander explains, "The 11-woman advantage in Kerala tells the essential story."[3] If all of India had Kerala's birth and child death rates, there would be 1.5 million fewer infant deaths in the country every year, and a dramatic reduction in population growth.

2. **Grassroots democracy** in Kerala included the free and fair election of a communist government in 1957. Their platform was land reform and the elimination of caste restrictions. Steady progress in

caste elimination was made. In 1969, the world's most successful land reform laws were passed, and 1.5 million landless peasants became entitled to the land they had worked. In 1987, a continuation of reforms returned 75 percent of state power to local decision-makers, putting in place one of the strongest grassroots democracies on Earth. People experienced the benefits of participation — democracy worked. More than 90 percent of eligible voters turn out for elections.[5]

Since 1957, voters have elected varying political parties, but support for the rural poor is steady. The communists did not try to control the means of production; instead, they created a level playing field not dominated by big business or government. More importantly, they worked to help the poorest of the poor. The result was a more equitable society and a drastic reduction in poverty. Thirty years after land reform, self-reliant, hard-working families have a secure home and land to grow food to partially feed themselves and to sell any excess in the market — the polar opposite to trickle down economics.

3. **A clear social agenda** was aimed at helping the poor and disenfranchised. Fair price shops, where staples are available to the poorest households at fixed prices, are within walking distance of every home in Kerala — 13,000 shops in all. Education and health care consume 65 percent of government spending. There are 174 arts and science colleges, 41 with government support and 133 privately financed. There were more females than males enrolled in the arts and sciences pre-degree, degree, and graduate courses in 1991 — a total of 82,538 women and 73,516 men.[6] Kerala has more libraries than the rest of India combined, nearly 5,000 in all. Health care centers are within three miles of nearly every home.[7] A self-employment scheme makes loans to individuals to start small businesses; the payment schedule is flexible and if the loan is fully repaid in 5 years, and the business is still open, a bonus of 25 percent of the original loan amount is gifted to the borrower. The self-employed pay little or no tax and have few regulations. Larger employers have to pay fair wages to men and women. Workers have the right to organize, and many unions exist.

The societal solutions discussed above — gender equality, grass-roots democracy, and a comprehensive social net — are all corner stones of a sustainable society. Kerala's public policy embodies practical, simple, and fair programs that could be adapted to local and regional governments worldwide.

Experiences

The psychiatrist R.D. Laing said, "We do not need theories so much as the experience that is the source of the theory."[8] One day I returned to my host family after a day of lectures to find Selvanose at the mortar grinding rice. A candle was lit in full daylight in the backyard. Shirt off, dress slacks still on, he quietly said, "Hi, Jim." I sensed a sacredness to this time, returned the greeting, and went to relax in my room. I later asked Molly why they don't take their rice to the junction where a machine will grind it in minutes. She said, "The quality is not the same as with the mortar and pestle."

I was starting to get a picture different from the ones in my college history books. Did ancient, tribal humanity suffer in a cruel world of toil, always hungry, huddled in caves, waiting to get eaten by some wild animal, or did they live on a fat, wild land, and see manual work as "bread labor" — a sacred part of daily life? In the ancient Hindu poem, the Bahagavad Gita, bread labor is a divine law which says that providing one's sustenance is a spiritual act of love; Leo Tolstoy and Gandhi both believed that bread labor creates the conditions necessary for a non-violent society independent of global markets.

One evening, four men in their 20s came by, as they often did. Around a candle on this still night, we talked and joked. Each of them had a repertoire of riddles and magic tricks, most of which stumped me. Along the street, candles lit neighboring porch steps, as families and friends closed the day together. I asked my new friends why Kerala had such a high quality of life compared to the rest of India, and one said, "People here like peace and a happy life." Another chimed in, "Kerala has a cooperative mind." This phrase seemed to summarize what I had been experiencing. The cooperative mind inhabited the 20 homes that surrounded the village green in our own distant past, where no laws or fences were needed. Each homeowner simply took their share and was satisfied. Consciously or unconsciously, this is what the people of Kerala do. If the entire world lived at their consumption level, 60 percent of the world's bioproductive space would be wild.[9]

I had always heard that the entire world wanted the American Dream. So I asked the young men what "things" they dreamed of. One said, "Maybe a bicycle." I probed, "Would you like a car?" They all chimed, "No, no." In the last decade, TV ownership rose from 0 to 13 percent in Kerala. In Jerry Mander's book, *In the Absence of the Sacred*,[10] he documents an organized resistance to the introduction of TV by the Dene of northern Alberta (Canada). Within years of its arrival, Cindy Gilday from the Native Women's Association had this to say:

> The effect has been to glamorize behaviors and values that are poisonous to life up here. Our traditions have a lot to do with survival. Cooperation, sharing, and non-materialism are the only ways that people can live here. TV always seems to present values opposite to those. I used to be a schoolteacher and when TV came to the villages, I saw an immediate change. People lost interest in the native stories, legends, and languages, which are really important because they teach people how to live.

In my brief time in Kerala, I saw evidence that television was beginning to have this effect. Time will tell if their culture is strong enough to survive the onslaught of advertising.

Practical Lessons

After learning about the radical reforms at a societal and individual level in Kerala, I was faced with the question: What practical lessons could North Americans learn from Kerala — beyond dismantling our televisions? Could any of these experiences be used to help fashion a sustainable life back home?

The Cooperative Mind

The cultivation of a cooperative mind is the most central lesson Kerala offers the individual. Kerala has systematically broken apart caste hierarchies over the last 100 years, and improving the welfare of the most downtrodden has become a state focus. During this same time, class stratification in high-income countries has become more pronounced. A 30-to-1 income disparity in 1960 between the 20 percent richest and poorest worldwide has expanded to 74 to 1 in 1998. It is unlikely congress will ever legislate that we tame our appetites and only take what we need from the global potluck; hence, it is up to each individual to voluntarily take less income to implement the cooperative mind.

Imagine this scenario. What would happen if every worker were to offer their services at a price as close to the average global income as practical given their particularities, such as family size, geographic location, etc.? In essence, this means setting the price for one's products or services according to their needs, instead of attempting to maximize profits (what the market would bear or as high of a salary as you can negotiate). Costs would come down. Each household could work just enough to support their basic needs, including a reasonable level of long-term security. By having lower incomes, individuals would consume less. As product prices fall, others can work less and earn less. The entire economy would gently slow down, yet everyone would still have their needs met. It simply takes each person limiting how much income they take and how much they consume. I'm not really suggesting communism. But I am suggesting a voluntary taming of the appetite. There's 6.2 billion people behind me in that line.

Take for example, the cost of a haircut in Kerala: 10 cents. The shop I visited was an 8' x 10' room. The barber's home life is materially simple, and at the end of each month, his family's needs are met. His family also grows food and he and his wife have sideline jobs. If he wanted an American lifestyle, 60 to 100 times more materially rich, his haircut would have to cost $6 or more, instead of 10 cents. When I charge beyond my needs, I cause others to charge more or work longer hours to afford my product. This begins an upward spiral of costs. Those who don't play the game lose, and inequity grows.

Earth Efficiency

When the world seemed infinite, wasting time was of greater concern than wasting resources. As we sail beyond the limits of what the Earth can sustain, the people of Kerala offer an alternative: Earth efficiency. In this New World Paradigm, humanity seeks to secure the most life quality from the fewest units of Earth used. In the Old World Paradigm individuals maximize consumer goods or wealth, while minimizing their investment of time.

If our designers, planners, and engineers shifted from a focus on time efficiency to Earth efficiency, and unleashed their creativity in this new paradigm, radical reductions would follow. And if we chose personal purchasing criteria for Earth-efficient products and services, they would tend to be simple, safe, readily available, local, low cost, ecologically friendly, used, recycled. These purchase criteria are easy to meet now because of the amount of perfectly good stuff thrown away or available second hand. While we still swim in excess, we have the leisure to develop truly sustainable local production of necessities. As we spend less, we need to earn less, thus better sharing the available employment, resources, and wealth.

Bioregionalism

In Kerala, many of the products were made locally from materials that came from the bioregion. For instance, while I was there, I commissioned a shirt to be sewn at a shop. The tailor worked in a 10' x 15' room, cleanly whitewashed, with two treadle machines, a table, four chairs, and a single rod to hang garments in progress. He brought me a tea from the vendor next door, took my measurements, and scribbled the amount of material needed on a scrap of paper. Several doors down, I purchased a hand woven (khadi) fabric made in Kerala, at a 20 percent discount (government subsidy to promote small business). Two helpers sized me up in detail. We chatted, laughed, and I returned in two days to a great-fitting shirt. The cost? 75 cents for the material and 75 cents for the stitching. Why so cheap? Like the barber, their shop and homes are simple. Because of the local raw material and labor sourcing, no transportation energy was required and no resources were consumed in advertisement and promotion. Here in North America, when we seek out bioregional products, we support those bioneers who are creating the alternatives to globalization. Protesting globalization is important, but so is living the solution.

This point took a while to sink into my process-engineer brain. I had worked for 12 years in manufacturing facilities and had taken the industrial approach as a given. Why does a shirt like that cost the American consumer $30? Strap on your seatbelt for a mini-tour of the shirt-making process in North America. Hovering over the cotton fields we see pesticides sprayed from planes, and chemical fertilizers applied with tractors. We see irrigation systems, large fuel tanks, machinery, buildings, and a big farmhouse. Two cars, two pickups, and two off-road vehicles are in the driveway. The 2,000-square-foot garage is full of tools, machines, and snowmobiles. We now fly to the corporate headquarters of the insurance company for the tractor, where we see executives behind oak desks who fly first class to meetings, eating business meals at fancy restaurants, lodging at five-star hotels. Next we see the storage, distribution and marketing for the tractor alone. Adding still more to the final cost of the factory-produced shirt are additional overhead demands including advertising, insurance, financing, and accounting.

In Kerala, most of this flow chart does not exist. The tailors are fair and offer a good product. When I passed by their storefront wearing my new shirt, we all felt good. A pleased customer was their advertising. They had no insurance, no telephone, no computer, and being self-employed, paid no tax. And, their work environment was healthy.

The Kani

I was eager to meet with Kerala's indigenous tribes, who continue to co-exist within the jungle, to see what I might learn from them. With an interpreter, I made two trips to Kani villages and made friends with Chendren, a man in his 20s. I returned a third time for a week. Chendren still knew how to hunt and gather. His village was spotlessly clean. Tidy thatched-roof homes stood amid a tropical evergreen rainforest. The creeks ran clear. The forest, I was told, contained 100 different tree species, eight times more than a typical North American forest. The birdcalls and sounds were so richly varied as to make the rest of rural-urban Kerala appear barren by comparison. Here I witnessed land and people in true harmony — before the domination of nature.

But the Kani are under pressure. Encroachment by loggers and farmers has forced them up against the mountains; areas where they had traditionally hunted and which are now protected as parks. Churches, schools and bars popped up at the interface — each looking for converts. Land schemes deeded parcels to tribal families, and then swindlers came in to exploit their holdings.

A 69-year-old grandmother, Chellamma, said through my interpreter, "As children, we had free range of the forests to gather tubers, nuts, and fruits — whatever we needed. We drank from the streams. The waters were very clean. We would sow wild seeds in the valleys for grain. Now there is a problem because each has a plot, and the areas for gathering are spread out. Now, people are forced to grow food and cash crops." With "private property," the areas for gathering become off-limits to others. She continued, "We are no longer allowed to enter the national forests. The wild pigs come down and dig up the tapioca roots." I asked if they had problems with the pigs before they started planting. She said, "They ate the forest tubers, like us, but there was no problem."

This experience shed light on our fight against nature. Monoculture agriculture creates what I have come to call the "candy-store effect." Native vegetation, the food of wildlife, is cleared to raise dense rows of ready-to-eat fruits and grains — "candy" to wildlife. Raids start, defense begins, and the battle is on. Wildlife often loses.

I asked Chellamma if she taught the children Kani culture. She said, "The children are away at school all day. When they return home, they're not interested in the tribal ways, hearing stories, or singing. The children have no time to go to the forest because of school." My time with Chellamma brought into question the whole idea of literacy programs and factory-type schools. For thousands of years, humans were educated in extended families. What is the effect of being separated from family and land and segregated by age during those formative years? Touted as romantic, to see children on their way to school, to me seemed sad, as were my own 13 years in what I considered to be prison.

If the only alternative is forced, colonial, factory, plantation or coolie labor, school is clearly better. But in these tribal areas, that was not the case. A child might wander the forests with Chellamma or Chendren learning healing herbs, wild foods, basket making, songs, poems, home construction, and spiritual practices. Chendren's father was an Ayurvedic doctor who knew hundreds of plants, and traveled throughout a wide region of jungle, gathering herbs to keep the villagers healthy. Before the age of 12, Chendren had extensive forest literacy. He was not plucked to attend a boarding school until his teens, where he stayed for five years. His older brother, Apicherrikan, called the school "tricksters." Education in rows has trade-offs; now, the tribal children are losing their forest literacy.

. . . . .

The Kani were just now facing the same situation that the Chumash and Dineh had 20 years after contact with the Europeans. Luckily, the Kani aren't facing outright warfare. However, swindlers, alcohol, factory-type schools and the clash between domination of nature and harmony with nature are eroding their traditional culture. Here, I had witnessed how people can live among elephants and lions — large, powerful, wild animals — without major problems; and how even a small monoculture of tapioca roots created conflicts.

Leaving Kerala

After my fellowship in Kerala had ended, I decided to spend two months in the Himalaya. On my way, the jungle called once more. I had learned that 10 years ago, the people of Kerala organized and defeated a dam project that threatened an intact evergreen rainforest called Silent Valley. This fact upset the notion that only affluent people can afford to concern themselves with ecology. Here, people making $300 a year defeated the proposed dam and created a multi-state biosphere preserve.

Once there, I met Somadas, a smartly dressed professional, who spoke good English and had a gentle, friendly way about him. He took me to meet his wife and two boys at their 12' x 14' home, a clean mud and brick structure with a thatched roof. They had no furniture or appliances, and all four slept on dried grass mats. Somadas' small pile of neatly folded dress clothes were next to similar piles for the three others. The kitchen had two earthen fireplaces molded into the floor to support cooking pots. Their total possessions could perhaps fill a few backpacks per person, yet there was no poverty here.

Tribals were considered below untouchables only 50 years ago in Kerala, and still are throughout India. In the context of Indian history, the union of Somadas and his wife is as much a miracle as Nelson Mandela becoming president of South Africa. Somadas explained that the tribes are matriarchal, so he joined her family. In this way his wife would be with her kin, who could best support her in child bearing and rearing. He said the women here have equal status.

In his wife's hamlet, we encountered the Mupan, or hereditary leader. Lean and muscled at 65, he stood up from his work on a stone building to offer a broad smile. The Mupan joined us for a stroll. I asked him how his people were doing. With sad eyes he said, "Our people have no way to live. Forests taken. Villagers encroaching all the time. The men leave to earn 50 rupees a day (US $1.00) in coolie labor. The little land we have, we have few options but to exploit. Traditions are out the window." I asked about their traditions. He pointed to the rugged peaks that rise from the jungle. "The mountain is the god of the tribal people — these are where our stories and songs come from."

Later Somadas explained that the Mupan is a gentle leader — no richer than the people are, just an honest family man. If problems arise, he will talk it out and maybe offer a punishment if necessary. If problems arise between hamlets, the Mupans will call a special meeting; otherwise, there is no government above the local hamlet.

· · · · ·

I have been warned, "Don't romanticize natives — their cultures are full of oppression." That may be true in some places, but it hasn't been my experience. Over the past 14 years I have lived, in total, a year's time in a dozen native communities. I traveled on foot or by bike, and slept outdoors or in their homes. I have seen some ugly things, most related to alcohol, outsider oppression, and recovery from genocide. But I have never felt threatened, and have received amazing generosity and hospitality. What has grown inside me is solidarity with their sovereignty issues. Whether tribals have anything to teach us, whether we like or dislike their ways, is not the point. They have an intrinsic right to decide their own future — but to do that they need their land base returned in large, generous amounts. To accept that tribal cultures should eventually be assimilated into modern society is ethnocentric violence; and selfishly, we may lose the very wisdom that could save us.

My day with Somadas clarified how simple and healthy life can be. Seeing him in his dress slacks, living as a tribal, opened a door for me. His willingness to embrace simple living and, after 20 years, to come to see its virtues, helped me realize that I can choose how I want to live.

. . . . .

From Kerala I took a train to the Himalaya to wander the wilderness. I needed to integrate the Kerala phenomena. In late May, I met a Frenchman and together we trekked over the snowy Shinkhun-La pass and in 13 days arrived in Padum, the capital of Zanskar, still inaccessible by road. From there, I went on alone for a month and a half.

After a night in a Tibetan Buddhist monastery, I left before sunrise with a hand-drawn map and 14 days of food. I was headed for the remote village of Shadi over a 17,000-foot pass. Near the summit, the snow's crust was warming, and every few steps I'd break through with my heavy pack. Each climb back to the snow's crust sent my heart racing, hungry for oxygen. In the blazing blue sky, panic struck.

Worn out, I reached the summit, marked by weathered prayer flags, and stopped for lunch. Looking down the long smooth valleys, all signs of humanity had disappeared. The valleys themselves seemed insignificant amongst this sea of Himalayan wilderness. My route headed into the heart of it. As I refueled the body, an idea came — to work my way to where the towering peaks shaded the snow. Sure enough, the crust was harder, and now gravity was in my favor. I followed an alpine valley below hanging glaciers, whose shear walls were colorfully lifted and folded. Several times a day I swam the milky torrents that intercepted my route.

One evening while sitting near a creek, rocks began rolling across my camp. I looked up, as four faces with curled horns looked down —

wild ibex! They said, "Break free the chains of domestication!" I said, "What?" They said, "Break free the chains of domestication! Don't submit to that shepherd's stick." Then they disappeared. As I sat there taking this all in, they circled around and came into full view, then pranced across a scree slope. Midway, two of them jumped in the air and did a stunt so surprising, I couldn't say what I had just seen. They landed, sure-footed, and jogged away.

Day seven, I arrived at Shadi. From a perch, the village's modest ecological footprint was visible — a cluster of homes surrounded by fields. At the village entrance, a monk invited me to join him for a visit. Inside the timber-and-earth home, a young man offered a bowl which was refilled many times with salt tea, sampa (roasted barley flour), and yak cheese. The monk and a mother and daughter spun wool as we spoke. Later, the daughter began churning butter. I was stuck by the similarity to the Dineh's lifestyle. Adapted to alpine deserts, Zanskar's matriarchal cultural practices have resulted in stable villages over millennia.

Having witnessed sustainability in action in the hot tropics and high mountains, I was eager to return home and begin a North American experiment.

THE GLOBAL LIVING PROJECT

On Morningstar Ridge, in British Columbia, Canada, 21 researchers were making history — the first known group attempt to *quantify* an equitable and sustainable lifestyle. The Global Living Project's challenge was to live good lives without drawing down planetary systems. For six weeks in the summer of 1996, the team monitored both consumption and life quality.

Upon arrival, the researchers emptied their backpacks onto a table and sorted the contents into various categories such as clothing, paper products, metals, and body-care products. They then entered the weights of each category onto a set of accounting sheets. Distance traveled to the research site was entered along with their means of transportation, be it bus, bike, foot, or plane.

Everything that entered or left the camp for the next six weeks was weighed and recorded. Food items were weighed and entered in one of

15 different food categories; vegetables, fruit, bread, rice, cereals, beans, and so on. To capture our total footprint, in addition to food, we tracked housing, utilities, transportation, consumer goods, services, wastes, and money spent. For transportation, we recorded the miles traveled, mode of transportation, and how many people shared the ride, as well as any repairs and maintenance. The infrastructure of our camp was measured, including common buildings, garden areas and garden tools. Then we estimated their life expectancy. For example, we figured out the amount of materials used to build the community hall that we shared and estimated an 80-year life. Wood was even weighed before making an evening fire.

Mathis Wackernagel was our scientific advisor from a distance and prepared the spreadsheets we used to track our progress. Yoshi Wada and Janette McIntosh from the University of British Columbia were on the team, and oversaw the footprinting process. Bill Rees visited the program and provided the necessary theory and big-picture importance of what we were doing. Dr. Alexander and his wife Anna were present to share their experiences in Kerala. Mark Dimaggio, a high school teacher who had taken a year sabbatical to develop a high-school curriculum based on footprinting came with his wife Sally and their children Kerry and Marcus. It was a rocky go at first, but we worked through the kinks.

At the end of the project, each team member knew their ecological footprint for living as we did during the experiment: three acres per person. This grand total was then compared to the average footprints of 151 nations based on the work of Rees and Wackernagel. Between 1996 and 2001, five teams of between 15 and 20 researchers participated in the GLP Summer Institute.

The Findings

The teams were able to maintain a high quality of life on a greatly reduced footprint. A summary of the findings over these years included:

- Equity among the planet's six billion humans is achievable in North America. The research team's ecological footprint averaged just over 3 acres per person, below the 4.7 acres available to each global citizen. A 3-acre footprint is below a person from China and above a person from India.

+ A strong majority of participants reported that their consumption was considerably lower during the Summer Institute compared to when they were at home. In comparison to the 3-acre footprint, the average Canadian uses 22 acres, and the average American uses 24 acres.

+ The team's goal was to use 20 percent of their 4.7-acre share, leaving 80 percent wild — i.e., using 1 acre each. To meet this goal of interspecies equity, the team would need to further reduce its footprint by a factor of three.

+ A clear majority of participants reported a higher quality of life during the GLP as compared to their life before the project.

How were the teams able to reduce their footprint to a level six times lower than the average North American, while increasing life quality? One primary factor was that GLP teams were the size of a traditional extended family and shared the infrastructures of a home. Participants shared one large community hall, garden space, kitchen, shower and two vehicles. This significantly reduced some of the big-ticket items — food, housing, transportation and utilities. Team members slept in tents (footprints would be higher in winter). The vehicles were used thoughtfully and sparingly. Trips were planned well in advance so that errands were combined, vehicles were full, and the most efficient vehicles were used first. Most of the vegetables eaten were grown locally or gathered from the wild. Fruits, grains, and beans were purchased in bulk from local, organic growers. Team members took turns riding bicycles to the organic grocer 14 miles away, always returning with heavily laden bike trailers. Other bike missions gathered fruits, berries and wild greens. The team ate very few dairy products and no meat. Consumer spending was minimized through creativity and distance from stores. For entertainment, they looked to each other and to the land. Researchers shared everything from recipes to yoga postures, songs to thesis papers.

Beyond the quantitative measures, the teams acknowledged the importance of the qualitative aspects of life. Each morning began with a period of silence, when individuals or groups could practice their chosen spiritual paths or simply have some quiet time. Some meditated, others prayed, some sang or went for walks in the forest, and some communed with their pillow till "last call" for breakfast. We joined hands in thanks and song before meals, taking time to honor those lives that were given so that we might live. Friendships deepened when participants prepared meals together or gathered firewood. Once a week we held a circle where a talking stick was passed.

The land itself was healing to many participants, most of whom came from urban areas. For many, it was their first time drinking water straight from the creeks, gathering and eating forest herbs, sleeping in a tent, and being relatively free from machine noises. The teams went into the mountain wilderness for up to a week's time with no agenda — other than to experience nature directly. At night we hung out around a campfire, played music together, or discussed experiences of the day. Participants were encouraged to pick a secret spot in the forest and visit it alone several times a week. This was a fearful experience for some, healing for others.

Quality of life was enhanced when individuals contributed to decisions. The teams learned and used a consensus process.

The study guide for the text *Your Money or Your Life* was used to open up and speak about our relationships to money, work, and consumerism. Conversations around values and how to become more aligned with them were often informal. These qualitative realms were documented in journals and teased out in group discussions and questionnaires.

The teams realized that urban living had certain advantages over wilderness living. For example, it was easier to get around by foot, bus, or bike in some cities. Shared, cooperative housing opportunities and community gardens are often possible in the city. Disadvantages include the high cost of housing, the large urban infrastructure for roads, utilities, and government, and pollution and noise. An "induced footprint" was also identified, where individuals found it difficult to resist the temptations of consumer culture, despite the inner knowledge that more is not necessarily better. Regardless of whether one lives in the city or the country, a dedication to reduce the use of fossil fuels and to live in smaller, more efficient homes were identified as important issues. Using products from within one's bioregion was found to reduce impact and create a deeper sense of belonging, a sense of home. Team members identified "most missed" items as baths, comfortable chairs and couches, sweets and goodies, and their friends and family.

Each team was comprised of educators, activists, and students, and ages varied from 2 to 72. The idea was to learn; from each other, from experts, and from the wilderness. With a total experience of living well with less, these individuals returned to their communities with insights, tools, and curricula for their students and peers. Following the GLP, many participants were able to integrate sustainable living skills into their urban homes and communities. On a "skills" level, participants started permaculture gardens, organized an organic school lunch program, gathered wild edible plants, and implemented energy conservation plans. Workshops in ecological footprinting were offered in schools and universities, and two masters theses were written. One participant sold his sports utility vehicle and downsized his home. Subtle yet powerful practices, such as giving thanks before meals, and regularly clearing the air to keep "issues" from building up, were used at home, building spiritual awareness and strengthening relationships.

At our yearly reunions, team members spoke of the difficulty of sticking with global living, especially without a supportive environment. It appears fairly easy for a person to walk into a more sustainable world, be it Kerala or the GLP. After a week or two of culture shock, folks just fit in. It seems much more difficult to slowly wean or to make the changes while living in the context of an unsustainable society.

To help with the transition back to their home lives, the teams employed a life energy allocation technique to encourage a balanced lifestyle. Inspired by legendary homesteaders and authors Helen and Scott Nearing from Harborside, Maine, life energy was roughly divided among:

- Bread labor — the work required to provide for our needs, such as gardening, cooking, cleaning and building projects.
- Personal growth — which included individual spiritual practices, exercise, art, hobbies, music, socializing, celebrating, walks

in the forests, workshops and lectures.

- Community service — which included assuming leadership roles, teaching or playing with children, community projects, wilderness protection, creek restoration, helping those in need, education and outreach.

I have found that simple living can be done in urban or rural places, each having benefits and difficulties. Although I never footprinted my life in San Luis Obispo, it was very similar in impact to my life in British Columbia with the Global Living Project. Our experiments so far have revealed that we can have a wonderful life, year-round, whatever the climate, while maintaining a three- to four-acre footprint. The tools outlined in Part II are intended to help you come to the same realizations.

PART II

THREE TOOLS

FOUR

SHARING THE EARTH

"Share the Earth" is an easy enough phrase to say. But as we explore more deeply this interconnected wild world, and experience the impacts of a complex global economy and then add in more variables, such as the needs of the unborn, we can soon be overwhelmed. It is not only a challenge to our scientific, spiritual, and ethical senses, but it also calls on the best of our unfettered intuition to come to grips with it responsibly. I find it helpful to remind myself : "I am one of six billion humans. My species shares paradise with 25 million other species. Each of these species has many thousands, or even billions in their population. How do I want to share Earth with all of this life?"

Although there are infinite ways to share, the easiest is simply to take less. This will be our foundation, or first step. We take less (or share more) when we:

- Earn less, taking less of the available work
- Consume less
- Make wiser choices
- Purchase local products.

You may be tempted to enthusiastically consume more than your share of available work and money and become a philanthropist, all for the joy of giving it away. But since this path is loaded with so many pitfalls, in terms of power dynamics and inner motivation, we'll keep our focus on all the possible ways of taking less. For now, imagine yourself back at that big potluck table, with all species, people, and future generations present. What is a reasonable share?

Through scientific observation, theories and experiments, we gain insights into natural phenomena and begin to ask questions such as:

- How much Earth is there?
- How much nature do humans use?
- How many species are there?
- What are the habitat needs of each species?
- At our current rate of resource use, how much will be left for future generations?

Once we've asked these questions, we can begin to look for answers. But after years of searching for scientific answers, I've discovered that science alone can't tell us how to share — something more is needed. This is where our personal ethics come in, to navigate us through the thousands of daily choices. Quite often, our moral decisions are heavily influenced by both the rational and the irrational — we engage our hearts as well as our heads.

Our intuition doesn't need a factual basis to know what to do; it is a way of knowing without the use of our rational minds. Intuitive information is like an internal compass, guiding us in considering the well-being of the whole. Does your intuition and spirituality influence how you share the Earth? Most spiritual paths include kindness, compassion, forgiveness, and reciprocity. If our scientific mind looks deeply into natural phenomena, while our spirituality embraces all life, and we pay attention to our intuition, our personal ethics will influence how we make day to day choices. As we get out of theory and down to practice, some ethical questions might be:

- Could Earth support all the world's people at my standard of living?

- Do other species or people suffer because of my lifestyle?
- Do good things come from each dollar I spend?
- Do other species have inherent value?
- Should my race, gender, strength, taxonomy, education, or birthplace allow me to consume more than others?
- Are wars being fought over resources that I use?
- Do I support corporations or industries that damage the environment or exploit workers in sweatshops?
- Is my lifestyle in alignment with my own values?

When I first began asking these questions, I realized that the subject of how I shared the Earth was rarely part of my decision making process. Yet when I took time to explore my values, I realized that this inquiry was deeply important to me. After beating myself up one too many times, I came to accept the process of living more equitably as a life-long endeavor to enjoy.

LIVING EQUITABLY

At the heart of radical simplicity is discovering how you would like to share the Earth. To help in this discovery process, we will go a level deeper and discuss three types of equity: interspecies, interhuman, and intergenerational.

Interspecies Equity

With the lightness of a butterfly Saint Francis of Assisi (1182-1226)[1] swept down to gently move an earthworm from the roadway. In prayers and canticles, he referred to Earth as mother, the wolves and birds as brothers and sisters — a non-anthropocentric communion. For Francis, mere existence granted each breeze or bug a spiritual fellowship worthy of ethical consideration. While St. Francis' spiritual and ethical treatment of all species was as radical then as it is now, nearly identical ethical and spiritual constructs have an unbroken lineage in countless indigenous cultures.

The vice president of the World Council of Indigenous peoples stated:"The Earth ... is the seat of spirituality, the fountain from which our cultures and languages flourish. The Earth is our historian, the keeper of events and the bones of our forefathers. It is the source of our independence; it is our mother. We do not dominate Her: we must harmonize with Her."[2] Chief Seattle, who died in 1866, forewarned of the end of living and the beginning of survival when the scent of man began to permeate the fragrant wild lands of his people.

In July of 1997, Stanford University biologist Peter M. Vitousek co-authored a paper on Human Domination of Earth's Ecosystems[3]. The report stated that:

+ No ecosystem is free of pervasive human influence.
+ Between one-third and one-half of the land surface has been transformed by human action.
+ Carbon dioxide concentration in the atmosphere has increased by nearly 30 percent since the industrial revolution began.
+ More than half of all accessible surface fresh water is put to use by humanity.
+ Approximately one-quarter of the bird species on Earth have been driven to extinction.

Chief Seattle's prophecy has come to be. With the current wars, ecological exploitation and poverty, one must ask what is next. The bad news is that we are not doing a very good job of sharing; in fact, the data suggests that humanity is dominating the Earth.

. . . . .

Ecological Overshoot of the Human Economy,[4] states that there are 28.2 billion acres of bioproductive land on Earth — the total surface area minus the deep oceans, deserts, icecaps and built-up land. When divided between six billion people, each person gets a 4.7-acre share — we'll call this area each person's "personal planetoid." But this assumes that humanity uses the entire planet's annual production. The question then becomes "How much of my 4.7-acre share do I want to use for myself and how much do I want to leave for other life forms?" You might think, "I want to share it all." A generous thought. But the reality is, you need to consume to survive. And what you use is not available for the deer, rabbits, or coyotes. For example, assume I am fenced into a one-acre garden with one deer and we eat the plants almost as fast as they grow, but don't deplete them. After 60 years, the land is still just as productive as it was when we entered. Generous me then invites a friend inside the fence. Now the plants can't keep pace with our appetites, and the land becomes depleted. Renewable "resources," or the planet's "bioproductivity," takes time to regenerate. They are only renewable if they're consumed at a rate slower than their annual growth or yield.

To get a scientific sense of this interspecies equity question, I cycled into the Carmanah Valley, an old growth rainforest of Vancouver Island, BC. The Western Canada Wilderness Committee (WCWC) had strapped rainforest platforms to an ancient Sitka spruce at 125', 150', 175', and 204' levels. I followed a boardwalk out of a massive clearcut into the cool wonder of cedars, hemlocks, firs, and these Sitka spruces, many of which were 200 feet tall and 20 feet around. The understory of ferns, skunk cabbage, and huckleberries, drenched in 200 inches of rain a year, was rampant and lush compared to the parched stumps of clearcut.

Here, I met up with entomologist Neville Winchester and his crew from the University of Victoria. Canada's first marbled murrelet nest had already been discovered, high in a Sitka spruce, as well as a tarantula-type spider — both old-growth dependent species. Neville described his study as assembling a biological inventory from the canopy down into the soil structure, and in the transition from forest to clearcut.

By the summer of 1993, Neville had collected 750,000 insects in five trees. Sixty new species had been tentatively identified, and he estimated there were over 200 new species to be confirmed, once they check the results with 62 identification experts. Neville said, "Since we really have no understanding of the full range of insect species that inhabit the rainforest, and since we have absolutely no idea how the ancient temperate rainforest ecosystem works, the last thing we should be doing is liquidating our last large intact watersheds."[5]

As I stared up through the spoked whorls, I wondered if my next photocopy run would extinct an unknown species? With a mere 1.5

million of the estimated 7 to 25 million species identified world-wide, caution is in order. And, with the current extinction rate estimated at 100 to 1,000 times faster than the natural rate,[6] humanity's current idea of sharing nature is deeply challenged.

Having looked closely at the species in just a few trees, let's approach the question of interspecies equity through conservation biology which looks at the needs of entire ecosystems. Reed F. Noss, a specialist in the field, has outlined four objectives that will maintain native biodiversity in perpetuity:[7]

+ Represent, in a system of protected areas, all native ecosystem types and serial stages across their natural range of variation.
+ Maintain viable populations of all native species in natural patterns of abundance and distribution.
+ Maintain ecological and evolutionary processes, such as disturbance regimes, hydrological processes, nutrient cycles, and biotic interactions, including predation.
+ Design and manage the system to be responsive to short-term and long-term environmental change and to maintain the evolutionary potential of lineages.

How much of Earth's bioproductive space should remain wild to uphold these fundamentals? To maintain a minimum population of 1,000 animals would require 242 million acres for grizzly bears, 200 million acres for wolverines, and 100 million acres for wolves.[8] Even the six-million-acre Adirondack Park, which contains the combined areas of Yosemite, Yellowstone, Olympic, and Grand Canyon National Parks struggled to support a reintroduction of lynx.[9]

To return the wolverines, mountain lions, and timber wolves to the park would require it to grow by thirty times. In truth, a successful reintroduction would require the cooperation of the people of New York, Vermont, New Hampshire, Massachusetts, and Maine, along with some delicate negotiations with New Brunswick and Quebec in order to meet the four fundamentals above. Reed Noss said that in order to preserve biodiversity and viability of species, between 25 and 75 percent of the total land area in most regions would need to be placed in protected reserves with buffer zones[10]. His analysis assumes that the reserves are interconnected with the larger landscape and other reserve areas of neighboring regions.

If the area outlined above was extensively restored, a 200 million acre (312,000 square mile) core area could be formed in New England and Canada. With a drastic reduction of roads and traffic, and a citizenry ready to co-exist with wildlife, these animals might make their way back down from Canada. Sound impossible? Living in British Columbia for seven years among grizzlies, cougars, and wolverines, I learned that coexisting is not rocket science, not costly, and not even difficult. But it would take a redesign of the human environment and a willingness to change habits.

Anthropocentrism, or the belief that humans are the primary measure of value, may be guiding more of our everyday decisions than we are prepared to acknowledge. A biocentric view, referred to as non-anthropocentrism or deep ecology, holds that the soil, spiders, winged and finned all have intrinsic value. When we think about interspecies equity, a more inclusive society is needed. But a society is made up of individuals, which is the place where changes begin.

Interhuman Equity

When we began defining global living, you were at a potluck buffet with six billion humans, the many life forms, and future generations all behind you in line. You had just filled your plate with that tofu burger and other low-impact delights. The grass was green and the sky blue. You found an empty seat with nine other friendly strangers; there was a girl from Uruguay, a just-married couple from Zimbabwe, a student from China, two brothers from India, a woman from the Slovak Republic, and a Mexican farmer with his son, who was in a wheelchair. You enjoyed a nice meal and got to know these interesting people.

But when the meal was over, you returned to the buffet to take what you need and want for the rest of your entire year. Now, how do you decide what is an equitable share among all the world's people? Will the student in China be able to afford tuition? Can the couple from Zimbabwe get sufficient food and shelter? What is a reasonable share that won't shortchange anyone? A strictly scientific approach might consider caloric intake, the climates of homelands, house designs, healthcare, and education — measures with a practical bottom line — to ensure all have a basic life-quality. This allocation based upon need would remove the biases of color, gender and power, and on average would provide equal shares for all people. You could assess your situation compared to the average world person. Perhaps life's been good and you could do well with less than others. Or, if you face hardships, you may decide to take some extra. So how much do you take?

The golden rule of "do unto others" has been around a long time and has an equivalent in all major religions. It seems unlikely that with 10 of us around a friendly table, we could go too far off course. Yet we have. Why?

Let's consider two hypothetical scenarios. After your green grass and blue sky dinner, the ten people at your table get a basket of money equal to ten sustainable, equitable shares of world Gross National Product (GNP). To determine how much is in the basket, we first divide the total world GNP — $29,340 billion — by six billion people for a $4,900 share. But because the total economic activity of humanity overshoots the globe's carrying capacity by 20 percent we adjust the share to $3,900. At this level of GNP, we still have humanity consuming the entire global bioproductivity. Let's say we scale back total human impact in terms of GNP by 75 percent to make room for the millions of other species. Each person would now have an annual equitable share of world GNP equal to $980. You begin to try to imagine living on $980 a year, gulp... and you freeze. Impossible!

The basket has $9,800, or 10 times the $980 equal shares. This money is laid out in bundles of 100 one-dollar bills. Now each draws a number from a hat. You draw first, and can take what you want. Everyone watches in silence. How much do you take?

Let's consider another scenario. All six billion people draw numbers, and it's your lucky day, you draw first again. With societal pressure removed, you approach a cash machine and are free to take out up to a billion dollars — you can transfer it to your account and no one will know. You know that $980 is a sustainable equitable portion. If you use more, others will have to use less. When the cash machine is near depletion, the last billion will get $100 each for the year. Dinner was splendid. You met some of your world neighbors, but now you are behind the curtain. The machine will pump out a billion dollars. It is between you and the machine. Once again, how much do you take?

These are the tough questions of global living. Some claim human nature is greedy, but if that were the whole truth, how can the historic and contemporary egalitarian societies be explained? Are they an anomaly, or a reminder of the potential of human kindness?

It is difficult to speculate just how equitable earlier societies actually were, but we can glean insights from historical encounters and contemporary egalitarian communities. For example, Russell Thornton's book, *American Indian Holocaust and Survival*,[11] estimated that in 1492, 1.8 million people lived in what is now called the United States. If we divide the biologically productive area of the continent's 1.79 billion acres by 1.8 million people, each person had 1,000 acres of productive land, and we know their footprints were a fraction of ours. Anthropologist Richard Robbins wrote of native North Americans, "Since there was little occupational specialization and little difference in individual wealth or possessions, relations were of an egalitarian nature."[12] Other written accounts offer support for this statement.

The Spanish priest, Bartholomew de las Casas, who accompanied Columbus on his initial journey to the new world, wrote about the Arawak of the Bahaman Islands: "They lived in large communal bell-shaped buildings, housing up to 600 people at one time...made of very strong wood and roofed with palm leaves... They lacked all manners of commerce, neither buying nor selling, and rely exclusively on their natural environment for maintenance. They are extremely generous with their possessions and by the same token covet the possessions of their friends and expect the same degree of liberality ... Endless testimonies ... prove the mild and pacific temperament of the natives ... But our work was to exasperate, ravage, kill, mangle, and destroy."[13]

. . . . .

The 1960s heralded the dawning of the Age of Aquarius, a hopeful symbol that the tides were turning — humanity was to usher in an age of harmony and understanding. Much awareness has been raised over the last 40 years, however the gap between the 20 richest and poorest percentiles has doubled. Income disparity stands at 250 to 1, measured in US dollars (74 to 1 using "purchasing-power parity," or "ppp").[14] The amount of raw nature needed to provide the one billion wealthiest people with an average of $25,500 worth of income could not be found within those countries' borders; in fact, it requires the entire Earth's annual yield. For the high-consumption twenty percent to take 250 times the GNP in US dollars than what lowest-consumption billion gets; no nation, no culture, no species is off limits. The World Trade Organization (WTO) and the General Agreement on Tariffs and Trade (GATT) — elite, undemocratic groups — have designed "legal" mechanisms to break down borders to ease raw material flows toward the industrialized world. The track record speaks for itself — a further concentration of wealth at the top.

In 1998, half of the 1.2 billion people who lived on less than $110 per year have stunted growth or mental retardation from insufficient caloric intake.[15] The poorest 3.6 billion — 60 percent of humanity — live on less than $520 per year. A third of the world's children suffer from malnutrition.[16] A Salvadoran peasant was quoted as saying, "You will never understand violence and nonviolence until you understand the violence to the spirit that happens from watching your children die of malnutrition."[17] Only 30 percent of the wealthiest billion report being very happy. In America, according to a poll of those earning $274 a day, 27 percent stated, "I cannot afford to buy everything I really need."[18] Living on $980 per year in North America might seem impossible; certainly it seems heroic.

Charles Gray, from Eugene, Oregon, author of *Toward a Nonviolent Economics*,[19] developed the concept of World Equity Wage (WEW) and capped his wage at $3.14 an hour, and worked no more than 20 hours a week. His voluntary "deprivileging" was motivated by a goal of sharing the available work and wealth with humanity and restoring the environment. When we met in 1995, he had already been living for 17 years on what he calculated to be the World Equity Budget (WEB), and averaged $1,190 in total annual living expenses from 1978 to 1993. He is a delightful, open-minded person and his book is an inspiration.

After 14 years of living on $5,000 per year (placing me amongst the wealthiest 17 percent of humanity), I know it would take a quantum redesign of my life and significantly reduced expectations of services to approach equity. I know it is hard in the context of an unsustainable culture, but every bit of societal level change, be it bike lanes, mixed zoning, or local organic markets will make the whole process easier.

. . . . .

As we make small steps toward better distribution of wealth, there are rewards. That girl from Uruguay might get the nutritional boost she needs and that couple from Zimbabwe might be able to set up their home. And you and I get to learn new skills and experience a life less centered upon things.

Intergenerational Equity

The year 1978 came and went. I was 20. It was a special year in both Earth's history and human history, and it passed without notice. It was the year humans claimed the entire sustainable yield of Earth. The overall system — the planet's capital if you will — would hereafter be drawn down. Before this day, if you consumed more than your average share, the wild ones paid the difference. After this day, if you consumed more, it came directly from another human's share, and at the expense of generations to come.

You and I might get to see the climax of this amazing spike of human impact; we are clearly riding a wild wave. The World Bank predicts that the doubling time to add the next billion humans might actually increase[20] — a first since we reached one billion. Population growth is slowing down. In the less industrialized world, women now have an average of four children, a clear drop from six only thirty years earlier. Demographers are uncertain as to how and why fertility levels have dropped and currently predict a peak population of between 10 and 11 billion.[21] If we assume the best, that these scientists behind their computers have a good crystal ball, then when I'm 92 in 2050, there will be 9 billion people. My $980 a year share of GNP will have shrunk to $650 and humanity will be overshooting carrying capacity by 88 percent. That is, if we don't somehow grapple with these incredibly tough issues and make some significant changes.

When my grandfather was born, in 1902, there were 1.6 billion people. On my father's birthdate in 1926, there were 2 billion. When I was born, in 1958, global population had risen to 2.9 billion. Now, 100 years after my grandfather's birth, we've added another 4.4 billion people, and the percent of fallow and wild bioproductive land has gone

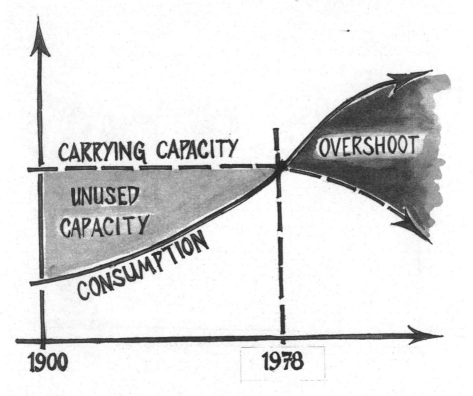

Figure 4.1: 1978 marked the year humans claimed the entire sustainable yield of the Earth. Thereafter, the overall system — the planet's capital, if you will — is being drawn down.

from 67 percent to a 20 percent overshoot. In the 150 or so years since
the Industrial Revolution, we've doubled the population 4 times and
doubled the size of the global economy 20 times.

A journey back 60,000 generations to the Rift Valley of what is now
northeast Africa — a period of 1.5 million years representing 99 percent of the human experience — the relatively small human settlements left the bulk of Earth's bioproductive space wild.

Intergenerational equity can be summed up as simply passing the
land on to the next generation with no degradation. How intensive-
ly do you want to use the Earth's bioproductivity? Do you wish to
leave a buffer, as in fallow fields, so that the unborn generations will
be assured a wild and bioproductive land? We know that the Earth

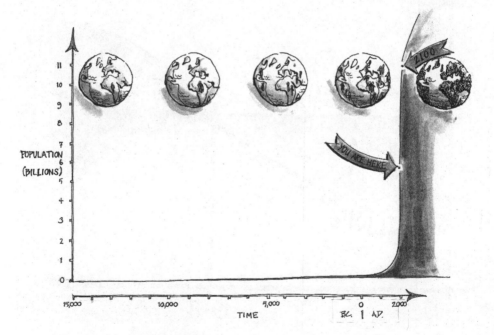

Figure 4.2: In the 150 or so years since the Industrial Revolution, we've doubled the population 4 times. At this rate, world population will peak in 2100
at 11 billion.

produces a tremendous amount of life each year. Currently, humanity takes 20 percent more than is produced, thus wearing down the Earth's systems. Might it be wise to scale back our annual take to help the overworked systems rebound? We can either err on the side of caution or gamble with our children's future.

FIVE

GETTING STARTED

The first step in creating your new lifestyle is the sustainability sweatshop. Once you've survived that, the creative process begins. Then, as you begin using the tools, old habits that serve neither you nor the world can die, leaving in their place a lifestyle of your own design.

At the end of the sweatshop, you'll arrive at your personal measurable sustainability goal. It is important to begin to taste and feel your goal. Like preparing to plant a garden, you dream about it, visualize it, and come to understand it in detail. Later in this section you will learn how to find out how big your footprint currently is. Then, as your footprint shrinks, you can see the amount of nature freed up in the process. Celebrate each increment! Time in nature can help keep the focus on the importance of returning precious habitat to the wild ones and will help keep your goal from slipping away.

In modern society, you will be lured away from your sustainability goal a hundred times a day. Keep your focus on porcupines and violets, not on numbers. Make friends with Afghans and Zimbabweans. Hang out with the youth that will inherit what we choose to leave them.

Witness the suffering caused by big footprints and the joy of a life in balance. Focus on making your life beautiful and part of the solution. Remember that billions of people still practice global living, as do wild beings. Teachers are everywhere. And worldwide, millions are tuned-in to radical simplicity. Chances are you can find people to scheme and dream with.

THE SUSTAINABILITY SWEATSHOP

Getting specific about sustainability tends to make people sweat, as they dig deep into ethical reserves. The sustainability sweatshop has been used in over six hundred workshops over the past six years, and consists of three parts:

1. Simple goal setting
2. Tough, sweaty goal setting
3. Cool down and visualization

Part One: Simple Goal Setting

Let's start with a simple exercise to get you into the rough ballpark of your sustainability goal.

Step 1. What percentage of the Earth's bioproductive spaces should humans use?

The remaining area would be left wild for the estimated 7 to 25 million other species to use. An answer of 0.2 means that humans use 20%, and 80% remains wild; an answer of 0.8 means that humans use 80%, and 20% remains wild.

10%	20%	30%	40%	50%	60%	70%	80%	90%	100%	humans use
0.1	0.2	0.3	0.4	0.5	0.6	0.7	0.8	0.9	1.0	my use
90%	80%	70%	60%	50%	40%	30%	20%	10%	0%	left wild

Step 2. Determining Your Goal

Simply multiply the decimal above by 4.7 acres (an equal portion of total planetary bioproductivity or your personal planetoid), to get your very own sustainability goal.

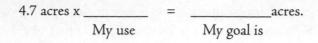

4.7 acres x _____ = _____ acres.
My use   My goal is

In rough terms, this number, in acres, is your goal. Now for a more in-depth goal-setting exercise.

Part Two: Tough, Sweaty Goal Setting

This is where you decide, in more detail, how you would like to share the Earth and what societal targets you would like to support. Think of this as your vision, how you would like to interact with the world. This is where science, ethics, intuition, and spirituality all help guide your answers. You might want to do this exercise in a quiet place out in nature. Remember that nothing is written in stone and there are no right or wrong answers. As time goes by you may wish to revisit this sweatshop, to see if you still want the same goals.

We will start with setting a personal time frame to achieve our sustainability goal. Too soon will be too hard, while too far into the future may be too late. One year, 10 years, 25 years, 50 years?

**In how many years do you want to achieve your sustainability goal?
Answer____**

For the rest of this target setting exercise, we will assume the greater societal goal for achieving sustainability to be 100 years from now. If you think that is too far in the future, realize that your approach will then have to be even more dramatic and quick.

Step 1. Interspecies equity

What percentage of the Earth's bioproductive space should humans use? Use your answer from Step 1 of the Simple Goal Setting above.

My use (enter decimal) ___

Step 2. Interhuman equity:

How much bioproductivity do you wish to use compared to what is available for each person worldwide? Choosing 0.5 means that you'll use half the global average available; 1 means perfect equality amongst humans; 3 means that you'll use three times the global average.

less than average	same	more than average
0.5 0.6 0.7 0.8 0.9	1	2 3 4 5 6

My use (enter decimal) _____

Step 3. Intergenerational Equity

At what rate do you wish to use your portion of the planet's bioproductivity? An answer of 1 means that nature just keeps pace with your use. An answer of 1.2 means that your use is 20 percent faster than the biological regeneration rate, leaving the next generation with depleted land. An answer of 0.8 means that you use your portion 20% slower than it regenerates — leaving fallow areas so the next generation inherits a less intensively-used Earth.

regenerating	max use	depleting
0.5 0.6 0.7 0.8 0.9	1	1.1 1.2 1.3 1.4 1.5

My use (enter decimal) _____

Step 4. Your overall equity factor

You may want a pocket calculator to do this next step, or you can sharpen your pencil for a little multiplication workout. You simply need to multiply "My use" from Steps 1-3 above together (in decimal numbers).

Interspecies Equity	Interhuman Equity	Intergenerational Equity	Overall Factor Equity
_____ x	_____ x	_____ =	_____

Example: 0.3 x 0.9 x 0.95 = 0.26

Step 5. Accounting for the Population Size

In this step you are asked to set the total human population goal that you would support working towards. We will assume this population goal will be reached 100 years from now. Please assume that any and all programs to reduce population would be totally voluntary and achieved though poverty alleviation, empowerment of women, and education, similar to the programs of Kerala.

A. For those who already have children: What global human population number would you support working towards over the next 100 years? If you support a global population goal of 1 billion people in 2100, your answer is a ratio of 6 (current population divided by desired population in 2100 or: 6 billion/1 billion = ratio of 6), corresponding to a total fertility rate (TFR) of 1; for a global population goal of 3 billion, your answer is a ratio of 2 (6 billion/3 billion), with a TRF of 1.4; for a global population of 6 billion, your answer is a ratio of 1, with a TRF of 1.8; and if you support a growth to 9 billion, your ratio is 0.66 (6/9), with a TRF of 2. **Answer (ratio from table below)_____**

Goal — Population in billions in 2100												
0.5	1	2	3	4	5	6	7	8	9	10	20	30
Ratio												
12	6	3	2	1.5	1.2	1	0.9	0.75	0.66	0.6	0.3	0.2
TFR Avg. # of children per family												
0.7	1	1.2	1.4	1.5	1.7	1.8	1.85	1.95	2	2.1	2.6	3

B. For those who have not yet had children: How many children do you want to have? Select the ratio from the table above that matches the completed family size (TFR) you would like. If 0 to 1 child, your ratio is 6; if 2 children, your ratio is 0.66; if 3 children, your ratio is 0.2. (By having one child you are contributing toward 1 billion in 2100. By having 2 children you are contributing toward 9 billion in 2100.) Another way to explain this step is: if the 2.9 billion people below the age of 25 each had 2 children, world population would reach 9 billion in 2100. Chapter 11 provides a more detailed analysis of these numbers.

Answer (ratio from table above)_____

Step 6: Calculate your Sustainability Goal

In this step, you multiply your overall equity factor times the population ratio you are willing to work towards. The amount of bioproductivity available for each person would halve if the human population doubles. Conversely, if the population reduces to one third its current size, then bioproductivity per person would increase by three times.

Bioproductivity available in 2000 acres/person "Personal Planetoid"	Overall Equity Factor (from Step 4 above)	Population ratio (from Step 5 A or B above)	Your Sustainability Goal acres/person
4.7 acres	x _____	x _____	= _____
For example: *4.7 acres*	*x 0.26*	*x 6 (1 child)*	*= 7.3 acres*

Part Three: Cool Down and Visualization

In summary, the sweatshop is intended to bring into focus the two primary sustainability factors that each person has control over:

1. How much you consume.
2. How many children you will have.

Society, your partner, or your family can try to influence you, but you are the one who ultimately decides. This is a good time to let your sustainability goal settle into your bones. For now, carry this number around with you and get used to it as a simple number. If your goal seems impossible, don't despair. Set some milestones for yourself — achieving it could take one year or 20 years. I've been working toward my sustainability goal since 1990 and still have work to do. The rest of the book will provide tools and strategies to ensure your success in this design challenge.

THREE TOOLS

If you are like most, your life is busy and you have unique considerations that will influence how you approach simplifying. That's where these tools come in; they'll help you focus on the specifics of your life. Let's explore their benefits and how we will use them.

Ecological Footprinting

Ecological Footprinting (EF) is a technique used to track the many flows of nature that support our daily life. If your bag of life's goodies comes from around the world, the footprint adds up your share of the oil rigs, roads, wheat fields and forests that go into your goodies. Can nature keep pace with your consumption?

Your Money or Your Life

Your Money or Your Life (YMOYL) is a book by Vicki Robin and Joe Dominguez which outlines techniques to track flows of money and time into and out of our lives. Through these techniques, you might manage to solve the mystery "Where did all that money go?" And in the process, you may start to question your values, and whether what you purchase actually enhances your life. This is where you begin to proactively design your life.

Learning from Nature

When we spend time in wild nature, we learn about the world directly. Relationships between salmon, cedar and grizzly bears will reveal themselves. We might be afraid to court the wild at first, but deep within, our bodies may also hunger for this connection.

WHOLE SYSTEMS

Taken together, these three tools are grounded in the evolving field of Whole Systems. Fritjof Capra, in his book *The Web of Life*, states, "The key to a comprehensive theory of living systems lies in the synthesis of two very different approaches, the study of substance (or structure) and the study of form (or pattern). In the study of structure we weigh and measure things. Patterns, however, cannot be measured or weighed; they must be mapped. To understand a pattern we must map a configuration of relationships. In other words, structure involves quantities, while pattern involves qualities."

Both the EF and *YMOYL* techniques will have you track your consumption of vegetables, electricity, gasoline, and insurance. EF tracks material quantities — pounds, kilowatt-hours or gallons — in essence, how much stuff. *YMOYL* keeps track of the financial costs of these items and the hours you spend (trade) each month working for these things, then questions how you feel about this trade. Patterns will emerge and at the end of each month you will know the following:

+ Your ecological footprint.
+ How your footprint compares with others' around the world.
+ The extent to which you are living within the earth's ecological capacity.
+ How much money you spent.
+ How many hours you traded for goods by consumer category.
+ How you feel about your trade of life for stuff.

These tools will not tell you what to do or what is right or wrong. They simply help you to see what you are doing and encourage you to do your own evaluation. Month by month your unique pattern of interpenetration of the world around you is brought into focus. Then the fun begins as you reinforce beneficial patterns.

Complete books exist on these tools, so we have included only the essentials here. This whole-systems approach will enable you to:

+ Assess and design your unique lifestyle.
+ Compare the impacts of certain activities, products, and technologies.

- Develop your own definition of sustainability.
- Set long-range personal and societal goals.
- Learn about the needs of people and beings.
- Develop a deep, respectful relationship with the natural world.

With an overview of our three tools and how they complement each other, we are ready to get into the specifics of our tools.

SIX

THE FIRST TOOL —
ECOLOGICAL
FOOTPRINTING

From the moment the alarm rings we are plugged into a global economy. After the third snooze, you beeline for the coffeepot. While it brews, you plug in a CD and wake up with a hot shower. You read a few headline paragraphs from the morning paper. You grab your keys, watch, wallet, and a banana and hop in the car to get to work on time. Have you ever puzzled over the impact or footprint of any of these activities? Ecological footprinting (EF) goes behind the scenes — just what does it take to make an alarm clock, grow a banana, construct a home, and operate an automobile?

A deeper look at that dark roast coffee is revealing. The beans are grown in cleared jungles that once sustained the local indigenous peoples, plants, and animals. Even shade-grown operations remove most of the canopy and the understory. Land is used to house the process facility, management and advertising firms, as well as the downtown store.

Additional forest land is needed to absorb the CO_2 emitted from the combustion of all the fuels needed to harvest, process, ship, roast, deliver, grind, and brew the beans. Somewhere on the planet, land was mined to make the metal for the machinery. Together, these items are embodied in the beans. In scientific sustainability lingo, the energy component of these processes is called embodied energy or energy intensity. What about the packaging, coffee pot, refrigerator, alarm clock, newspaper, clothes, electricity and car? Can you see how the global economy makes it difficult to trace our footprints? Thanks to Bill Rees and Mathis Wackernagel, who have been developing and refining the technique for over a decade at the University of British Columbia in Vancouver, and at Redefining Progress in Oakland, California, the seemingly unmanageable has become manageable.

The feedback provided by footprinting is less direct than the dry tangle of a clearcut forest. But if we take time in nature, we will directly experience who gives their lives for our consumer products. Feedback is useless if it doesn't affect our choices: for instance, if our eyes see a cliff, then we ride over the edge anyway, what good was the visual feedback?

Choices are the bottom line. How might our footprint have changed if instead of a delivered paper, we listened to the radio, instead of a banana, we ate a local apple, and instead of driving to work, we bicycled?

Ecological footprinting can be used to design a lifestyle, a business, or an institution in alignment with our personal or collective value system. If 100 people designed with EF, we would see 100 creative solutions. We will now go deeper into how a footprint is determined.

FOOTPRINTING SCIENCE

Ecological footprinting measures the amount of bioproductivity that an individual or a nation uses in a given year. Your footprint is the amount of bioproductive land and sea area in continuous production to supply all you use and to absorb your wastes, using prevailing technology.

Sustainability can occur when humanity consistently draws on planetary yield more slowly than it regenerates. When humanity drains the planet's bioproductivity faster than it replenishes, ecology is damaged. When this trend continues over time, the planet's capacity to support life is destroyed. Footprinting is what takes the guesswork out of sustainability. It allows us to measure our progress.

Ecological Footprinting is now used worldwide in diverse applications. The World Wildlife Fund (WWF) International employed EF in its *Living Planet Report*, a comprehensive overview of planetary sustainability. The footprints of 151 nations are calculated with a robust methodology developed by Redefining Progress. A nation's imports are added to domestic production, then exports are subtracted yielding national consumption. This calculation is done for more than 200 categories, such as cereals, timber, fish meal, coal and cotton. The European Parliament Directorate General for Research published a detailed report examining EF as a tool for government. The Earthday Network's year 2002 international celebration launched a website to calculate an individual's footprint using an electronic version of the quiz included in this chapter (see Figure 6.7). The United Nations *State of the World Population 2001* report incorporated Ecological Footprinting concepts. A curriculum based upon EF, called *Ecovoyageurs*, has been created and distributed to 5,000 elementary and middle schools in Canada. The applications continue to grow.

The EF analysis is based on data published by United Nations agencies[1] and the Intergovernmental Panel on Climate Change.[2] The system we will use to track footprints was developed by Mathis Wackernagel, Diana Deumling, Chad Monfreda and Ritik Dholakia at Redefining Progress. For more information on the science of EF refer to the books *Our Ecological Footprint*[3] and *Sharing Nature's Interest*[4]

WHAT'S IN A FOOTPRINT?

There are many calculations behind the footprint system; however, it is quite easy to use. If numbers aren't your cup of tea, don't let this section scare you off. You won't have to go beyond basic arithmetic.

A footprint is all about how we impact the land. But lands are incredibly diverse. Most valley bottoms were once prime wildlife habitat with deep rich soils that fueled giant trees, dense shrubs, and herbs with an incredible bioproductivity. These valleys are now typically farms, housing developments, and industrial sites. At the other bioproductive extreme are deserts, full of cactus, sage, coyotes, and buzzards; however, they grow only a small fraction of the biomass of the valley bottom. Lands with very low bioproductivity such as deserts, icecaps, and deep oceans aren't included in the analysis.

Figure 6-1
FIVE ASSUMPTIONS
Five Assumptions Behind the Ecological Footprint Calculations

1. It is possible to keep track of most of the resources people consume and much of the waste they generate.
2. Most of these resource and waste flows can be measured in terms of the biologically productive land areas required to maintain these flows. (Those resource and waste flows that cannot be measured are excluded from this assessment).
3. These different areas can be expressed in the same unit once they are scaled proportionally to their biomass productivity. In other words, each particular acre or hectare used can be converted to an equivalent area of world-average land productivity.
4. Since these areas stand for mutually exclusive uses, and each standardized hectare or acre represents the same amount of biomass productivity, they can be added up to a total — this total represents humanity's demand.
5. This area of total human demand can be compared with nature's supply of ecological services since it is also possible to assess the area on the planet that is biologically productive.

(Source: *The Living Planet Report*)

The results of EF underestimate human impact and overestimate the available biological capacity. The analysis includes current agricultural practices as if they caused no long-term damage to soil productivity. Some activities such as fresh water collection and the release of solid, liquid, and gaseous wastes (apart from CO_2) have not yet been included because of insufficient data. Additionally, nonrenewable activities that systematically erode nature's capacity to regenerate have been excluded such as the creation of plutonium, polychlorinated biphenyl's (PCBs) and chlorofluorocarbons (CFCs); species extinction; aquifer destruction; deforestation and desertification. Our hope is that as you take to radical simplicity you will phase out their use.

There are seven types of bioproductive land considered in the footprint:

- **Cropland,** or arable land, is the most productive type of space. It grows food, animal feed, fiber, oil crops, and rubber. There are about 7.8 billion acres (3.18 billion hectares) of cropland worldwide.

Figure 6.2: The seven types of bioproductive land considered in a footprint are cropland, pasture, forest land, sea space, built-up land, fossil fuel and wilderness land.

- **Pasture** is the land where animals graze, providing meat, hides, wool and milk. This category is less productive than cropland, and includes both lightly forested areas and arable land used for pasture. Worldwide there are 4 billion acres (1.62 billion hectares) of land used as pasture.

- **Forestland** is used to provide timber for buildings and furniture, wood fiber for paper, and fuel wood. Forests comprise 12.75 billion acres (5.16 billion hectares).

- **Sea space** comprises the areas of continental coasts that provide 95 percent of the fish caught. This area of 2.1 billion acres (0.84 billion hectares) is 8 percent of the total ocean surface.

- **Built-up land** is the area that accommodates the infrastructure for homes, government, business, transportation, capturing solar, wind and hydro energy, and industrial production. This area totals 1.48 billion acres (0.6 billion hectares) of land worldwide.

- **Fossil fuel land** is the forest area needed to sequester (or absorb) the CO_2 added to the atmosphere from burned fossil fuels. A second calculation method is used by Redefining Progress to determine the land area needed to yield an equivalent amount of plant-based fuel that provides results similar to the CO_2 method. Since the oceans absorb about 35 percent of the emissions from burned fossil fuels, EF only accounts for the 65 percent that remain. This fossil fuel land can provide habitat, however the intensity of absorbing high levels of CO_2 dominate this area's function.

- **Wilderness land** is that which is protected from human use. The bioproductivity is primarily available to non-human life. Currently only 3.5 percent of global land area is protected in parks, reserves, and wilderness, however, many of these areas include parks and wildlife reserves where significant human activities are still occurring.

Each item we consume requires one or more of these types of land. For example, a commercial carrot requires cropland, built-up land for storage and sales, and fossil fuel land for the chemical pesticides, fertilizers, and fuels used in the processing and shipping.

If you had a one-acre garden that supplied all your food, would your food footprint be one acre? Maybe. If your plot's soil was of average world bioproductivity, then yes, your footprint would be one acre. However, if your plot was decent arable land, its productivity would be 2.2 times average; if it was closer to pasture land it would be half the average. We call this proration equivalence. Once lands are scaled according to their productivity, they can be added together. (See Figure 6.3 below.) The table also lists the acres available to human of each type of land if divided equally, again, assuming we take the whole enchilada.

Figure 6.3
BIOLOGICALLY PRODUCTIVE SPACE

Land Type	Equivalence Factors	Biocapacity acres/person
Arable	2.2	1.31
Pasture	0.5	0.67
Forest	1.3	2.12
Built-up	2.2	0.25
Sea	0.4	0.35
		Total 4.7

Calculating Footprints

In the simplest terms, you multiply the amount of an item you consume in a month by what we call a footprint factor (ff), and you have your footprint for that item.

(Amount per month consumed) x (ff) = ecological footprint (EF)

- Amount can be pounds or kilograms, gallons, quarts or liters, miles or kilometers, square feet or square meters, kilowatt hours, dollars. You just need to pick either metric or standard and stick with it. (You can divide the number of square yards by 4,840 to get acres, and divide the number of square meters by 10,000 to get hectares.)

+ The ffs translate the amount you use per month into the land area, in square yards or square meters, kept in continuous production to supply that flow of product.

+ An EF is always an area, whether in square yards or square meters, acres or hectares.

The scientists at Redefining Progress do a lot of number crunching to generate a footprint factors. You only need to multiply the ff by your monthly gas use for instance to know your gas footprint. The four steps in creating a footprint factor are listed below for you to have a sense of how they are generated.

Step one: The yield data is gathered from the Food and Agriculture Organization of the United Nations (FAO).[5] For example, how many pounds of carrots, cotton, or lumber can be sustainably harvested from one acre of land in a year?

Step two: If the product used energy in its production, then add to step one above the fossil energy component. This includes all the energy necessary to make possible the final consumption of this raw material or manufactured product. A structural consumption multiplier accounts for the energy consumed by government to purchase public goods and services.

Step three: To the results of steps one and two above, a correction factor is applied that will calibrate the overall footprint system of this book to data generated from the more robust national accounting system of *The Living Planet Report.*

Step four: This step factors the total of each land-use type; — arable, pasture, forest, built and sea — for its productivity when compared to the average productivity of all biologically productive land and sea space on Earth. Once this step is complete, land amounts can be added together. For those interested, the details behind these calculations can be found on the Household Ecological Footprint Calculator that can be downloaded from <www.redefiningprogress.org>.

This book includes footprint factors for nearly 100 common items, further sorted into categories of food, housing, transportation, goods and services, stocks, and wastes. Because there is such a variety of goods and services, the ffs used are calculated from national average yields using average production methods. This book aims to strike a balance between simplicity and accuracy, but errs on the side of being a conservative underestimate.

HOW BIG IS MY FOOTPRINT?

This chapter will offer several methods to determine the size of your footprint. The easy methods are less accurate but provide a quick answer, so that in less than half an hour you'll have an estimate. However, to make it this simple, some assumptions had to be made that may or may not apply to your life. To get a more accurate footprint assessment requires more commitment from you, both in record keeping and in calculating. Often, the tough things we undertake have big payoffs, and this is certainly the case here.

To actually achieve your footprint goals may take years. I suggest becoming fluent with all the tools and working through the entire book. The key element to achieving sustainability is for you to enjoy the process; this way, you'll stay with it over time.

How Big is my Paycheck?

An initial footprint estimate can be based on the correlation between a person's footprint and their paycheck. This method might not seem very accurate, but because of the degree to which most North Americans engage in the global economy, the correlation is stronger than you might think. Nearly 40 percent of baby boomers have less than $10,000 saved for retirement[6] — after 30 years, earning an average of over three-quarters of a million dollars.[7] Where did the rest go? I don't know where it went. It's just gone. On average, we spend what we earn, and in a global economy, the things we buy carry a big footprint.

You could maintain a large salary and live simply. A footprint is really created when you spend the money or consume stuff or services. If you save your earnings or make lots of donations, you may not correlate with the table below. Generally, though, the more income we have, the easier it is to take that vacation when we feel a need to get away. With more income, additions to the house or a second house might just feel natural; for many of us, we spend simply because we can.

The World Bank maintains yearly data on per capita Gross National Product, which is a close approximation to per capita incomes, and Redefining Progress calculates the footprints of 151 nations. If we plot footprint versus income, a strong correlation is evident. So, for a first crude approximation of your footprint, find yourself on the table below. If you tend to consider the environment in your purchases and actions, you may be on the low end of the range.

Figure 6-4
FOOTPRINTS AS THEY CORRELATE TO INCOME

Income (GNP/capita)	Footprint
$100,000 and up	40 to 60 acres
$50,000 to $100,000	30 to 50 acres
$30,000 to $50,000	25 to 40 acres
$30,000 and up (Europe and Japan)	15 acres and up
$25,000 to $30,000	20 to 30 acres
$20,000 to $25,000	18 to 22 acres
$15,000 to $20,000	14 to 20 acres
$10,000 to $15,000	12 to 18 acres
$5,000 to $10,000	5 to 15 acres
$2,500 to $5,000	3 to 13 acres
$1,000 to $2,500	2.5 to 6 acres
$500 to $1,000	2 to 5 acres
$100 to $500	1.5 to 4 acres

Sources: World Bank, *World Development Indicators* CD-ROM, World Bank, 2000.

Chambers, Nicky, Craig Simmons, and Mathis Wackernagel, *Sharing Nature's Interest: Ecological Footprints as an Indicator of Sustainability*, Earthscan Publications, 2000.

This book is focused on the decisions that you have direct control over, and income is one of them. Those who don't have their basic needs met may focus on how to get more income. Once you have enough, though, deciding to take less will open opportunities for those in need. In an overcrowded world, sharing the available work is an important ethic.

Choosing less income goes against the grain of modern society, where more is seen as better. In fact, there is no cultural or legal restriction on how much we take, and because our incomes provide a culturally based sense of worth that is rarely challenged, choosing less is difficult. Additionally, we may enjoy the comfort, safety, and privilege our incomes provide — money equals power in a global economy. Who gets our money and who doesn't? The more we earn, the more we control. Money buys things beyond necessities and luxuries; our dollars can

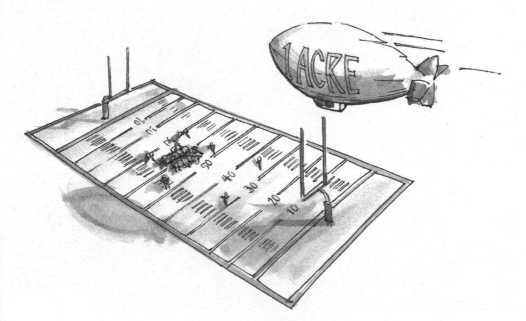

Figure 6.5: To get a sense of scale, one acre is slightly smaller than a football field. 1 acre = 4,840 square yards, and one football field is 5,330 square yards.

influence politics and negotiate our way through tax laws or legal difficulties. Money buys services, security, and healthcare. When money can
buy such influence, the fundamental ideal of democracy — that all
voices have equal value and effect — becomes an unachievable myth.

QUICK FOOTPRINT QUIZ

Redefining Progress has created a quiz to quickly assess your impact.
With these twelve questions, a reasonable estimate is reached. For an
online, international version of this quiz, with other country and language selections and a dynamic interface, visit <www.myfootprint.org>
For more information on the Ecological Footprint, visit
<www.redefiningprogress.org>. You can also get a pencil and paper and
take the quiz right here.

Figure 6.6: Ecological footprinting goes behind the scenes — just what does it
take to make newspaper, grow a banana, brew a cup of coffee, operate an automobile?

Figure 6-7
ECOLOGICAL FOOTPRINT QUIZ

© Redefining Progress, July 2002.

Calculate your Ecological Footprint
Ever wondered how much "nature" your lifestyle requires? You're about to find out. This is a very basic quiz to calculate a quick and relatively accurate Ecological Footprint for an individual living in the US. The Ecological Footprint Quiz estimates how much productive land and water area you take up for the resources you consume and the waste you generate. After answering 12 easy questions you'll be able to compare your Ecological Footprint to what other people use and to what is available on the planet.

Please answer as honestly and accurately as possible.

Instructions
Circle your response, and the number in each column that corresponds to your answer.
Enter the circled number from each column into the SUBTOTAL boxes below each column. Calculate the footprint for each section by multiplying your numbers as shown. Enter the subtotals from each section under "QUIZ RESULTS." Add up your subtotals to get your total footprint.

Caution
This quiz may surprise you, shock you, or make you think. Please remain calm ... but not too calm!

FOOD
Q1. Animal-based Food
A plant-based diet generally requires less land, energy, and other resources. As with all food, the size of the footprint largely depends on how it's grown. Look for "free range" animal products that have been produced by local, small-scale organic or sustainable farmers.

How often do you eat animal-based foods? (Beef, pork, chicken, fish, eggs, dairy products.)

Never (vegan) .... a. 0.46
Infrequently (no meat or eggs/dairy a few times a week) .. b. 0.59
Occasionally (no meat or occasional meat, eggs/dairy daily c. 0.73
Often (meat once or twice a week) .... d. 0.86
Very often (meat daily) .... e. 1
Almost always (meat and egg/dairy in almost all meals) .. f. 1.14

Q2. Locally Grown Food

A significant portion of the energy involved in the food system is spent on transporting food from harvest to market, and for processing, packaging and storage. Growing food yourself or purchasing locally grown, in-season, unprocessed food can greatly reduce the need to expend energy in food production. Shopping at farmers' markets or buying directly from farmers is the best way to ensure that you are purchasing locally grown food, and to minimize your food footprint.

How much of the food that you eat is processed, packaged and not locally grown (from more than 200 miles away)?

Most of the food I eat is processed, packaged
and from far away .... a. 1.10
Three quarters .... b. 1
Half .... c. 0.90
One quarter .... d. 0.79
Very little. Most food I eat is unprocessed,
unpackaged and locally grown .... e. 0.69

> Subtotal (1) — food footprint:
> 5.5 x Q1 x Q2 = __3.6__ acres
> *Example: 5.5 x 0.86 x 1 = 4.7 acres*

SHELTER (Simplified, for full version see <www.myfootprint.org>)
Q3. How many people live in your household? (Used to calculate your share of living space.)

1 person .... a. 1
2 people .... b. 2 *(circled)*
3 people .... c. 3
4 people .... d. 4
5 people .... e. 5
6 people .... f. 6
7 or more people .... g. 7

Q4. House or apartment size
The average living space for a US household is around 1,500 square feet.
What is the size of your home?

2,500 square feet or larger .... a. 2.9
1,900 – 2,500 square feet .... b. 2.2
1,500 – 1,900 square feet .... c. 1.7
1,000 – 1,500 square feet .... d. 1.2
500 – 1,000 square feet .... e. 0.7
500 square feet or smaller .... f. 0.2 *(circled)*

Q5. Which housing type best describes your home?

Free standing house .... a. 1
Multi-story apartment building .... b. 0.8
Green-design residence .... c. 0.5 *(circled)*

Q6. Do you use energy conservation and efficiency measures throughout your home?

No .... a. 1
Yes .... b. 0.75 *(circled)*

> **Subtotal (2) — shelter footprint:**
> 5.1 x (2.6/Q3) x Q4 x Q5 x Q6 = 1.2 acres
> *Example: 5.1 x (2.6/2) x 1.2 x 1 x 0.75 = 6.0 acres*

TRANSPORTATION
Q7. Public Transportation
On average, how far do you travel on public transportation each week?

200 miles or more . . . . a. 17.29
75-200 miles . . . . (b.) 8.47
25-75 miles . . . . c. 3.09
1-25 miles . . . . d. 0.89
0 miles . . . . e. 0

> **Subtotal (3) — public transit footprint:**
> 0.05 x Q7 = ,42 acres
> *Example: 0.05 x 3.09 = 0.2 acres*

Q8. Car
The average car-driving American travels about 14,000 vehicle miles per year, or 270 miles per week.

On average, how far do you go by car each week (as a driver or passenger)? If your answer is "0-10 miles" for Q8, enter "0" in the subtotal box and skip Q9 and Q10.

400 miles or more . . . . a. 1.91
300-400 miles . . . . b. 1.43
200-300 miles . . . . c. 1
100-200 miles . . . . d. 0.55
10-100 miles . . . . (e.) 0.12
0-10 miles . . . . f. 0

Q9. How many miles per gallon does your car get?
If you don't own a car, estimate the average fuel efficiency of the cars you ride in.

More than 50 miles per gallon . . . . a. 0.31
35-50 miles per gallon . . . . b. 0.46
25-35 miles per gallon . . . . (c.) 0.65
15-25 miles per gallon . . . . d. 0.98
Fewer than 15 miles per gallon . . . . e. 1.54

Q10. How often do you drive a car with someone else, rather than alone?

Almost never . . . . a. 1.5
Occasionally (about 25%) . . . . b. 1
Often (about 50%) . . . . c. 0.75
Very Often (about 75%) . . . . d. 0.6
Almost always . . . . e. 0.5

> **Subtotal (4) car footprint:**
> 4.0 x Q8 x Q9 x Q10 = _.156_ acres
> *Example: 4.0 x 0.55 x 0.98 x 1 = 2.2 acres*

Q11. Air travel
Every year, Americans fly an average of 4.7 hours per person on commercial airlines. This is roughly equivalent to one round trip flight between Washington, DC and Chicago each year.
Approximately how many hours do you spend flying each year?

100 hours (approx. 1 coast-to-coast US
roundtrip each month) . . . . a. 20
25 hours (approx. 2-3 coast-to-coast US
roundtrips each year) . . . . b. 5
10 hours (approx. 1 coast-to-coast US
roundtrip per year) . . . . c. 2
3 hours . . . . d. 0.6
Never fly . . . . e. 0

> **Subtotal (5) air travel footprint:**
> 0.3 x Q11 = _.18_ acres
> *Example: 0.3 x 5 = 1.5 acres*

GOODS
Q12. Compared to people in your neighborhood, how much waste do you generate?

Much less . . . . a. 0.75
About the same . . . . b. 1
Much more . . . . c. 1.25

QUIZ RESULTS:

(1) Food Footprint _3.6_ acres .... Enter from Subtotal (1)

(2) Shelter Footprint _1.2_ acres .... Enter from Subtotal (2)

(3) Public Transit Footprint _.42_ acres .. Enter from Subtotal (3)

(4) Car Footprint _.16_ acres .... Enter from Subtotal (4)

(5) Air Travel Footprint _.18_ acres ...... Enter from Subtotal (5)

(6) Mobility Footprint _.76_ acres .... Add (3) through (5)

(7) Goods Factor _.75_ .... Enter from Question 12

(8) Shelter + Mobility _1.96_ .... Add (2) + (6)

(9) Goods and Services _1.323_ acres ...... Multiply (7) x (8) x 0.9

Your Total Footprint = _6.883_ acres ..... Add (1) + (2) + (6) + (9)

Example:

(1) Food Footprint	4.7 acres
(2) Shelter Footprint	6.0 acres
(3) Public Transit Footprint	0.2 acres
(4) Car Footprint	2.2 acres
(5) Air Travel Footprint	1.5 acres
(6) Mobility Footprint	3.9 acres
(7) Goods Factor	1
(8) Shelter + Mobility	9.9
(9) Goods and Services	8.9 acres
Your Total Footprint =	**24 acres**

In comparison:
The average US Ecological Footprint is 24 acres per person

Your footprint measures _____% of an average US Footprint.

Formula = (Your footprint/24) x 100

Worldwide, there exists 4.7 biologically productive acres per person.

Therefore, if everyone lived like you, we would need _____ planets.
Formula = Your Footprint / 4.7

US Footprint Averages (acres/person)
Food Footprint: 5.5
Shelter: 5.1
Mobility Footprint: 4.3
Public Transit: 0.1
Motorbike: 0.01
Car: 4.0
Air Travel: 0.3
Goods & Services Footprint: 8.6
Average Total Footprint: 23.5

To arrive at your food footprint, the quiz sums up arable land, pasture, sea space, and land areas to sequester CO_2 from the energy expended to grow, process and transport the items. Your choices in the food arena make a sizable difference depending upon your diet. If you purchase only organic food, your impact will shrink further still.

Your goods and services footprints are determined based upon the size of your food, shelter, and mobility footprints. This result considers average lifestyles, and estimates your use of appliances, clothing, electronics, sports equipment, toys, computers, communications equipment, household furnishings, and cleaning products.

The quiz includes services like water, sewage, garbage, telecommunications, education, healthcare, financial services, entertainment, recreation, tourism, military, and other governmental services. As you can see, we attempt to capture many items in a simple quiz, and depending upon your actual lifestyle, your EF could be higher or lower.

Your mobility footprint includes many of the impacts that result from walking, cycling, taking trains, driving cars, and flying. Included in this estimate are areas needed for roads, manufacturing of vehicles, motor vehicle departments, police, insurance, and forests needed to absorb CO_2.

Your housing footprint includes yard area, the energy and materials for constructing the building, and the energy to operate it.

. . . . .

How did your results compare using the two methods of this chapter? In the next section, you'll find the Footprinting Calculator, which will introduce you to the deluxe version of footprinting, with which you can determine even more precisely the impacts of your choices.

THE FOOTPRINTING CALCULATOR

Which has a bigger footprint, snail-mail (postal service) or emails, paper or plastic, beef or soybeans, flying or driving? Each day we are faced with streams of choices. How do we know which ones have a smaller footprint? Certain decisions are so clean-cut , like comparing a 30-pound bicycle to a 2,000-pound single-occupancy automobile. But which footprint is bigger: commuting six miles daily in a car that gets 50 miles per gallon with four people on board, taking the bus, riding a horse, or cycling? This is where you play with the tool, learn its limitations, and see how to make thoughtful estimates. Some of you may be frustrated that every item you consume isn't on our tables. Others might find the detail we have here too much. Because of the plethora of consumer choices and our intentional limit of fewer than 100 items, you will need to find the item that best fits. The system requires you to make assumptions and educated guesses. You might need to do a little digging around for information. Be patient, give it a try; what you will begin to uncover is the five, ten or twenty items that make up the bulk of your footprint. This is what you are after, not decimal place exactness. Once you have a baseline, then month by month, or day by day, you can see how your choices matter.

Footprinting Language

It will help to familiarize yourself with the charts in Appendix B. Tables B.1 through B.4 are used to calculate the footprint of all inputs or flows into your life, Table B.5 is used to calculate the footprint of those inputs that stick around for more than six months, and Table B.6 is used to calculate the footprint of the outputs or wastes from your life.

Jargon control has been engaged, but like any new endeavor, understanding a special meaning for a few words is needed.

Figure 6.8: A typical household embraces a wide array of stocks, makes use of many flows, and generates all sorts of wastes.

Categories: There are six categories of consumption: food; housing; transportation; goods and services; stocks; and wastes. Each has its own chart.

Items: These are the predetermined listings under each category (for example, vegetables, bread, flour, and so on are listed under food).

Flows: Consider anything you purchase that is completely used up within six months as a flow item. Examples of flows are: eating out, electricity, lotto tickets, water, gas, palm readings, plane trips, postage, bus, food, phone, insurance, massage, and so on.

Stocks: All long-lasting goods that you currently own or buy that last for more than six months are stock items.

Cars and Houses: Although your car and house are stocks, they are treated in a special way. The impact of making a car is accounted for when you record fuel use. If you own two or three cars, account for them by the weight per month (after you factor in its useful life and the number of users) on Table B.5 under "Metal." Similarly, for your house, the ff is based on the standard average North American home.

Wastes: These are the items that you recycle or throw in the garbage. All kitchen scraps are assumed to be composted.

Using the Calculator

The first thing you will want to do is make a few copies of Charts B.1 through B.6 in Appendix B.

Step One

Find the item that best matches the item you want to footprint. A banana goes under veggies, an alarm clock under computers and electronics, the cappuccino machine under small appliances, a newspaper under paper and cardboard, and a novel goes under durable paper. Some items require you to find the most similar material. An aluminum canoe goes under metal, a wooden one under furniture, a PVC canoe under plastic, but what about a fiberglass one? I'd put it under plastic.

For items such as pet/cattle feed, look at the ingredients and estimate the rough percentages of the two or three biggest components (e.g. 33% rice, 33% beans and other pulses (soy), 33% turkey). Hay that is for horses can go under straw.

What about items that are made of several materials such as the handles of your pots, bike tires and saddle, lawn mower tires? Look at the ffs of the different materials. For example, the ff for metal is 397 and plastic is 331. Because the factors are close, it is safe to put the entire weight under the primary component. A leather couch with a wood frame could be estimated by percent weight of leather (ff = 2,119) and wooden furniture (ff = 483). You might err on the side of bigger footprint.

Now that you have found the best matching item, on to step two.

Step Two

Enter the amount you use in a month in the "Amount used per month" column, with the exception of your living area. To calculate your housing footprint, simply enter the area of your share of the entire home that you live in on Table B.2. (e.g. 100% of bedroom area, 25% of the kitchen, living room, and office areas, and 50% of the bathroom, garage and shed).

To determine the footprint of flying once a year, divide the hours of the roundtrip flight by 12 to get a monthly amount of time on the plane, and enter this on Table B.3.

To find the footprint of buying a computer that will last for three years, divide its weight by three years and again by 12 months and enter this amount on Table B.5.

If you want to know your food footprint but you only measured your consumption for five days, simply multiply your amounts by six and plug them into the calculator. Weekly amounts, multiply by four.

Step Three

Now multiply your "Amount used per month" by the footprint factor (ff) and you have your ecological footprint (EF) for that item.

Fine Tuning the Calculator

What if an item doesn't really match up that well with the footprint factor given? In this case, the calculator can be fine-tuned using Tables A.1 through A.6. Say your food is all grown locally, or your house was made from timbers from your land, or your neighbor built your furniture with little or no machines or fossil fuels. You can reduce the energy footprint factor by some reasonable percentage. Take a look at the column labeled "energy footprint factor" and "land footprint factor" on Tables A.1 through A.6. Together they add to make the ff. In other words:

$$\text{footprint factor (ff)} = \text{energy footprint factor (eff)} + \text{land footprint factor (lff)}$$

In some cases, you can either scale back the energy footprint factor or eliminate it altogether. You can make your own measurements, question the grower or manufacturer, or make an educated guess.

Notice that the third column on each table, "average per capita use in the US" will give you a rough idea of how your consumption compares to the average for that item. (In some cases this figure is less useful; for example, the 1.2-gallon figure listed for propane on Table A.2: Monthly Housing, is averaged out by per capita use, including all the people who don't use propane.)

Making Comparisons

In this section we will go through each category (food, housing, transportation, etc.) and compare a few choices in each. If the item you want to calculate has no green attributes such as being local, organic, or made with little or no fossil fuels, then you will only need Tables B.1 through B.6. If you purchase lower impact products, use Tables A.1 through A.6, as already mentioned.

Food

Let's start by using Table A.1: Monthly Food Footprint Factors to compare dietary choices. For example, one pound of veggies a month has a footprint of 33 square yards (63 square meters), breads have a monthly footprint factor of 128 square yards (235 square meters), and cheese is 503 square yards (926 square meters). Since all these items are measured in pounds, the ffs alone offer the footprint comparison. Pound for pound, cheese has an EF 15 times that of veggies. Take a look at the fifth row down on Table A.1, "beans and other dried pulses." They have an energy ff of 19 and a land ff of 233 for a total ff of 252. But remember, they are dried, so once cooked they will weigh three to four times more. Although their dry weight ff is 7.6 times that of veggies, once rehydrated their ff is only twice that of veggies for equal amounts of edible food. If you are monitoring your monthly footprint, as we will in the next chapter, just record the amount of dry beans used each month. To calculate the footprint of a single item, for example, two pounds of coffee per month, simply multiply (2 x 512), for a footprint of 1,240 square yards (0.2 acre).

Comparison One

Let's see the difference between a tofu, beef, and chicken burger. We can simply compare the factors, in which case:

a. Tofu is derived from soybeans, so use the "beans and other dried pulses" ff = 252. The dried beans are soaked and turned into soy milk, then congealed into cakes and pressed, resulting in a finished product about three times the weight of dry beans, reducing the ff by three times to 84. To get a pound of tofu, one-third pound of beans are used.
b. Beef: ff = 1,180.
c. Chicken: ff = 335.

A tofu burger's footprint is 4 times less than a chicken burger (335/84), and 14 times less than a beef burger (1,180/84).

Now let's say you raised the chickens in your backyard and grew their feed manually, so there were no fossil fuel inputs. How does this chicken burger compare to a packaged tofu burger?

a. Tofu — still 84
b. Chicken — 185 (only the land component of the ff)

Comparison Two

How about a comparison between buying produce consisting of veggies, potatoes, and fruit at the supermarket versus growing them yourself versus purchasing them locally? If you were to eat 50 pounds a month, here is how you would make the comparisons.

(a) **Supermarket vegetables.** Table A.1: Monthly Food gives an ff for veggies, potatoes and/or fruit, assuming average yields and embodied energy (energy to produce and ship), of 33. Energy accounts for 18, and land, 15.

$$EF = 50 \text{ pounds per month x } 33 \text{ (ff)} = 1,650 \text{ sq. yd.}$$
$$\text{or } 0.34 \text{ } (1,650/4,840) \text{ acres}$$

(b) **Home-grown veggies.** Let's assume that you use no outside inputs such as chemicals, fertilizers, or manures. Further, we will assume your tender care and use of on-site green manures produces yields equivalent to commercial operations. In this case, it would be reasonable to assume your veggie footprint factor to be approximately the land component or 15. In other words, set the energy footprint factor (eff) to zero.

$$EF = 50 \text{ pounds per month x } 15 = 7,50 \text{ sq. yd.}$$
$$\text{or } 0.15 \text{ } (750/4,840) \text{ acres}$$

So, by growing them yourself, fossil-fuel free, you reduced your produce footprint by a factor of 2.2. But if you buy or truck in inputs of organic matter or manure, you will want to include them. You could use the straw ff on Table A.2: Monthly Housing and estimate the volume of your material compared to a fluffed straw bale. Because the ff is for dry weights and your materials might be wet, volume is one way to go. If you buy packaged inputs, they will already be weighed for you; you just need to select the best fit for your ff. What about leaves and seaweed? It is up to you, but my mind says that nature has a use for everything. That seaweed on the beach is part of the ecosystem and is not going to waste there; leaves build forest soils. You could estimate their volume compared to an untied straw bale. On the other hand, leaves from a cemetery might serve little ecological function in the landfill.

(c) **Local veggies.** Estimating their footprint takes either a bit of research or an educated guess. It might be reasonable to assume the land footprint factor to be the same: 15. Some operations might get more production per acre either because of their great soil, knowledge, love, or fertility inputs. Yields can vary widely, but to keep it simple, assume the ff = 15. If you discover your local farmer to be a full chemical commercial operation, the only real savings is the transportation. In this case, you might reduce the energy footprint factor by 25% from 18 to 14. So you add together 17 and 14 to get a total footprint factor of 31. In this case,

EF = 50 pounds per month x 31 = 1,550 sq. yd. or 0.32 acres

If your local organic farm uses few machines and you bicycled to get the produce, set the energy factor to zero and the footprint would be the same as growing them yourself. If you drive to get them, to keep your accounting simple, you might set the energy factor to zero and account for your total gas burned each month separately. If you want to make the comparison more exact, you will soon see how to estimate the footprint for making, say, four car trips a month to the farm. If the farm is organic, but you see a lot of machines in use, and lots of neat bags of soil amendments piled high, perhaps take 50% off the energy factor.

By supporting local farms and eating in season, you are saving significant amounts of nature. As you learn more about the growers, you can fine-tune your factors. If it all seems too complicated, just use the footprint factors (ffs) on Tables A.1 through A.6.

(d) **A home-grown approach.** As an alternative method to footprint home-grown produce, you could measure your garden area and your yields. But to use this method, you will have to multiply your garden area by an equivalence factor. This will compare your garden to world average bio-productive space. As a rough guide, to get your garden footprint, multiply your garden area by three for good soils, by two for fair or average soils, and by one for poor soils.

Remember that all Earth's bioproductive area is "1." If you don't do the above multiplication, you can't add your garden footprint to your other data without an error.

Estimate your soils based on the land as it was before it was converted to garden. If you transformed sandy average soil to good soil, use the average soil equivalence factor. If you truck in inputs, account for them as you go.

For example, a friend of mine, Hank, harvested 2,000 pounds of vegetables from a garden that is one-seventh of an acre or about 700 square yards, on soils that were average (an equivalence of 2).

- To get his garden footprint, we multiply 700 sq. yd. x 2 = 1,400 sq. yd.
- To convert to acres: EF = 1,400 sq. yd. x 1 acre/ 4,840 sq. yd. = 0.29 acres

To determine his very own ff:

Step one: Convert his yield to pounds per month per square yard:

$$\frac{2,000 \text{ lb./yr.}}{700 \text{ sq. yd}} \times \frac{1 \text{ year}}{12 \text{ months}} = 0.238 \text{ lb./sq. yd./month}$$

Step two: His ff = 1/yield x equivalence factor (1/0.238) x 2 = 8.4

Let's compare his yield to standard practices. From Table A.1: Monthly Food Footprint Factors, we see a land ff for veggies, potatoes, and fruit of 15. Through love, skill, and hard work his garden is nearly twice as productive as commercial practices.

Housing

Comparison One — Sharing

Let's begin by comparing the footprints of different sized living spaces. Table A.2: Monthly Housing Footprint Factors lists the per-capita average living space at 582 square feet. Notice how the footprint factor reduces with the age of the home. What is the footprint of a 20-year-old 1,200-square-foot home inhabited by by one, two, or four people? Simply multiply the number of square feet per person by the ff.

EF for one person: 1,200 x 12.2 = 14,640 sq. yd. or 3 acres
Shared by two people: 1,200/2 x 12.2 = 7,320 sq. yd. or 1.5 acres
Shared by four people: 1,200/4 x 12.2 = 3,660 sq. yd. 0.75 acres

Comparison Two — Caring

Now let's see the benefits of extending the life of your home though care and maintenance from the average 40-year life to 80 years. Most homes go through many remodels, overhauls, termite infestations, additions, or are torn down and replaced. We will assume that your home has never been remodeled or infested, just well cared-for. At 60 years, it has had two new roofs and complete paint jobs and is still in good shape. It could last another 20 years without a major restoration. For a simplistic comparison, assume you accounted for the roofing materials, paints, and other maintenance supplies separately. Just your housing footprint in the above three examples would be halved to 1.54, 0.75, and 0.375 acres respectively through caring. The paint and roofing could go under "plastic products" on Table A.5: Monthly Stocks, which has an ff of 331. If the materials weighed 1,500 pounds and lasted 25 years, the additional footprint for maintaining your house would be:

1,500 lb./25 years/12 months to get a per-month weight of 5 lb.
Then multiply this by the ff for plastic:
    5 x 331 = 1,655 sq. yd.
If four people shared the home improvement:
    EF = 1,655/4 = 414 sq. yd. each.

Comparison Three — Conserving

Most of us get our electricity from the grid. The grid refers to a distribution network taking power from different generation facilities. On average, in the US, what comes into your house will be 88 percent fossil and nuclear, 10 percent hydroelectric, 1.5 percent biomass, 0.4 percent geothermal, and 0.1 percent wind. Aside from producing your own power, the best way to reduce your footprint is to reduce your monthly usage. To consider the footprint difference between incandescent light bulbs and compact fluorescent bulbs, assume you have twenty light bulbs and each is on one hour a day. The incandescent bulbs are 75-watts each. What footprint savings would result from switching to 10-watt compact fluorescent bulbs?

(a) **Incandescent.** To find out how many kilowatt-hours (kWh) you would use in one month, multiply 20 bulb-hours x 75 watts x 30 days = 45,000 watt-hours.

To convert to kWh, divide by 1,000 and you get 45 kWh. From Table A.2, we see the ff for grid electricity is 31. So:

EF = 45kWh x 31 = 1,395 sq. yd. or 0.3 acres

(b) **Fluorescent.** Now with 10-watt compact fluorescent bulbs multiply 20 bulb-hours x 10 watts x 30 days = 6,000 watt-hours or 6 kWh.

EF = 6 kWh x 31 = 186 sq. yd. or 0.04 acres

Comparison Four — Combining

Home heating is typically among the top five footprint items. Assume you heat with oil and use 760 gallons a year or 63.4 gallons per month. Table A.2: Monthly Housing gives the ff for fuel oil as 389 sq. yd./gal. Your footprint is:

EF = 63.4 gal. x 389 = 24,660 sq. yd or 5.1 acres

There are many ways to reduce the per person footprint of heating:

+ Have more people share the home. Just by getting one housemate, you halve your heating footprint.
+ You can lower the thermostat, turn it way down when you leave for work, and close rooms not in use.
+ Weatherstrip doors and windows and caulk any drafts. A bigger project would be to increase insulation. Regular maintenance of the heater will also save energy.

Until these improvements are made, you won't know how much you will save. But if your home is drafty and thinly insulated, and you don't actively conserve, reducing your heating footprint by one third to one half is possible without getting a housemate. For a radical change, say you do all of the above and go from 63.4 to 35 gallons per month and have four people in your home, your heating footprint could become:

EF = 35 gal. /4 people x 389 = 3,400 sq. yd. or 0.7 acres

Transportation

Let's find out just how big a footprint our transportation choices involve.

Comparison One — Average car use in the US

From Table A.3: Transportation Footprint Factors, we see that the average American uses 37 gallons of gas each month. The ff is 500, so:
EF = 37 gal. x 500 = 18,500 sq. yd. or 3.8 acres

With an average fuel efficiency of 20 mpg, this fuel will take you 738 miles a month. If you have a ten-mile roundtrip commute each day, by the end of the month, 200 of your miles are commuting miles. What are the other 538 miles used for? Let's assume 240 miles are for visiting family and friends, or three 80-mile round trips. 100 miles are used for joy rides and 98 miles for shopping. Lets see how your footprint could shrink if you exploited multi-modal options.

(a) **Carpooling.** Say you carpool to work with three others in a car that gets 50 mpg. The 200 miles is divided by 50 miles per gallon for a total of 4 gallons used. Now you divide this by four people to get 1 gallon each.
EF = 1 gal. x 500 = 500 sq. yd or 0.1 acres
(b) **Bus.** Say you took the bus for the 240-mile family visits. Use the ff for "Bus, inter-city" from Table A.3: 4
EF = 240 x 4 = 960 sq. yd. or 0.2 acres
(c) **Bicycle.** Your joy rides were by bicycle. Negligible footprint.

(d)**Combining.** Let's say you combined shopping trips, did some by bike, and reduced the miles driven to 10 per month. Your car gets 50 mpg, so fuel use is 0.2 gallons (10 mi./50mpg)

EF = 0.2 gal. x 500 = 100 sq. yd. or 0.02 acres

Now for your new, reduced total:

EF = 500 + 960 + 100 = 1,560 sq. yd. or 0.3 acres

Compared to the average EF of 3.8 acres, this example has nearly 13 times less impact.

Comparison Two — Automobiles

If you were after a one-acre footprint, and allocated 0.1 acres (484 sq. yd.) to gasoline for a 50-mile-per-gallon car, how many miles could be traveled each month? Ready for a little algebra? We want to find the amount of gas that, once burned, has an EF of 0.1 acres.

EF = Amount x ff

We multiply both sides by 1/ff to get:
Amount = EF/ff
Amount (#gal/month) = 484 sq. yd. /500 gal. /sq. yd = 1 gal.
1 gal. X 50 mpg = 50 miles per month

If on average, two people shared the ride, you could go 100 miles a month by car and maintain a 0.1-acre transportation footprint.

Comparison Three — Cross-country Travel

What would be the footprint to travel across America once a year by plane, bus, train, car, bike or horse? Assume the journey is 6,000 miles round trip. Use Table A.3: Monthly Transportation and divide your journey by 12 months to input monthly flow data into the table.

(a)**Plane (economy class):** EF = 14hr. /12 months x 5,216 sq. yd. [ff/hr] = 6,085 sq. yd. or 1.3 acres
(b)**Bus:** EF = 6,000 mi./12 months x 4[ff/mi.] = 2,000 sq. yd. or 0.4 acres

(c) **Train:** EF = 6,000mi. /12 months x 17[ff/mi.] =
   8,500 sq. yd or 1.8 acres

(d) **Car (20 mpg):** EF = 6,000 mi./12 months/20mpg x 500[ff/mi.] =
   12,500 sq. yd. or 2.6 acres

(e) **Car (50 mpg):** EF = 6,000mi. /12 months/50mpg x 500 =
   5,000 sq. yd. or 1 acre

(f) **Bicycle:** Assume the trip takes three months, and your footprint
   will be equal to the amount of additional fuel you feed your body.
   Assume your yearly food intake will increase by:

   1.5 lb./day x 3 months x 30 days/month = 135 lb. yr.

Because you make this trip once a year, divide by 12 to get a monthly increase in food:

   135/12 = 11.25 lb./mo.

If this food is one-third veggies and fruit, one-third bread and one-third noodles and cereals, you would consume 3.75 pounds of each per month.

   EF (Veggie and fruit) = 3.75 x 33 [ff] = 124 sq. yd.

   EF (Bread) = 3.75 x 128[ff] = 480 sq. yd.

   EF (Noodle and cereal) = 3.75 x 118[ff] = 443 sq. yd.

   EF (Total increase in food) = 1,047 sq. yd. or 0.22 acres

(g) **Horse:** 6,000 mi./100 mi. per day = 60 days

   Option A. You need to feed the horse year round, so the EF is its
   monthly food requirements: 30 days x (2.25 lb. soy + 12.75 lb. cereal) = 67.5 lb. soy + 382 lb. cereal

   EF = 67.5 X 252[soy ff] + 382.5 x 118 [cereal ff] = 62,145 sq. yd.
   or 12.8 acres

   Option B. Someone else fed the horse for 10 months, and during
   the trip it grazed on grasses. In this case, we remove the fossil fuel
   component (eff) and use the lff for cereals.

   EF = 2 months/12 months x 450 lb. cereal/month x 118[cereal ff]
   = 8,850 sq. yd. or 1.8 acres

Stocks, Goods and Services

Comparison One — Snail mails or E-mails?

Now we are in a position to compare snail mails to emails. To make this comparison, use Table A.4: Monthly Goods and Services and Table

A.5: Monthly Stocks. Stocks are goods that last longer than six months. I will make some assumptions, but if you have your own data, go ahead and try running the numbers for your particular situation. Let's say that you will send 100 communications per month.

(a) **E-mail**: Assume that you use the computer mostly for email. It weighs 90 pounds and will last four years before either breaking down or becoming obsolete. Your computer ff, found on Table A.5: Stocks is 1,325.

Amount per month = 90 lb./4 years/12 months = 1.9 lb./month

EF (for the computer) = 1.9 lb./month x 1,325 = 2,484 sq. yd. or 0.5 acres

Now consider the footprint of your phone line and Internet provider. Assume the Internet connection costs $15 per month and the Internet portion of your phone bill is $3 for a total of $18. On Table A.4: Monthly Goods and Services, you will find the ff for telephone is 13.

EF (for the phone/Internet portion) = $18/month x 13 = 234 sq. yd. or 0.05 acres

Assume the computer is on one hour a day. At 250 watts per hour, it uses 7.5 kWh/month (250 watts x 1 hr. x 30 days). The ff for electricity, found on Table A.2: Monthly Housing, is 31.

EF (for the electricity portion) = 7.5 kWh x 31 = 233 sq. yd. or 0.05 acres

Finally, let's assume that you used one half-pound of paper, or about 50 sheets to print certain e-mails. The ff for recycled paper, found on Table A.6: Monthly Wastes, is 194.

EF (for the printing portion) = 0.5 x 194 = 97 sq. yd. or 0.02 acres

The grand total EF for emails with these assumptions is: 3,048 sq. yd. or 0.68 acres

(b) **Snail Mail**: Now we will compare the footprint of sending 100 one-page letters per month by regular mail. A ream of 20-pound letter size paper, 500 sheets, weighs five pounds. We will assume that you do a draft for every letter and will use 200 sheets. The weight for paper per month is: 200/500 x 5 lb. = 2 lb.

And we will assume the envelopes weigh another pound. The paper footprint is:

EF = 3 lb. x 194 (ff) = 582 sq. yd. or 0.12 acres

Next, we will determine the footprint of the mail service from Table A. 4: Monthly Goods and Services, assuming that two pounds are domestic and one pound is international. This footprint is:

EF = 2 lb. x 60 (ff) + 1 lb. x 300 (ff) = 420 sq. yd or 0.087 acres

The total EF for snail mail is: 582 + 420 = 1,002 sq. yd. or 0.2 acres

Surprise! For this set of assumptions, emails have more than three times the footprint of snail mails.

Wastes

For wastes, we can compare the footprint of zero recycling, 100 percent recycling and reusing your own packages. We will assume that you generate a similar quantity of recyclable materials as the average person does.

Comparison One

You throw it all away. All potentially recyclable materials are tossed and your footprint is figured from Table A.6: Monthly Wastes using the ff for garbage:

EF = (21 lb. + 1 lb. + 2 lb. + 5 lb. + 5 lb.) x 481 =
16,354 sq. yd. or 3.4 acres

Comparison Two

You recycle every container. The individual ffs are on Table A.6: Monthly Wastes.

EF = 21 lb. x 194 + 1 lb. x 83 + 2 lb. x
335 + 5 lb. X 69 + 5 lb. X 68 = 5,662 sq. yd. or 1.2 acres

Comparison Three

You bring your own packaging and only purchase from a bulk food store. At the end of each month, you recycle two pounds of failed plastic bags and containers. The ff for recycled plastic is 96.

EF = 2lb. x 98 = 196 sq. yd. or 0.04 acres

As you can see, the choices we make result in dramatic footprint differences. In many cases, without any new technology or "green products" we can reduce our footprint. Take some time to play with these charts. Once mastered, you can make estimates rather quickly.

FOOTPRINTING

Now that you've run through some exercises, we're ready to begin footprinting your life. Month by month you will monitor progress toward the sustainability goal arrived at in the Sustainability Sweatshop. I suggest reading through this entire section before you begin.

The process you are about to start requires a commitment similar to an evening night class or learning to operate a computer for the first time. You will need about five to ten hours a month for the first two or three months. After that, the time should halve. I recommend you ensure that this is a good time for you to begin; by giving it the time it deserves, success in achieving your goals is more likely. And the time you invest now will return thousands of hours over a lifetime.

If this is too busy a time in your life, enjoy reading the rest of the book, and clear a future space when it will work.

What You'll Need

Following is a list of things you should have handy before you begin.

+ A weigh scale. A bathroom scale will work for most items, but for lighter purchases, a more sensitive kitchen scale or a hook scale (used for weighing fish, carried by sporting goods stores) is useful.
+ A pocket calculator.
+ A tape measure 10 to 25 feet long or a rope marked off with masking tape at one-foot increments.
+ Copies of the charts and worksheets from Appendix B for the months you commit to the process: Tables B.1 through B.6 — two copies of each (enough for two months); Tables B.7 and B.8 — four copies of each; and Tables B.9 and B.10— one copy of each.
+ Your utility bills, telephone bills, checkbook register, credit card statements, and receipts as needed.

- Pencils, erasers, and scrap paper.
- Two pieces of scrap two-by-four, 12 to 18 inches long, to be placed on the scale where your feet would go. Then you can put a cardboard box, a bin, or a laundry basket on the scale and still read the dial. If needed, a 4-to 5-foot-long two-by-four can be placed on the scale with two of the four legs of a piece of furniture lifted onto it. Double this amount and you have an approximate weight of that piece.
- A box, bin, or laundry basket.

If you have a computer and would like to use a spreadsheet, you can download one from <www.redefiningprogress.org> or <www.globalliving-project.org>. You will need a spreadsheet program capable of running Microsoft Excel (version 4 or newer). I will do my best to keep the spreadsheets available, but I can't offer any long-term guarantees.

A Few Questions

Questions may arise as you begin your personal footprinting process. Here are some common questions and answers.

- **Will the footprint factors change over time?** Yes. Each year the Food and Agriculture Organization (FAO) updates their yield information and the footprinting science becomes more accurate. This book contains the most updated figures at the time of publication. You can check the spreadsheets on the websites periodically to see if significant changes have affected the calculations.
- **We buy food as a household. What should I do?** Say there are four household members and you all eat more or less the same amount and kinds of food; you can simply divide the food footprint by four. If there is a remarkable difference in diet between household members (for example. you are a vegetarian among folks who eat meat and dairy), just exclude items you don't eat. If someone is an athlete, his or her portion of food is probably larger. You'd want to factor this in.
- **Can we footprint as a couple or household?** Yes you can. At the end of each month, just divide your total footprint by the

number of household members. However, keep in mind that if others aren't committed to the process, it could be frustrating to get their data, and, unless you are joined at the hip, your daily choices will differ. With this caution, go for it if it feels right. With a little extra bookkeeping you can track communal and individual footprints and total them at the end of each month.

+ **Should I include business expenses?** No. Double counting would result. Say you sell encyclopedias door to door. I buy a set and mark it on my footprint table under durable paper. The energy footprint factor (eff) of durable paper includes your travel fuel. If you then include the travel on your table, the trip would be counted once by you and once by me. As a rule of thumb, include everything *you* pay for.

+ **What if I buy used items?** Estimate how far into their useful life they were when you took ownership. Say the clothes are broken-in but still have lots of life — use 50 percent. If I save stuff from a landfill, I could rationalize a negative footprint; alternatively, I can still "claim" a portion, reasoning that just because this culture is wasteful, I shouldn't get a free footprint ride. Another example is carpooling or hitchhiking — you can count it as a bus trip or receive it as a gift — it's up to you. There are no eco-police!

A final reminder: stick with one measuring system. You can use metric or US standard measurements, providing you are consistent. (Appendix A contains a table of common conversion factors.) Take a moment to leaf through the worksheets and tables in Appendix A and Appendix B to familiarize yourself with the system.

Step 1: Flows

What flows through your life in a month? Each item purchased that will be used up within six months is recorded on Table B.7: Worksheet 1 — Monthly Flows. You will want to take a copy of this worksheet wherever you go. Fold it up, stick it in your wallet or purse, and keep a pen handy. Take it out each time you buy gas, a meal, go to the movies, etc. Purchases that need to be weighed can be done on your scale that is ready and waiting. If you just returned from the market, your receipt might list all the weights you need. You can total them up item by item, or sort by item, toss them into the laundry basket, and take a measurement. You can get a more accurate measurement of light items with a kitchen scale or a fish scale. If you use the fish scale, you can use a plastic grocery bag to hold the stuff you want to weigh.

Step 2: Taking Stock

Taking stock is a time to tune into your material surroundings and appreciate all that you have. What you are after is a complete list of everything you own that can be listed under the 10 different items on Table B.5: Monthly Stocks Footprint. You will weigh them, estimate their useful life and number of users, assign a dollar value, and ask yourself if you really need or want each of these items.

Figure 6.9: Various types of scales can be used to weigh your flows and smaller stocks.

There are many reasons why this is an important and useful step. For starters:

+ Each item took bounty from nature and had wastes associated with its production. This is where we tally all that up and remove some of the guesswork from your footprint assessment.
+ The impact of your choices will come to light.
+ You will deeply encounter your possessions. You might be very happy with the level of material you tend to buy – that is not for anyone else to judge. Alternatively, you may have moments of reckoning. The sooner the better! Let it be a time of spring-cleaning and freedom by coming face to face with it all. Many of us have no idea where our money goes. This is where you find out.

Figure 6.10
SAMPLE MONTHLY FLOWS WORKSHEET
From March 1, 2003 — March 31st, 2003

Item	Description	Measurement per Person	Cost	Income
Veggies	fruits and veggies	12 lb.	$15.50	
Bread		2 lb.	$4	
Milk		2 qt.	$1.55	
Recycled Aluminum		1 lb.		
Paycheck				$284.00
Recycled Glass		5 lb.		
Recycled Paper		20 lb.		
Eating Out	dinner	$12	$12	
Gas		8 gal.	$10.95	
Firewood		450 lb.	$10	
Entertainment	movies	$6	$6	
Entertainment	disco	$10	$10	
Eating Out	dinner	$15	$15	
Paycheck				$284.00
Electric	grid	310 kWh	$42.95	
Veggies		$25 lb.	$23.50	

- The trends of how you spend money and consume nature will emerge. Is this the trend you want in your future?
- This step can heighten an appreciation for what you have.
- Consumer culture says "things" will get you a sexy partner, bring you happiness, make you free, set you apart from others, etc. Have any of your purchases accomplished these things? What stuff bought on impulse lays idle in your closet, attic, or garage? Let this sobering information direct your future purchases.
- How much clutter do you have? Could you reduce your living space and save cleaning time, money, and footprint? Perhaps you can take a smaller place or find a housemate? Could you pay down the mortgage by selling the clutter?
- "Things" can clog your physical, mental, and spiritual space. They may trip you up in more ways than you think — worry, wishing, guilt... and they can distract you from your non-material or spiritual self.

In the grand scheme of things, this step — taking stock — is often a catalyst for change. Have some fun with it. Choose some good music. Fill the house with the smell of muffins baking and make a day of it! And if you begin to run out of steam, save the pilgrimage to the attic, storage shed, and garage for another day. If you don't want to weigh your stocks, then don't; you could treat Table B.5: Monthly Stocks as you would the other five charts, taking the footprint hit as you buy each item. Your footprint will fluctuate month by month and after a six-month period you can calculate your average footprint, and if you own a housefull of stuff, you might be underestimating your footprint by 5-20 percent. If your initial inventory of stock items doesn't change, you can use the same weight/month figure for each item, month after month. If weighing your stocks is out of the question, choose yourself from one of the descriptions below to get an estimated number of acres for your stocks.

Stock Estimates

A. You live in a house that is 3,000 square feet or larger and have a vacation house. Your large garage holds an SUV and some of the following: a small convertible, a motorcycle, a pleasure boat, a snowmobile, an ATV, a mountain bike, a kayak. You have several of the following: a storage unit, a workshop, a music studio, a finished basement, an extra apartment, a recreation room. You have lots of electronics, possibly a big screen TV, the latest audio or visual equipment, a computer with accessories, and a variety of musical instruments. The kitchen rivals Martha Stewart's and the library spans time and topic. Your stuff would fill a full sized 18-wheeler moving van and weighs about 17,000 pounds. Your "Stocks" footprint is approximately 15 acres.

B. Your home is in the 2,000 square foot range, not grandiose, but comfortable. Your home is well-stocked with what you need, some luxuries and a little more clutter than you would like. You have an extra car and your recreation is partially motorized, but you enjoy your sailboat or canoe. Your toolshed includes a workshop, riding lawn mower and room for hobbies. Your electronics are up to date including a high-speed Internet connection. That tractor-trailer is somewhat more than half full with 12,000 pounds of stocks. Your "Stocks" footprint is approximately 8 acres.

C. This lifestyle is similar to the one above, though with a bit more frugality. The house is 1,000 square feet, you don't keep the extra car, but you still enjoy the boat. You hold onto your things longer and don't always need the newest computer upgrades. You are very comfortable and lack for little in your material world. A good-sized U-Haul truck could move your 9,400 pounds of stocks. Your "Stocks" footprint is approximately 5.5 acres.

D. This lifestyle shares a 700 square foot home and combines frugality with reducing the amount of stuff in your life. You have a decent library, computer, older stereo, tools and toys but you still have room to host a dinner party. You are into human-powered recreation and have a good supply of camping equipment. Your 4,000 pounds of possessions could be moved with the help of a couple of friends with pick-up trucks making a few trips. Your "Stocks" footprint is approximately 2.5 acres.

E. You don't feel the need to own much — just the basics. You share a 400 square foot space that is uncluttered but has little room for more. You do have a laptop, 10 boxes of books, a boom box, a juicer and enough tools to fix your old car, bicycle, do home repairs, and garden. If you need something, you look for it used, make it, or borrow it from a friend. All of your stuff could be packed into one medium-size van. Your "Stocks" footprint is approximately 0.66 acres.

When you're ready to get started, here is how it works. With a scale and a copy of Table B.8: Worksheet 2 — Monthly Stocks, and Table B.5: Monthly Stocks Footprint in your hand, pick a place to begin, any place — let's say your bedroom. You are looking for all articles that last more than six months.

Figure 6.11
TIPS FOR WEIGHING STOCKS

WEIGHING STOCKS

Furniture: Have a friend or two lift one end while you slide the scale underneath. Double your measurement. For a table or bed with legs, place a 4 or 5 foot two-by-four on the scale, zero it, rest two legs on it, and double your measurement. A chair can be balanced on one leg. Get creative. If you don't want to empty a bookshelf, find a piece of scrap wood similar to the shelves and weigh it. If it is four feet long, divide its weight by four and you have the weight per foot. Now measure the total footage of shelves including upright members and multiply by your weight per foot. If the china cabinet looks like too big a project, leave it for next week. Keep moving.

Major appliances: Some have funny weight distribution, so you might want to weigh the right side, then the left side and add them together. (Figure 6.12 provides a list of weights of common appliances in case you don't want to weigh yours or they are built in.) If your appliances are energy efficient, the benefits will show up in the lower monthly flows of gas or electricity.

Clothes and textiles: If you don't want to sort your clothes by cotton, wool, and synthetic, you could make some estimates; for example, are they mostly cotton? If so, you could count them all as cotton without much error. You could also estimate the average life expectancy of all your clothes, then weigh a representative three-foot section of clothes off your closet rod, figure a per-foot weight and then take a linear measure of your closet.

Durable paper and files: You can use a similar trick. Weigh an average three-foot pile of books, divide by three and then multiply by the total length of all your bookshelves. These tricks make the job go fast and if you do them carefully, your answer will still be meaningful.

Here are the steps to filling out Table B.8: Worksheet 2 — Monthly Stocks.

Step A

Weigh each item. Any items made of the same material that have the same number of users and a similar useful life can be weighed together. For example, only you use your cotton tee shirts, jeans, sweats, underwear, socks, sheets and towels, and you estimate them to last five years. Place the two-by-fours on the scale, set the empty laundry basket on top, zero the meter, and fill it with these items. You will need a little help from a friend for your furniture. While your dresser is empty, weigh it too. Don't weigh every drumstick and knick-knack unless they are valuable and you have a collection of them. If you have less than five pounds of a long-lasting item, you can group it with other articles of the same material or "item" or exclude it.

Step B

For each line item, record the number of regular users. If you and your husband share the bed, but he rarely uses the computer, record two for the bed and one for the computer. If your living room is shared by four household members, record four for each item in the room. If only you use the espresso machine, record one.

Step C

Estimate the useful life in months for each item. Some well-built pieces of furniture can last 100 years. Others might only last 10 years. If you like to get new furniture every five years, consider this in your estimate. If you bought it used and figure it was 15 years old and you will stretch it another 15 years, record 30. Do you get a new computer every 2 years or 8 years? Factor in how you tend to use things.

Figure 6.12
WEIGHTS OF MAJOR APPLIANCES

Appliance	Weights in Pounds		
	small	medium	large
Refrigerator	77	166	347
Microwave	28	42	68
Range	103	166	234
Dishwasher	80	90	120
Clothes Washer	80	156	193
Clothes Dryer	114	121	145
Chest Freezer	115	150	220
Air Conditioner	72	133	163
Hot Water Tank	130	180	250
Gas Furnace	114	146	176
Oil Furnace	250	315	410
Wood Stove	225	350	493

Step D

To get the weight per month, divide the weight by the number of users, then divide that figure by the life expectancy measured in months. For example, (35 lb / 2 users) / 24 months = weight per month.

Step E

Estimate the item's current dollar value. How much would you get for these items if they sold at a yard sale, in a consignment shop, or through a local classified ad? You might estimate your 5-year cotton all together, your 20-year wool together, and the 50-year wool carpet by itself. Don't bog down. Pretend the crowds are coming at six in the morning and you need to put a sticker on it now. The intention here is to estimate your net worth, which includes the value of everything you own. If you have homeowner's insurance, you might have a list already. Adjust the prices from the replacement value to the value that you could sell it for.

Step F

As you encounter each article, ask yourself if it is clutter. Under the clutter column write "yes", "no" or "some." You might use this as a time to make a big pile of things you are ready to unload and save yourself the recording work. To unload items you can:

- Have a yard sale, or go to a swap meet or flea market.
- Bring items to a consignment shop.
- List them in a "penny-wise" paper.
- Make a poster with a list of items for sale.
- Put them in your front yard with a "free stuff" sign.
- Take it to Goodwill or a thrift store.
- Donate it to charity.
- Give it to friends.

Have fun with the downsizing. Try not to throw out perfectly good things, as this wastes precious nature.

Again, try not to bog down or get too sidetracked unless you are having fun with it; an entire bedroom or living room can be done in two to four hours with the help of a friend. If you are excited by the process of taking stock, do it all in a whirlwind, making quick estimates. Or, you can pace yourself and do a meticulous job, footprinting a room each week. If you are busy now, plan to do your stocks over the next few months — they aren't going anywhere until you decide they are. You can begin recording your flows right away and slowly fill in your stocks table.

Figure 6.13
SAMPLE MONTHLY STOCK WORKSHEET
Worksheet 2: Monthly stocks from March 1, 2000 — March 31, 2000

Item	Description	Weight	# of Users	Life Exp. (Months)	Weight/ Month	Cost or Value	Clutter?
Cotton	Clothes & Towels	55 lb.	1	60	0.92	$50	some
Wool	Sweaters & Blankets	18 lb.	1	120	0.15	$50	no
Leather	Shoes & Jackets	12 lb.	1	60	0.2	$75	some
Computer	Pentium	95 lb.	2	36	1.32	$1,200	no
Electronic Equipment	Radio & Stereo	65 lb.	2	96	0.34	$300	no
Furniture	Kitchen Table	80 lb.	4	240	0.25	$100	no
Glass	Kitchen Ware	200 lb	4	120	0.42	$50	lots
Major Appliance	Refrigerator	222 lb.	4	120	0.46	$300	yes
Major Appliance	Dishwasher	167 lb.	2	120	0.7	$150	yes
Metal	Pots & Utensils	45 lb.	4	240	0.05	$200	some
Cotton	Towel	8 lb.	4	36	0.05	$10	some
Durable Paper	Magazines	50 lb.	2	24	1.04	$0	lots

All articles that you record on Table B.8: Worksheet 2 — Monthly Stocks will end up on Table B.5: Monthly Stocks Footprint, so use the same item names on the worksheets as are used on the charts. (for example, furniture, small appl., durable paper). This will make it easy to transfer worksheet totals to the charts. Remember, the long-lasting stock items are converted to monthly figures.

When measuring each article, choose between either the US standard or metric unit of measure indicated for that item. The footprint factors are formulated for those measurement units only. For example, don't use ounces when pounds are asked for. Make a point of double-checking your units of measure now and again, until you get the system down.

If you later get rid of the dishwasher, put a line through it on Table B.8 and retotal your "Major Appliance" items for the next month. If you get a new computer, add a new article to Table B.8 and retotal as above. If you throw the dishwasher in the trash, list its weight under garbage that month and cross it off your stocks list. Don't worry about the food in your cupboards or your toiletries. You will record them as flows as you bring them into your home.

Step 3. Determining Your Footprint

At the end of each month, total the amount of stocks and flows for each item and place the figures on Tables B.1 through B.6. For example, add all your weights of veggies, potatoes and fruit from your monthly flows worksheets and record the total on Table B.1: Monthly Food Footprint in the "Amount used per month" column. Then do the same for stocks. For example, add together all "weight per month" entries on Table B.8: Monthly Stocks Worksheet for cotton, and record that number on Table B.1: Monthly Stocks Footprint in the "Amount per month" column. Multiply the "Amount per month" by the footprint factor for each item and put the result in the EF column.

Total the footprint of all items on Tables B.1 through B.6 and place the totals on Table B.9: Monthly Totals, then add categories 1 through 6 to get your footprint.

Divide square yards by 4,840 to get acres, and divide square meters by 10,000 to get hectares. Place your footprint on Table B. 10. You did it! You now know your ecological footprint. Treat yourself to a long walk in the forest — you deserve it! And appreciate that you can now begin working your way toward your sustainability goal. Our second tool, *Your Money or Your Life*, will strengthen all that you have done so far and help tremendously with the process of shrinking your footprint.

SEVEN

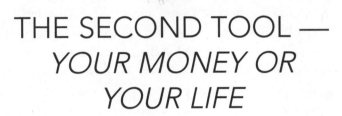

THE SECOND TOOL — *YOUR MONEY OR YOUR LIFE*

S peaking of *Your Money or Your Life*, by Vicki Robin and Joe Dominguez, the late Dartmouth professor and sustainability scientist Donella Meadows said, "This book is not only profound, but subversive." Profound because it is honest and makes good sense. Subversive because ordinary people nod along with its premise: that less is more.

The comprehensive nine-step program from *Your Money or Your Life* (*YMOYL*) has helped thousands of people transform their relationship with money. People who use the method report spending less and saving more. Through assessing their fulfillment and values as related to their consumption, readers have been able to free up time for family, hobbies, their spiritual life and service work.

If you are already following the nine steps, great; you are way ahead of the game. If *YMOYL* has been on your reading list or is gathering dust on your bookshelf, perhaps now is the perfect time to start the program. If you don't have *YMOYL* — don't worry; *Radical Simplicity* contains an abbreviated version of what you need to get started with the first five steps. Having said that, if you want the full benefits of the nine-step program, *YMOYL* is essential.

YMOYL asks you to keep track of every penny you spend and then figure your monthly totals for food, housing, transportation, and so on. Additionally, you are asked to inventory every item you own and assign a monetary value to it. This probably sounds familiar, as we did these steps in the last chapter while determining our footprint. You are then shown how to determine how much of your time — or life energy — you spent to obtain everything you consumed that month. A self-evaluation process follows, in which you ask yourself if the trade of life energy for stuff was worth it, and if the purchases were in alignment with your values. Month by month you will track your earnings and money spent. As your savings grow, you will also track the interest income you receive each month. When the amount you spend per month equals your monthly interest income, you are free from paid employment for the rest of your life.

THE NINE STEPS OF YMOYL

The nine-step program is really about building a lifestyle based in whole systems; understanding that the whole of your life is greater than the sum of the parts. It is about mindfulness. You will know it is working when you cut your friends' hair, get rid of credit cards, blanket your television, get out of debt, brown bag your lunch, vacation locally, have tea with your neighbor, meditate or pray, and save more money than you ever thought possible.

A whole-systems life could happen for you through the magic of the universe — tomorrow. But say it doesn't. You might then decide to take on the full nine-step program.

THE FAMILY OF FULFILLMENT CURVES

We often get on the treadmill without much prompting while in high school. We happily join in our culture's preoccupation with stuff, egged on by a barrage of advertisements. Once out on our own, we feel an excitement to set up our first home. We begin to acquire the basics of survival: pots and pans, a toaster, a desk, a bed and so on. Each new item brings a good deal of fulfillment.

Once out of college, with our first real job and a few credit cards, we set out to acquire some comforts. Yes, to have a car that you don't need to park on a hill just in case the battery finishes dying — that feels good. Zero percent financing, who can resist? The boom box that survived many dorm-room dance parties gets upgraded as your CD collection expands. Proper oak bookshelves now hold your reading list and you feel grounded. As you acquire comforts, chances are your fulfillment grows, but not by the leaps and bounds of your survival phase.

With your first promotion, you are now in the market for some luxuries. This time you will choose the color and style of your car, one that matches your personality. You add on a sunroom and fully remodel your kitchen. Within hours of being in the new car, the new-gadget buzz wears off and the stress of working overtime and handling other people's problems returns. Organizing the plumber, electrician, and cabinetmaker has your nerves shot and you and your partner have a quarrel. "We never go for walks on the beach anymore." You never notice the point of transition, but your playful laughter and spontaneous eccentricity now needs to fit into a weekly planner. You are now on the slippery slope of beyond enough. You have too much of the things that don't bring fulfillment and not enough of the things that do.

Authors Vicki and Joe have pinned the point on the fulfillment curve where you peak — where you have what you need, you enjoy what you have, but there's no stressful excess. You have enough. To discover your own unique enoughness point is a vital step in the process of *YMOYL*.

Four Qualities and Six Realities of "Enoughness"

When we locate our unique enoughness point, several qualities can enter our life:

1. **Purpose.** Less distracted with things, our higher purpose can rise above the background noise of society.

2. **Accountability to Earth, society, our family, and ourselves.** We can decide not to let consumer addiction ruin our life, our marriage, or the planet.

3. **An internal yardstick.** This means that we nurture a profound understanding of how much is enough, independent of our country of origin and aligned with our values of what is fair and sustainable.

4. **FI.** In *YMOYL*, the term FI is used to mean *financial integrity*, *financial intelligence* and *financial independence*. Financial integrity means being <u>responsible</u> for the implications of the money that flows through our life; our spending is aligned with our values. Financial intelligence means <u>spending our life energy wisely.</u> Financial independence means having <u>saved enough</u> to meet monthly expenses from interest income. After this happens, expenses associated with work can decrease.

These four qualities can lead to six realities:

1. **Peace of mind.** With your financial house in order, fear and anxiety of not having enough fades. There is space to explore your spiritual path, space to grow.

2. **Out of debt.** Never to return.

3. **Savings.** With savings, you will feel secure that, should an unforeseen illness or emergency arise, your life will not fall apart.

4. **Skills.** With your extra time and freedom, you develop new skills that make simple living more fun and easy. You can now swing a hammer and hit the nail, you can fix your own bike, and you can grow your own vegetables.

5. **Community.** With more of yourself available, you get involved. You might even meet some of your non-human neighbors.

6. **Income.** Having located an enoughness point independent of societal pressures, obtaining sufficient income now becomes, in the words of Thoreau, "a pastime, not a hardship." Wanting to feel secure is a very basic human need; security can mean money in the bank and insurance, but it can also mean dear friends and a bountiful garden.

When we participate in the global economy, we become global citizens. What we think we need is often not determined by our inner sense; instead, we compare ourselves to our neighbors or to what the advertisers tell us we should have, or to the only life we have ever known. The five steps in this chapter will help you define for yourself how much is enough.

A synergy builds when these six realities enter your life. You feel more confident to walk your path — one that serves you, as well as the greater world, and is of your own design. Where you have the time for friends, family, and walks on the beach.

In reality, your financial house is also your ecological house. How you consume is typically the largest interaction you have with all life. This is where you decide other creatures' fate — who lives and who dies. Every product, every dollar, is really nature: life forms and landforms consumed, killed, or devoured for our wants and needs. There is no escaping this. Footprinting helps us to have a global reference for our enoughness point, measured within the context of all life, all people, and future generations.

WHY IS THIS TOOL SO TIMELY?

For 14 years, I have been working and searching for ways to achieve a peaceful, sustainable human existence on Earth. *YMOYL* still stands out to me as one of the most hopeful tools and trends.

We all stand at a crossroads — one road is faint, forested, and intriguing. The other is a four-laner clogged with traffic, mortgages, and plastic baby toys. As loan debt rises, corporations are ready with open arms, credit cards, and fat paychecks. It is a time to search the soul.

If you're stuck on the treadmill, you might be spending too much time on four-laners and decompressing in front of the television to ever realize that alternatives are possible. Some people end up trying the alternatives without sufficient available energy and/or skills to succeed, and become discouraged, puzzled by their failure to achieve their goals. What we are after is to learn to stop an approach that isn't working and find a better route. Mastering these tools might seem like a lot of work, but the effort will be more than worthwhile. Imagine yourself in 20 years reflecting back on your life. A year of dedication now will be as far away and forgotten as your last year of junior high school. But if that year frees the next 50 years to fulfill your wildest dreams, it could be the most profound year of your life.

Perhaps you're already a simple liver. You have taken the time to set your ecological house in order and are now ready for the next steps. Now what? Do you want to help bring back salmon to your watershed; create a farmers' market; protect a threatened landscape; work with inner-city youth? Do you dream that the next generation will be free of war and exploitation? Perhaps you and your friends have been scheming about something positive, a needed venture, a new movement or a community building activity. Imagine if a group of ten people with a host of skills and big hearts were freed from much of the 40-hour workweek. How much more possible might your collective vision be?

YMOYL prepares you to be available when called to task. We are facing challenging times. But if we use our newfound freedom to serve, while fully coming alive ourselves, then big changes are possible. YMOYL speaks a language that transcends politics, religion, and pop culture, and speaks to people's best sense of what is good and right. That language brings people together instead of causing further divisions; it must be a language of inclusion, compassion and common sense. Some simple and powerful assumptions behind YMOYL are:

- People are good and want to do what is best for all.
- By not shaming or blaming ourselves or others, a better environment for growth is created.
- We will make incremental, but radical changes when we see how we ourselves will benefit.
- What's good for me is good for the planet.

The assumption is that when we come alive and speak an inclusive language, fulfilling our biggest dreams becomes more possible.

THE MAKING OF A MOVEMENT

The entire voluntary simplicity movement has had incredible success so far, and is still in its infancy. Here are a few headline clips to give you a sense of its potential as a bigger mass movement.

On November 6, 1995, *Time* magazine reported, "Surprise! The gurus who promote the pleasures of unadorned living are busier (and richer) than ever. *YMOYL* has grossed $3.5 million and sold 350,000 copies in just three years. In that time, Robin has given more than 600 press interviews, plowed through two 10-city book tours, appeared twice on Oprah and co-conducted financial seminars around North America. Before the book was written, she hadn't been on an airplane in 20 years ...They have put the profits they have netted into a charitable foundation."

People Weekly ran a story in November 1992 that told Joe Dominguez' story of growing up in Harlem, where he delivered groceries at the age of 8. "A gifted student, he left the City College of New York to work as a messenger at a Wall Street brokerage firm." He soon became a technical analyst. In the later 1960s, Joe put his program in motion. "Living frugally, he saved all he could, charted his income and expenses and focused on the day when his investment earnings would exceed his spending. Five years later, in 1969, the moment arrived." With $80,000 squirreled away at age 30, he quit — never to work for money again.

Even with the authors suggesting people get their book from the library, it has sold 800,000 copies to date, and remains in the top 1,000 list after 30 months on the *Business Week* best-seller list. A poll sponsored by the Merck Family Fund indicated that 82 percent of Americans agreed with the statement "We buy and consume far more than we need." Earlier we cited a poll whereby only 30 percent of the wealthiest billion report being very happy and of those earning $274 a day, 27 percent stated, "I cannot afford to buy everything I really need."[1] Some are realizing that money can't buy love, that their excess material might even stand in the way of their dreams. A powerful awakening is underway; is the tide turning? As government and business push patriotic consumerism, people's better sense is to scale back.

As early as 1993, *YMOYL* enjoyed great success, making the *New York Times* best-seller list four times. "This is not a fad," Joe Dominguez insisted. "It's a philosophy upon which this country was founded. It's about squeezing the buck until the eagle grins." And what were the sales gimmicks of these gurus of frugality? In a prominent box under a snapshot of Vicki cutting Joe's hair was a list titled, "Frugal Tips From the Experts:"

+ Buy what you need but don't "go shopping"
+ Take care of what you own
+ Do it yourself
+ Anticipate your needs
+ Get it for less
+ Buy it used
+ Pay off your credit-card balance
+ Walk or bicycle to do errands

The *Boston Globe* posed the question "What is the gift for the person who has everything?" "How about nothing," suggested Vicki Robin. "I'm encouraging people to give each other time," she said.

SUCCESS STORIES

On May 24, 1995, The *Wall Street Journal* reported on Kees Kolff, a physician, and Helen Kolff, a former teacher who used *YMOYL* to cut expenses by 20 percent. They retired from paid employment two years after starting the program. "Now we have the freedom to do the kind of work we want without thinking of compensation," said Ms. Kolff, who planned to help environmental groups. She continued, "There are lots of things that need doing that just don't pay." As for Mr. Kolff, "It's not that I don't love my work as a physician. I do. But over the past few years, I've become more and more concerned about the health of the whole system, as well as the health of individuals. Now I'd also like to think of myself as a physician to the planet."

In a September 21, 1995 *New York Times* article, Gloria Quinones of East Harlem said, "I feel free. I've broken out of that loop and I don't want it back." She left a $74,000-a-year job to raise her sons, Diego 10 and Julian, 14. The family now lives on her husband's salary as a public school teacher. In the same article, Kathryn and Thomas Henchen of Holmen, Wisconsin were reported to have reduced their combined monthly expenses from $2,500 to $900 in 14 months, while they paid off their mortgage of $50,000. Kathryn said they use their added time to enjoy each other's company, see family and friends, garden and appreciate nature.

. . . . .

In the next section, we will discuss some of the different ways you might consider applying this tool.

WAYS TO USE THIS TOOL

As a graduate of *YMOYL*, you will need only a fraction of the income you thought you needed. In this new world, opportunities multiply like rabbits without weasels. Here are some examples of approaches possible with this tool.

Financial Independence

To become financially independent means that your interest income equals what you spend. Work for money is now optional. Further, it means that you take responsibility for your actions and live in accord with your values. If you are a company lifer, you may decide to retire early. This can open a job for the under-employed, save the company money, and give you time to do your heart's work.

Periodic Financial Independence

The late David Brower spoke of a Green Cross — to heal the Earth. He encouraged people to make a commitment to serve the Earth instead of serving in the military. To accomplish this, you could save enough money through reducing your demand to dedicate a year or two to the Earth. As a student of *YMOYL*, you will overflow with ideas to support yourself in a spartan fashion — a boot camp of your own design that is full of discipline and rigor and that works for your highest ideals. Locate an organization you resonate with and learn about their projects and volunteer opportunities. Volunteer on a project or two and if there is synergy, offer a year volunteer commitment. Chances are, if you do quality work and are dependable, positive, honest, and dedicated, you will get an awesome reference and maybe even job offers. What have you got to lose? If you follow your heart, good things will follow. They might even chase you.

Flexible Work

A flexible work schedule has allowed many people to integrate simple living into their lives. Once you spend less, you may simply transition to part-time work. There is a growing trend to work from home. With the Internet, all sorts of small businesses can happen from many a small town where housing is still affordable. Sharing a workspace and freedom from a commute will save money, time and footprint. Some people may feel isolated at home, while others will be jazzed to be with their partner, kids, gardens and community.

A Job You Truly Believe In

You may be one of the fortunate people who love your work and are fulfilled by your contribution. Why change anything then? Maybe you don't need to. However, say, for instance, that you could live on half the money. Why not take a salary cut and hire another person so more good works can happen? Or, with lower salaries, your products could become more affordable, enabling others to also earn less.

Restorative Employment

We can restore the health of the whole ecological and social system through our employment. Few jobs today are even in the ballpark. However, it is within human capacity, both technologically and ethically, to leave the Earth in better shape each day. By relearning to operate within ecological laws, in balance, we can improve the health of the system. When we grow organic food, protect habitat, restore damaged land and redesign cities to be car-free, we restore Earth.

Each of us will decide how this tool will best fit in with the whole of our lives. Regardless of how we apply this tool, the first five steps of the nine step program will be the same.

THE FIRST FIVE STEPS

Becoming conscious of how we use our life energy and consume nature takes considerable focus in the beginning, like learning to ride a bike.

But with practice, the monitoring of our monetary and biophysical impact will become second nature. All you will need to get started is:

+ One copy of Tables C.1 through C.6, Table C.7: Net Worth Worksheet, Table C.8: Real Hourly Wage (RHW).
+ The Tables B.7 and B.8, Worksheet 1 — Monthly Flows and Worksheet 2 — Monthly Stock; and Table B.9: Monthly Totals, which we began using in the last chapter.
+ A calculator, pencils and scrap paper.

Step 1: Making Peace with the Past

Determine how much money you have earned in your lifetime. It's not that hard. Sum up all income to date — on the books, off the books, gifts, capital gains, tips, etc. Enter the amount in Life Earnings on Table C.7: Net Worth Worksheet.

So, what have you got to show for it? To calculate your net worth add together your liquid assets and fixed assets, then subtract everything you owe (liabilities). Your list of liquid assets includes all your cash, bank accounts, stocks, bonds, mutual funds, life insurance cash value, etc. Enter the amount on Table C.7: Net Worth Worksheet as liquid assets.

Most of your fixed assets will have already been listed and assigned a value from the footprinting exercise in the last chapter. So, total the value of all items on Table B.8: Monthly Stocks Worksheet, and add to this the market value of your house(s) and car(s). Enter the amount on Table C.7 as fixed assets.

Your liabilities include all loans (bank, school, friends, car, mortgage, and so on), credit card debt, unpaid bills, etc. Enter the amount on Table C.7: Net Worth Worksheet as liabilities.

Net Worth = (Liquid Assets + Fixed Assets) - Liabilities

The purpose of Step 1 is to get a clear picture of how powerful you are at bringing money into your life, and instill confidence and facilitate goal setting. This step will also help you to identify clutter and visualize simplifying your life. Some of you might do this step and realize you could retire from paid employment immediately. If your picture is less rosy, if you are deep in debt, take a deep breath and a walk in the forest. The bright side is that you have seen the reality of your situation sooner rather than later. This might ignite some bold changes in old patterns. Remember: guilt, fear, and anxiety won't help.

Step 2: Being in the Present

When we earn money, we are trading our precious life energy for dollars. Our real hourly wage is often much less than our salary because we have many expenses related to our job that we do not get paid for, such as commuting, meals out and child care. Additionally, our 40-hour workweek is much longer if we include the time spent commuting, costuming, and sitting zoned out in front of the TV after a stressful day. Table C.8: Hourly Wage versus Real Hourly Wage (RHW) will walk you through the calculation of your Real Hourly Wage (RHW). This step can generate powerful insights by enabling us to see how much of our life we trade for each dollar we earn.

Keep track of every cent that comes into and goes out of your life. Table B.7: Worksheet 1 — Monthly Flows and Table B.8: Worksheet 2 — Monthly Stocks are where you record these amounts. Again, anything that is used up within six months is recorded under Flows, while items that last more than six months are recorded as Stocks. These are the sheets that you fold and carry around with you for both footprinting and YMOYL.

The purpose of Step 2 is to allow you to become aware of the true price at which you are trading your most precious resource — your life energy — and to demonstrate clearly what you are trading that energy for.

Step 3: Where Is It All Going?

At the end of each month, total the amount of money you recorded for each item. For example, add together all your veggie expenses, all your gasoline expenses, all your entertainment expenses, etc. on Table B.7: Worksheet 1 — Monthly Flows. Record the total for each item on Tables C.1 through C.6. For example, the "veggies" total goes on Table C.1: Monthly Food — YMOYL and "gasoline" goes on Table C.3: Monthly Transportation. On Table B.8: Worksheet 2 — Monthly Stocks , total only any new additions to the cost column of this month's worksheet for each item, and enter those amounts on Table C.5: Monthly Stocks — YMOYL, in the dollars spent/month column for each item.

Total the dollars spent within each category, (e.g. total "Dollars Spent per month" on Table C.1: Monthly Food — YMOYL) and enter in the sub-total box at the bottom of Tables C.1 through C.6. Transfer these totals to Table B.9: Monthly Totals.

To determine the hours of life energy you traded for each item on Tables C.1 — C.6, simply divide the dollars spent/month by your RHW (Real Hourly Wage). Enter your result in the hours of life energy column for each item. Total your income for the month from Table B.7: Worksheet 1 — Monthly Flows and record on Table B.9: Monthly Totals.

The purpose of Step 3 is to demonstrate the balance between income and spending patterns, and create a picture of how you are actually living, by determining the hours of life energy you have traded and what you received for it.

Step 4: Three Questions That Will Transform Your Life

This is the core of the *YMOYL* program. It is working when you walk into the store with one item on your list and walk out with only that one item. On Tables C.1 through C.6, you ask yourself three questions of each line item.

1. Did I receive fulfillment, satisfaction and value in proportion to life energy spent?
2. Is this expenditure of life energy in alignment with my values and life purpose? Refer to the footprint and hours of life energy traded for each item.
3. How might this expenditure change if I didn't have to work for a living?

For each line item, use one of the following marks, mark a "-" if you do not receive fulfillment in proportion to the hours of life energy spent in acquiring that item, if that expenditure is not in alignment with your values and purpose, and/or if the expense could diminish if you were not working for a living. Mark a "+" if you believe that upping this expenditure will increase fulfillment, will demonstrate greater personal alignment, or will increase after Financial Independence. Mark a "0" if that line item is just fine on all counts.

Figure 7.5
SAMPLE TABLE C.1 MONTHLY FOOD

Item	Dollars/Month	Hours of Life Energy	Fulfillment	Alignment	After FI
Veggies	$54	8.3	+	+	+
Bread	$30	4.6	0	-	-
Flour, Rice	$73	11.2	-	0	+

The purpose of Step 4 is to clarify your earning, spending, values, purpose, sense of fulfillment and integrity; to help you discover what is "enough" for you and render yourself immune to advertising. You'll be able to create a map of your interactions with the planet and use solid information, intuition and ethics to guide your lifestyle.

Step 5: Making Life Energy Visible

In this step, you will create a plot of your total monthly income, total monthly dollars spent, and your FI income from interest-bearing accounts or investments. You may want to make a poster-sized version and post it where you will see it every day.

The purpose of Step 5 is to show the trends in your financial and ecological situation, and give you a sense of progress over time. This step will also provide feedback on your changing sense of fulfillment, as you become more aware of the impact of your spending, in turn providing inspiration and stimulus to stay with the program.

. . . . .

Some aspects of Step 6: Valuing Your Life Energy will be explored in later sections of this book. For now, congratulations! You have worked through the entire epic journey of tracking life energy and footprints. I encourage you to stay with it until you reach your sustainability goal.

EIGHT

THE THIRD TOOL — LEARNING FROM NATURE

The landscape speaks to us constantly. Books and teachers can help us learn from nature, but are no substitute for a shimmering beach or a lonely desert. Hopefully, there is a magical, wild place near your home, accessible by foot, pedal, or bus; an undomesticated corner passed over and for now forgotten, where you can take time regularly to learn from nature. What draws your attention? Is it the morning canopy singers? The edible plants in a nearby field? Whose tracks are on the sandbar today? Maybe you're not curious now and need time to wander. Each of us learns differently — your curiosity will tell you where to start. The most important thing is to be with nature on her terms.

COURTING THE WILD

The ideas in this section are nothing new. Many great books and resources are available about being in nature. What I'd like to offer is a suggestion: that however you enjoy being in nature, consider upping your dosage. Like those doctors who recommend saturation levels of vitamin C, I'm suggesting spending one or two hours of each day in nature. Not only as a fun exercise, but also as a way to remain sane and grounded in a stressful world; as a way to continually expand our compassion for all life. Eat the wild plants; know the birds by their song; sense the approaching storm; see the first buds swell.

The tools discussed up to this point can help us, but nature can inspire us. For a culture alienated from wilderness, coming to feel comfortable and intimate there will take time and experience. But, by "courting the wild" we might be influenced by a beautiful and powerful force that moves us to live according to our values and visions.

Wherever you live, chances are you can find passionate people who have dedicated their lives to understanding nature. They will tell you more than you may want to know, unless you find the one who specializes in what you're hungry to learn. Then you will hope they keep talking. By following your intuition, you will find books, people, and events to accelerate your learning.

Some activities in nature are utilitarian, yet they lure us out into her beauty. Most people I've hunted or fished with do it for solitude or to be in nature with their good friends. Putting food on the table is secondary. If done responsibly, living more directly from nature can reduce our overall impact. We see who gives their lives for us to live. Alternatively, you might be interested in a non-utilitarian time in nature — time to wander, meditate, or learn the flowers. Follow your own inspiration.

Fear of Nature

When I was 20 years old, I was afraid to be in the forests. I was scared of wild animals and of other men stronger than I was. I had a 12-gauge shotgun in the house and two bullets on the dresser. I hunted and felt I had the right to defend myself. If someone came into my camp or house, I thought at the time, I'd blow him away. It took a long time to be able to sleep unarmed in a tent and not feel vulnerable. After many nights of not being threatened, I have finally relaxed. Getting rid of the TV, so saturated with violence, has helped. A year after I got rid of the

TV, I sold the gun. Some fears are healthy, but after 24 years without a TV or a gun, I realize that my fear was irrational.

After overcoming a deep fear of the outdoors, I have slept hundreds of nights in wild lands without a weapon or a tent. Many times I have seen or tracked grizzly bears, black bears, cougars, wolves, coyotes, elephants, buffalo, tigers, karapu korunga, wolverine, moose, and rattlesnakes. All these animals could kill me, yet I've never been seriously threatened.

Are you afraid to be in nature? Are you afraid of men, lightning, being cold, or wildlife? It pays to be prepared and learn survival skills on easier adventures where there is more margin for error. Work up to wilderness expeditions – you'll gain confidence as you go. Your life is more endangered in an automobile than in nature, but knowing that won't help overcome the fear. It takes experience. Below are some suggested ways to learn from nature.

BEING IN NATURE

Secret Spot

The Wilderness Awareness School in Duvall, Washington uses the "secret spot" as a place to begin learning. The idea is this: you locate a spot in nature that invites you in. Then you return for an hour each day for a year. It is best if the spot is close to home so you can cycle or walk there. Are you wondering, "What am I going to do for an hour in the same spot every day?" You can sit quietly and observe what's going on. Your hearing or sense of smell might heighten if you close your eyes. Try taking ten minutes to focus on each sense: sounds, sights, smells, touch and intuition. While you sit quietly, what birds come in? What animal tracks, webs or feathers arrived since yesterday? What interactions between species do you notice? How do you feel in relation to this place? Maybe you want to let go of thoughts, plans, and worries and remain present to each passing moment. You can keep a journal, write poems and stories, or make detailed observations. Draw a map of a 20' by 20' area; learn every plant and animal there.

Walking Meditation

Thich Nhat Hanh, a Vietnamese Buddhist monk, encourages a walking meditation together with a breathing meditation for calming the mind and body. He states, "Walking meditation means to enjoy walking without any intention to arrive. Usually in our daily life we walk because we want to go somewhere. Walking meditation is different. Walking is only for walking. You enjoy every step you take. The Zen master Ling Chi said that the miracle is not to walk on burning charcoal or in the thin air or on the water; the miracle is just to walk on earth. You breathe in. You become aware of the fact that you are alive. You are still alive and you are walking on this beautiful planet. That is already performing a miracle... You walk as if you kiss the earth with your feet, as if you massage the earth with your feet."

Owl Walk

This slow walk is best done in bare feet. Keep your head level and eyes straight ahead. Open your peripheral vision as wide as possible. Before you shift your weight, feel the ground with your forward foot to make sure you can transfer your weight there. Keep your posture very straight and knees flexible and slightly bent. Open your senses widely as you go. Stop if you can't take it all in. Occasionally stop and look over each shoulder, then continue. Try to become invisible to the forest. This type of walking has gotten me home many nights in the forest when my flashlight batteries went dead.

Vision Quests

There are many types and forms of vision quests. They are typically taken solo and involve fasting in a place free of human influence. Their duration can be from 24 hours up to 40 days. You don't have to fast, but if you do, it will be an entirely different experience. Fasts, vigils, dreams, ceremonies, prayers, exertion (long runs, bikes, or climbing mountains) — each opens us to distinct planes of being.

It is best to have guidance from an elder, your family, or close friends when you depart and when you return. It can be an emotional time and it is good to have prearranged support from someone who understands and supports you and what you are doing. You can also have a friend check your status during the quest. You can leave a daily note or move a stone from a pile in an agreed-upon fashion. If you have problems, they will notice and take action. You can quest with a group of friends where each picks a direction and stays in silence the whole time. You can establish a central place to do a daily silent check in. You might arrange to have a sharing circle before and after.

DOING IN NATURE

Day Walks

Just a plain and simple walk in a park or through the forest is a great way to learn from nature. You don't need a big agenda. Do you need to burn off steam or calories? Then go for a run, a walk, or a climb. By moving, you will see and feel larger patterns of the landscape. Relationships between sun, moisture, hills, plant communities, and animal trails will unfold. You may spook grouse, songbirds, and deer, although most animals will flee before you arrive.

Tracking

The tracker learns to unravel a mystery. Are there brown needles or a coat of pollen in the track? When was the last windy day? When was the last rain? If you do the same trail each day, you will learn how tracks age under different conditions. Is the print a domestic dog or a coyote? Was there a human print near the dog print? Are the tracks similarly dusted with needles? If so, it might be a domestic dog. Was its gait steady? Then it might be a coyote.

If you practice tracking in the winter, your summer tracking will improve. Beaches and swamps are easier, but with practice, you can track where the clues are subtle.

Overnights

There is something magical about sleeping outside. The fresh air, all the plant smells, and the bird and animal activity make this a rich experience. Even a tent in the backyard can connect you with the non-human communities that surround you. Moon cycles are noticed. As the season progresses you will hear each newly arrived migratory bird.

Human-powered Activity

Out biking, the larger patterns of the landscape will begin to make sense. Being in a canoe, you will silently slip through some of the most productive ecological systems. On cross-country skis, you can access quiet, remote terrain where few others enter. Consider exploring the many human-powered modes of transportation when going to spend time in nature; to be in nature, yet not harm her in getting there, is surely a modern challenge.

Harvesting Wild Foods and Medicines

This is an excellent way to invite the forest into you. Wild edible plants grow in parks, forests, and even in your yard. Many originated from Europe or Asia, but many are indigenous. Some are common weeds. Get a few books on wild edible plant identification, or go on plant walks with people who know their stuff. Learning the plants can be liberating. Just to know that I can feed myself almost anywhere has released a big fear; the fear that if we don't buy into mainstream culture we won't be fed. Some plants take acquiring a taste for; they may not be what we want to eat at times, but they will provide for our needs.

Harvesting Fuel and Fiber

Gathering firewood can tune you in to the forest ecology. For years, I had cut dead trees for firewood. Then I realized that, for 20 years, others had done the same and now there were no snags (standing dead trees) for cavity-nesting birds. Instead, I began to cut trees that were blocking the sun from our garden and the southern side of our home. By cutting these trees, I no longer needed a truck to haul them, used less firewood and grew more food.

Abundant fibers can be gathered for making baskets, mats, or even clothes. Cedar bark was used extensively for hundreds of household objects by First Nations peoples. Nettles can make strong twine and clothes. Cattail can be made into mats or cordage. Willow and bamboo can be made into baskets.

Harvesting Fertility

The fertility of nature is something to be admired and gently gleaned. Gathered seaweed, leaves, and pruned greens can be added to the compost pile or mulched into the soil. Have you noticed how the forest floor will be sparse in early spring and an impenetrable jungle by early summer? Some of these plants are edible and others make great green manure. To use them as green manure, make alternating layers of greens, browns (straw, wood chips, or dried leaves), kitchen compost, and soil in your compost heap. Often I get sufficient greens from maintaining trails and pruning trees and shrubs that encroach on the garden.

Vegetable Gardening

It seems the longer people garden, the better they succeed, and the less they claim to know. Many forces of nature are out of your control and affect your production — it's very humbling. Gardening gets you outside more and paying attention to the weather, insects, and soils. And gardens can be designed to be less intrusive and problematic for wildlife. I'm a big believer in fences; if rabbits, deer, and porcupines never get a taste, both you and they will be happier. Although you might tolerate raids of your garden, your neighbors might kill the intruders. If you fence and defend one small area, you can leave the rest natural and enjoy the wildlife there, and see how they live naturally.

STUDYING NATURE

Watersheds

Every inch of land and water that feeds a certain creek, stream, or river is part of the watershed. A major watershed may include all land from mountaintop headwaters to the sea. As rivers snake through a landscape, they race or meander, are rocky or muddy, narrow or wide. They create a wide range of ever-changing habitats, including wetlands, flood plains and lakes. Nutrients are washed down from forests to the sea to feed aquatic life. If the waterway is passable by salmon, nutrients will be returned upstream when the salmon spawn and die, feeding bears, wolves, otters, eagles and the forest floor. We all live in a watershed.

Imagine you are a drop of water from a hard rain. How would you move across the landscape? Where would you end up?

Identification and Behavior

Field guides for birds, animals, insects, plants, soil or geology are a great way to learn from others who have dedicated their lives to understanding nature. Knowing names will enable you to compare notes with others. If you study the behaviors of birds for instance, you will begin to learn about the properties of plants that are used for nests, the seasonal migrations, what foods are available, and how and where they mate. You will start seeing bigger patterns of interactions.

Ecology

This is the science of the relationships between organisms and their environment, which includes how you relate to the landscape. Do you live in a forest, grassland or desert? How would your behavior change in each? Are you near the ocean or fresh water? What are the relationships between the redwing blackbird and the cattails? How do sun exposure, latitude, elevation, soil, weather patterns, and precipitation affect plant and animal communities? By being out in nature, you will begin to understand migrations of birds, whales and butterflies. What is the first flower to bloom in a wetland near you each spring? What insects will pollinate these flowers? What birds overwinter near your home?

You could spend your entire life studying your 20 foot by 20 foot secret spot and not know all the relationships between the living things there. From the soil layers to the canopy, there are thousands of species. To simply know their names is one thing, but to know why they are there and what they are doing is a broad field of study, mostly unknown. Who passes through your secret spot each year? What did they bring and leave behind? How has this piece of land changed over the last 20,000 years? How has the land been treated over the last 500 years? Ecology is where you put all the information together to paint a multi-dimensional picture of the landscape over time.

Biomimicry

Biomimicry is the conscious copying of examples and mechanisms from natural organisms and ecologies. Through in-depth study and observation of ecological systems, humans can attempt to replicate certain self-regulating ecological relationships into human habitat designs. The full extent of complex relationships between the thousands of life forms on each square foot of living Earth may never be fully understood or appreciated by humans. However, by using nature itself as a database for design examples, your human ecology can serve ever more indigenous functions.

AT HOME IN NATURE

After some time in relationship with nature, the land just might enter our bones. I can often get off the bike, walk into the woods, and find a patch of nettles for dinner. I can't tell you how I knew they would be there. Smell, terrain, plant associations all might be clues, yet my mind doesn't engage — my body just finds them. After seven years at our mountain home, a mile and a half from a paved road, I sensed the approach of guests five minutes before they would arrive. I didn't practice. Without the bark of dogs, weed whackers, and streams of cars, the forest language permeates the body and mind.

Earth bonds are ancient. Before the current age of agricultural monocultures, humans lived in landscapes full of biodiversity, and interpenetrated with thousands of species. We learned from them, they learned from us, and we evolved together. Diversity brought balance and health. Our bodies and souls grew to expect connection with all life.

Surrounded by concrete, steel, and glass, we suffer in many ways. As we sterilize our surroundings, we kill the beneficial organisms along with the "pests," creating an unstable system. With short life cycles, the unwanted organisms mutate, then thrive in the altered environment. Humans are robust survivors, but when certain other robust survivors want to live in or on our bodies, they can make us ill. We might respond with stronger chemicals, creating more disabling diseases.

How do we turn the tide and live in biodiversity again? Beginning at home, a section of lawn or pavement can be planted with natives that used to grow there. Even a small natural area will begin to attract birds, mammals and butterflies. This can begin a restoration process.

It becomes difficult for us to understand the needs of other beings when we are isolated from the web of life. Restraint comes from an appreciation of nature's specific needs. There is no other way.

I was invited to join a Chumash man, Cho' Slo, when he performed a specific ceremony that hadn't been done in years. It was a winter solstice vigil where we stayed awake for four days and four nights, all the while tending a central fire — dancing, singing, sweating and sitting in silence. The sticks that were used to tend the fire were yucca stalks that had been colorfully painted with Chumash symbols by the participants. Over four days all the painted stalks had been slowly burned as we took turns tending the fire. The fire represented our inner fire; the stalk, our attachments, pride, or lack of humility. By tending the inner fire, we prepared for our next year's cycle of living, ideally with less illusion and in more complete harmony with our true nature and the natural world.

I stayed awake the best I could for four nights and days under the sky. At 33 years old, I didn't know that the stars circled the North Star. For the first time in my life, I watched the Big Dipper, Cassiopeia, and Orion making their route. Since that ceremony, when I walk the forest at night, I notice the orientation of the path I am on relative to the North Star. Then during the day or on cloudy nights I might remember the North Star's position, relative to specific locations along that path — slowly building an internal compass.

In summary, the more time you are in nature, the more it enters your being. I enjoy being in nature with others, but there is a special quality to being alone. Pets and friends draw me to their own sights and smells, some of which I would miss. But alone, a certain intensity magnifies the land's voice. It is clearer. The subtlety of my own senses and instincts can be followed directly. A healthy diet of time alone and with friends in nature can ground the whole process of reducing your impact.

PART III

INTEGRATION

NINE

APPLYING THE TOOLS

The purpose of everything we've done so far is to begin the shrinking process — of footprints and of money spent — while freeing up more life energy. In this section, you become the architect of your lifestyle design and work toward the sustainability goal you defined in the sustainability sweatshop. If a gulf exists between your measured footprint and your goal, some of the strategies and principles of this chapter might help produce the reductions you are after.

Using the three tools — EF, *YMOYL* and learning from nature — yields a phenomenal body of information specific to your life. This information provides guidance in the shrinking process. At this point, you should know:

* Your sustainability definition, and when you hope to achieve it.
* What population target you are willing to support or how many children you would like to have
* The footprint of your lifestyle choices.
* How much life energy you trade for things and experiences, and whether your choices were worth the trade and aligned with your values.

♦ A bit more about your surrounding landscapes and ecology. Hopefully you feel more at ease exploring them. You might have some ideas for restoring your backyard to a native habitat and you may have begun making consumer choices that have less impact on nature.

That's a lot of information! Just by staying with the process of using the tools, month after month, your footprint might shrink without a serious design effort. Those three questions of *YMOYL*, where you tune into fulfillment, values, and how life might change once off the treadmill, are meant to help you develop an internal yardstick. Now is a good time to notice how you respond to advertisers and societal pressure. Most of us will go through four common stages when taking on this challenge:

1. Unconscious unsustainability
2. Conscious unsustainability
3. Conscious sustainability
4. Unconscious sustainability

It can take years to proceed through the above four stages. And you may backslide along the way. That's okay. Living simply in the land of plenty is not that easy. At times you might be tempted to just forget the whole thing; some of the strategies in this section can keep the process alive and progressing.

GETTING STRATEGIC

Because each of us is inspired differently and makes different lifestyle choices, we each need to design a plan suited to our situation. What works for me won't necessarily work for you. One approach is to look over your data in more detail and identify where large reductions are possible and areas where you feel excited to make changes.

Big-ticket Items

Footprinting shows where the big leaks are. Careful study of your monthly charts will reveal where to invest your energy to give the Earth the biggest break — these are your big-ticket items. Each month, use Table B.11 to list some of the big-ticket items in your current footprint. Remember to make a copy of Table B.11: Big Ticket Items and Low Hanging Fruit, so you still have a clean original for future use. Making changes in these areas could take time and planning. Skills may need to be learned and family members included in your decisions. Trust yourself to move quickly when the time is right or slow down if your spouse is feeling threatened or if the children are planning a mutiny.

Low-hanging Fruit

On Table B.11 you can also list "Low-hanging fruit," which refers to changes you are ready to make NOW or in the near future. They are often habits we never think about, that don't really help us out; we just leave the faucet running while we brush our teeth or leave lights on in the house because ... "I don't know why. I just never thought about it." No big change is needed — you might bring used bags with you to the grocery store, or instead of a gym membership, you cycle to work on a slightly longer but peaceful route. You'll find yourself saving money on gas, parking, or the gym. Again, tap into the creativity of your household in identifying low-hanging fruits. Novel solutions have a better chance of working if the needs of all household members are considered.

. . . . .

Say you find out your footprint is similar to the average North American's. You've made your monthly lists of big-ticket items and low-hanging fruit, and after six months, you have made considerable changes, but still your house is much bigger than needed and your job has you stuck with a big commute. You may feel trapped; it may be time for some deep breaths and a relaxing walk on the beach. Trust your intuition. North Americans change homes and jobs quite frequently. Stick with the process. Get in touch with your deeper values and callings. New opportunities might arise that previously you would not have considered, but can now embrace. You may be able to carpool or use public transportation until you find a smaller, less expensive home that is easier to heat and within walking distance from work. Make it a win for the entire family. For example, learning to have fun as a family living simply can come gradually by having positive experiences on camping trips. Brainstorm as a family on ways to reduce the big-ticket items. Trust in open communication, kindness, and understanding. Keep it fun and light.

For example, you might choose to focus on three items each month. Pick ones that you are most inspired to work on, when the timing is right in your life. If you are part of a household, perhaps each member can pick an item to task-master for the month. A brainstorm or discussion can happen to gather ideas from the household on how to reduce energy use, garbage, or chemicals on the lawn. The ideas can be quickly jotted down, regardless of how far-out they might seem. Try setting a ground rule that forbids shooting down others' ideas, no matter how crazy they seem; this can start a rapid flow of creativity that might otherwise be inhibited, and at this point, you're just looking for ideas.

If the person who ends up taking on a certain item has all this input, and then is empowered with the freedom to come up with a reduction plan, they might enjoy the design process even more. You can develop a detailed plan to move toward your sustainability goal, with a date in mind when you will meet it. Make these lists monthly and post them on your refrigerator or somewhere equally visible to all members of the household. Milestones can be set along the way, and you can review your progress each month.

You might be after a more casual approach, in which case you could use Table B.11 to list a few big-ticket items and low-hanging fruits each month. Review your filled-out monthly footprint and money charts (Tables B.1 through B.6 and C.1 through C.6) to identify them.

Then, answer those three monthly questions posed in *YMOYL*. Look over where you indicated +, -, and 0 on Tables C.1 through C.6. Write out your lists of big-ticket items and low-hanging fruits each month and allow your subconscious to do the work. Just by identifying them, you might make different day to day choices.

THE TRIPLE BOTTOM LINE TEST

As you get into the process of radical simplification, you might discover that when you set out to shrink your footprint, you also end up saving time and money. During my engineering career, I had bought into a certain set of cultural myths. First, I believed that clothes washers, computers, riding lawn mowers, and cars save us time. Second, I believed that "economy of scale" would make products cheaper — therefore, shop at Mall Wart. Third and last, I had heard that environmental protection is expensive, so, expect to pay more for "green" products and organic food. The first two, I more or less agreed with, but this last one was too counter-intuitive. How could it cost more to reduce impact? Doesn't it cost money to destroy nature or make pesticides? Leave off the pesticides, it should cost less, right? Well, a trip to the health-food store upheld the myth: a bag of organic chips or carrots did cost more than the supermarket variety, but I remained skeptically puzzled as to why.

I began doing a systems analysis on this question and deciphered this puzzle into an accounting problem. The costs of products from large manufacturers are often kept artificially low until they eliminate competition . Because they control so much wealth, they can influence public policy to get low-cost access to energy, land, toxic disposal sites and raw materials. Often, wasteful, polluting, inefficient processes are located where few environmental regulations exist and low wages can be paid. If these large-scale manufacturers had to be responsible for the implications of their processes, their products would be more expensive, and possibly more so than most bioregional products. What you don't pay over the counter you pay in taxes, dirty air, dead animals, polluted water, clearcut forests, sweatshops and strip-mined lands. Small-scale bioregional producers, although their products might use less energy and materials and create less waste because they wield less political influence, don't get big tax breaks and bailouts or discounted access to resources. Although small businesses are often over-regulated, some of the worst polluting can be done by small, irresponsible outfits. Still, local products typically reflect a truer total cost. Myth #3 was called into question. I returned to the first two myths regarding conveniences and economies of scale.

I had purged my life of many "conveniences" and bought little from stores offering the "economies of scale." Yet my expenses were lower and I had more free time than ever. If these myths were true, why wasn't I toiling away?

As I evaluated my recent lifestyle changes with this crude engineer's "systems analysis," I discovered that simple living activities often saved time and money, and further reduced my footprint. So much so that this test formed a first-level filter that I came to call the triple bottom line. If an activity passed the test, continuation was likely. As an example, let's put our transportation choices to the triple bottom line test.

If your daily travel is up to a 20-mile round trip, cycling could pass the triple bottom line test. It is easy to imagine how a bike can save money and footprint, but time? In urban areas, trips under three miles are often just as fast on a bike. When the time to park and walk to the final destination is included, time is saved. Add in an even larger factor — the time spent at work to pay for the car — and the amount of time you save skyrockets. On average, people spend almost one day a week (or about an hour and a half a day) working to pay for their vehicles. You could work four days a week, commute up to ten miles each way by bike, and still save time. Ivan Illich determined that the average American male driver spends 1,600 hours a year (30 a week) on car-related activity. That includes time to work for it, care for it, sit in it, and talk about it. Excluded from this 30-hour-per-week estimate is the time spent in hospitals, traffic courts, and garages, not to mention the time spent watching car commercials or researching for the next automobile purchase. In the year Illich did his experiment, the average male traveled 7,500 miles a year, yielding a five-mile-per-hour actual rate of travel.[1] A bike can go 10 to 20 miles per hour and can be bought used for $100 and maintained for $25 a year.

How about money and footprint? In *Divorce Your Car*, Katie Alvord reports: "Cars gobble more than a sixth ($6,200) of the average US household's budget for out-of-pocket expenses, which include vehicle purchase, taxes (for police, registration, emergency response, highways, parking, etc.), maintenance, fuel, registration and insurance. Add to that the costs to the environment and society that are paid from general fund moneys, not user fees. This category includes such things as road construction and maintenance, law enforcement, emergency response, parking real estate and structures, fuel production and clean-up subsidies, congestion costs from loss of productivity, medical and other crash-related costs, pollution, wildlife deaths, and sprawl. These external costs have been estimated to be between $9,927 and $15,053 per car per year."[2]

The footprint of a six-mile daily round-trip commute is:

+ By bike (area to grow the calories expended): 167 square yards, or 13 paces by 13 paces
+ By bus: 3,060 square yards, or over a half-acre
+ By car (20 mpg, single occupant): 4,500 square yards, or almost an acre

There are also less tangible yet significant potential benefits to cycling, such as decreased stress level, lower medical bills and improved attitude, health, and productivity. You might meet more interesting people, see more wildlife, hear more birds, and have a lot more fun. As you set out to tackle your big-ticket items, you might find many alternatives that meet the triple bottom line test.

Improving Energy Efficiency

Some of the modern super-efficient appliances, products and homes can pass the triple bottom line test. But it is worth doing the analysis because some may save energy, but still not reduce overall lifecycle footprint. Some "green" products may be so costly that you trade many hours of life energy paying for them. And if our behavior is such that we carelessly drive twice as far because our car is so fuel efficient, the benefits can easily evaporate. That said, some well-constructed, efficient products used sparingly can save time, money and footprint.

As an example, let's compare an energy-efficient refrigerator to a typical older model. The refrigerator is the single biggest power consumer in most households. We will spread the appliance's manufacture and disposal (garbage) footprint over its useful life. Then we can add in the monthly energy use to get a monthly comparison.

Say the refrigerator is ten years old and has another ten years of life. It weighs 200 pounds. The manufacturing footprint factor (ff) for major appliances is found on Table A.5 to be 994. Used for 20 years, its footprint would be:

$$200 \text{ lb.}/20 \text{ yr.}/12 \text{ mo. x } 994 = 828 \text{ sq. yd.}$$

To find the monthly footprint of the energy use, we multiply the ff for electricity, 31, times the monthly kWh usage. Finding this information might not be so easy. You could turn off all your circuit breakers except for the fridge and unplug anything else on that circuit overnight or while you're away and record the change in your electric meter, and the time between readings. This will be a little lower than actual usage if you never open the door. I found the following energy usage information on the web and calculated the energy footprint below:

+ A typical model made in 1990: EF = 75 kWh/month x 31 = 2,325 sq. yd.
+ A one-door manual defrost: EF = 54 kWh/month x 31 = 1,674 sq. yd.
+ A 2-door frost-free: EF = 165 kWh/month x 31 = 5,115 sq. yd.
+ A small one-door model: EF = 36 kWh/month x 31 = 1,116 sq. yd.
+ An inefficient 1973 model: EF = 150 kWh x 31 = 4,650 sq. yd.
+ A Super Low Energy Vestfrost: EF = 27 kWh x 31 (ff) = 837 sq. yd.

Based upon this information, it is not a given that an old refrigerator is inefficient. An older manual defrost or small-sized refrigerator that is well cared-for might be quite efficient.

The appliance's garbage footprint is determined by dividing its weight by the months of life expectancy (we translate a once-in-20-years event, throwing away the refrigerator, into a monthly figure) and then multiply by the ff for garbage, 481:

$$\text{EF} = 200 \text{ lbs.}/20 \text{ yr.}/12 \text{ mo. x } 481 = 401 \text{ sq. yd.}$$

Total monthly footprint for the 1990 vintage model kept for 20 years:

EF = 828(Manufacture) + 401(disposal) + 2,325(electricity)
  = 3,554 sq. yd.
For a single door manual:
EF = 828 + 401 + 1,674 = 2,903 sq. yd.
And for the Super Low Energy model:
EF = 828 + 401 + 837 = 2,066 sq. yd.

In this case, the super energy-efficient appliance offers a 42 percent footprint reduction compared to a the 1990 vintage model. But if the old refrigerator is a single door, manual defrost, the footprint savings reduces to 29 percent. In this case, you could open the door less often, clean the coils, repair any leaky gaskets and put it in a cooler location, and possibly make up some of the 29 percent reduction and save a bunch of clams.

Efficiency's Caution

My psychology regarding efficiency is interesting. When we arrived in Maine, my parents graciously loaned us a 50-mpg GEO to help us get settled. Because it was so efficient and always available, I burned three times the gas I typically do before I took notice. When I finally checked the footprint, I realized the 10 gallons of gas a month, even after splitting it with my partner, still equaled 0.5 acres. Efficiency needs to be coupled with a conserving reverence in order to yield an overall benefit. I remembered why I prefer not to keep my van street legal: I'd just use it more. Why? Because it's there.

GUIDING PRINCIPLES

The process of reducing your footprint and working toward your sustainability goal can be aided by some guiding principles. Because principles are not specific, they can open up a wide range of choices, which can be helpful, especially in a world of incredible variety. Below are some practical, scientific, and spiritual principles that you might find either useful or inspiring.

Good Old-fashioned Principles

Earlier generations of Americans honored frugality and responsibility, basic values of such cornerstone importance that I will risk being repetitive and discuss them here. They include:

Sharing: Share with another person and halve your impact; with four people, quarter the impact. Sharing your sandwich is a kind gesture, but won't reduce your footprint if you then eat something else. If you share tools, cars, bicycles, housing and heating, you will be reducing footprint.

Caring: By doubling the life of a possession, you halve its footprint. Quadruple its life and you quarter its footprint. Your possessions are Earth's bounty transformed. Take care of them. A bicycle can last a lifetime with regular maintenance if kept locked and out of the rain.

Conserving: Conserving often simply takes awareness. For example, an average of 26 percent of food is wasted in America. You can turn off lights that are not in use, turn down the heat when you leave the house or go to bed, and take joy rides on the bike. Try making good lists and shopping less frequently.

Cooperation: Consider not only what is good for you, but also what is good for the Earth and other people.

Attitude: Positive attitude and willingness open the heart. Shrinking your footprint out of a love for all life will feel great to you and inspire others. But if you start feeling like a victim or a martyr, reconsider your attitude. If you feel a grudge of resentment coming on, back off and go for a walk and reflect on what's happening inside. Expressing fears and doubts is healthy; becoming fixated on fears, regrets and doubts will burn you and your friends out.

Permaculture Principles

Permaculture, a word coined by Bill Mollison, "is a contraction not only of permanent agriculture but also of permanent culture." In his book, *Introduction to Permaculture*[3], he explains: "On one level, permaculture deals with plants, animals, buildings, and infrastructures (water, energy, communications). However, permaculture is not about these elements themselves, but rather about the relationships we can create

between them by the way we place them in the landscape." A few principles that can assist in shrinking footprints and saving money are:
Location: By setting up our homes in walking or cycling proximity to food, employment, friends, family and recreation, we will save huge amounts of nature over the course of our lives. Where location is concerned, a "category 1 design flaw" is the most serious of flaws (for example, building your house on a floodplain or next to toxic waste incinerator). For my partner and I, living 3,000 miles from our families was our category 1 flaw. It was not a pretty choice to face year after year — polluting the air by flying, or not visiting with family. And because most of us will spend more of our life energy working to pay for our housing than any other item, it is worth exploring alternatives. If for some reason you decide to move, you could establish criteria for location selection, such as:

- Is housing affordable?
- Can I grow food there?
- Is the area safe for our children?
- Will I have a social network of family and friends and enough like-minded people to help keep me inspired?
- Are the streets safe for cycling and walking?
- Can I access nature under my own propulsion?
- Is it a decent place to nurture my life's work?
- Are the air, land and water healthy?
- Will I want to be there in 50 years?

By placing ourselves where we want to be, we can plant fruit and nut trees. We can pull the tires and shopping carts out of the creeks. We can pick up groceries for our elderly neighbors, shoot hoops with the boys, and someday run for the school board.

Each element or action performs many functions: For example, if you build a pond in your garden, it stores water, provides wildlife habitat, is aesthetically pleasing, and attracts frogs to eat the slugs. If you make friends with your neighbors, you can drive less to visit distant friends; when you have too much zucchini and tomatoes, you can pass them over the fence; and you will develop a sense of community. They might water your garden when you're away or cook chicken soup when you're sick. If they need a cup of flour, they will knock on your door instead of driving to get it. You can share tools, cars, dinners and stories.

Work with, not against nature: If you plant native plants, including edible and medicinal ones, you can recreate the original ecology of your yard. When established, they need little maintenance and no watering. They attract indigenous insects, mammals and birds.

Problems are opportunities: Say you are growing tired of weeding the garden. Many of the common garden weeds are edible and nutritious. Plants such as soopalallie, alder, clover, lupine, and legumes might be considered weeds, however they "fix" nitrogen, meaning nodules develop on the roots which store this volatile gas, which is essential for the manufacture of proteins.

One year I had a terrible slug problem. I collected a hundred a night, apologized, then drowned them in a covered garden bucket and left it in the sun. I fed the smelly slug soup to the tomato plants and they grew to be seven feet tall, producing a generous harvest. At first I had resented the slugs; but I came to be grateful that they brought me out under the stars to experience the night's magic, and then provided perfect fertilizer for my plants — a cold, nasty wind can be great when it's spinning a windmill.

Diversity strengthens the system: Indigenous ecology, languages, and cultures are incredibly diverse, which contributes to their resilience. I was told in a sweatlodge with the Dineh of Arizona that all ways of sweating are right — they respect cultural diversity. And so there are many ways to live equitably. Take a garden example. Say your entire livelihood depends upon one crop or one product. What if a drought, bug or fungus destroys your crop? Diversity enables long-term security. Forest ecology, when not manipulated or over-harvested, exhibits a natural ebb and flow of bugs and disease. An infestation might affect certain age groups or species, but not all. Left alone, the more resilient individuals within a species will be strengthened.

Stacking: A forest garden is a permaculture system that mimics a forest ecosystem. It includes edible roots and tubers below the soil, perennial herbs above. Above and around the herbs are berries, above which are fruits and nuts. In this type of garden, the three dimensional spacing (stacking) can offer greater combined yield than monoculture row crops. Compared to row crops, it offers much more habitat and food for other species.

Spiritual Principles

As with the good old-fashioned principles, by putting spiritual principles into practice we move toward our sustainability goal. Common among diverse traditions are these basic principles:

Kindness: Being kind to all life is a choice we can make in every moment of every day — doing as little harm and as much good as we can, given our situation.

Compassion: By putting ourselves in others' shoes we may understand their struggle. The roots of the word compassion are "to suffer with;" by practicing voluntary radical simplicity, we will better understand the situation of the world's low-income people. Most spiritual traditions extend compassion to all life, the Earth as a whole, and the beholder (this means you!).

Love: The intense concern a mother has for her child, and the child for its mother is one example of unconditional love. Most of us entered this world in the space of love. When the child no longer relies on its mother for nourishment, warmth, and safety, the Mother Earth takes over meeting most of our needs. This space of intense concern can be extended to all life.

Responsibility: When we love others and the Earth we will naturally want to be accountable for our influence on their welfare. In a global economy, truly being accountable for the implications of even our smallest actions is a tall order. If we transition to a bioregional lifestyle where we see the results of our choices and we cultivate a love for all life, we might be more willing to be accountable.

Limits: Self-imposed limits and restraints are part of a spiritual life. We can grow to love limits as they focus our energy into positive, helpful activities that do no harm.

Fascination: To see the wonder and miracle of even the seemingly common things helps us appreciate our brief time on this planet. We draw a breath... and then another... What a miracle!

It just might be that humanity has natural tendencies towards love, kindness, fairness, and fascination. If you feel these tendencies within and act on them, your simplifications might become simpler.

These strategies and principles can help us make underlying shifts in the way we live our lives. If we can stick with global living long enough, we might get to where we experience unconscious harmony. Living your life according to your values and principles just feels good. The tools are there to provide feedback throughout the process. For one person, the motivation may be saved money; for another, saved Earth; for another, more free time; for still another, creating conditions for world peace. Tune into your own motivation. Try not to be afraid to experiment, take measurements, and tune into your intuition. And, be ready for surprises.

TEN

THE WISEACRE
CHALLENGE

work that you like is not work

*A path without a heart is never enjoyable. You have to work
hard even to take it. On the other hand, a path with a heart is
easy; it does not make you work at liking it.*

— Don Juan

Thesis 2

One thesis of this book is that it is possible to live on very small
footprints. This by itself has little appeal; I could sit on a
couch and eat macaroni and cheese until I die. What does
have appeal is having a great quality of life on a small footprint. This is
the Wiseacre Challenge — to become expert at getting the most from
the least.

A wiseacre is someone who, even with a thousand people telling
them they are foolish and idealistic, and that their actions are futile,
still attempts to live by their own standards. She hasn't taken on a life
of radical simplicity to prove a point or to shame others, for she knows

164

how tough it is to live this way in America. Her life just feels good, and it works for her. The "wise" part of "wiseacre" means paying attention to that inner sense of what is right. The "acre" part refers to knowledge of spatial limits. On a finite planet, how much is enough?

The wiseacre faces a seeming dilemma everyday. If she consumes as an average North American, she will receive support from her culture; if she consumes according to her own standards, she might be the oddball. But that's okay; oddball or not, she is now willing to make sacrifices for planet Earth.

In taking on the wiseacre challenge, how much should one consume? The word "should" implies an ethical choice. That means it is up to you and you alone to decide. No one else can decide your ethics for you. The questions of the Sustainability Sweatshop were intended for you to develop your own sustainability goal. In the Sustainability Sweatshop, we considered two well-known pieces of data. One was the bioproductive surface area of Earth — 28 billion acres.[1] The other was the human population — slightly more than 6 billion. The bioproductive space divided equally between all humans defined your personal planetoid — an equal portion of the bioproductive space, or 4.7 acres per person. But that's with humans using the planet's entire productive space. There are different opinions on how much of the bioproductivity humans should use, reflecting different worldviews. A "deep ecologist" might argue that humanity should use no more than ten percent. A supporter of economic growth and technological salvation might argue humans should use it all.

What is your worldview? What portion of your 4.7-acre share of this stupendous planet will you use for yourself, and what portion will you leave for the other species? In the Sweatshop, you were encouraged to be visionary. Instead of contemplating what rate of destruction you are willing to tolerate, what picture of a sustainable future, in your heart of hearts, are you willing to work towards? This is your sustainability goal. The process of getting there is your Wiseacre Challenge.

This book makes the case that it is possible to live according to one's personal values, with an awareness of the limits of a finite Earth. Others are doing it and we can too.

Bold changes in perception, attitude and actions are needed. But the technical and practical aspects have been known for tens of thousands of years. The difficult part is to understand why to even bother, and then to feel motivated to do it. We've looked extensively at "why and how" throughout this book; we've offered examples and tools. This chapter makes the challenge tangible, but the motivation is fully up to each of us.

WHO LIVES ON ONE WISEACRE?

Redefining Progress calculated <u>India's</u> average per-capita footprint at two acres. In the remote rural and tribal areas the footprints are lower than average, according to development experts who consider these people "disadvantaged." According to the World Bank's Year 2000 CD-ROM, India's average annual GNP per capita was $440. The highest 20 percent earned $1,005 per capita while the lowest 20 percent earned $176. In Chapter 8, we showed that income and footprint have a strong correlation. If the average person earning $440 per year has a footprint of two acres, then the 20 percent poorest earning $176 per year would have a footprint of about 0.8 acres ($176/$440 x 2 acres = 0.8 acres) This means that roughly 200 million (20 percent) of India's one billion people live on less than one acre.

Both in India's tropical south and cold northern Himalayan regions, I was invited to stay the night, share a meal, or have tea in many rural and tribal homes. These people had the basics of healthy food, shelter, and a dignified degree of self-reliance. Tougher to measure was the quality of their lives — qualities related to culture and community. Many still had extended families. The youth were involved in village life and elders, were not in nursing homes. I saw no police and felt no danger. The people didn't appear stressed and took time to engage with an unplanned visitor. There was plenty of fun and laughter. The work I saw people doing looked healthy — it contributed to the family's needs. Outside pressures were apparent, but the fabric of their existence was still holding together. The ecology was relatively intact in the tribal areas and up north in Zanskar. Few were overweight, and most had sufficient exercise from working. Automobiles and all the associated pollutants and dangers were absent from the remote villages. The intrusive sound of machinery was rare, as were overflights of planes. I sensed a general peace and harmony.

Experiencing Poverty

You could say I am romanticizing what I saw. However, I could tell stories from traveling in India by bike, foot, and bus where I did see poverty. Sad and harrowing situations. Cardboard shelters lined the streets of Bombay. Street vendors washed their pots in the sewer. People went to the bathroom in the creeks. Beggars with leprosy stretched out hands missing most fingers. Two overweight upper-caste women in white saris got stuck in a bus entryway while trying to force their way onto the bus after walking past dozens of women with babies in their arms begging for food.

In the foothills of the Himalayas, in Himachal Pradesh, children played in the snow with holes in their sneakers, no socks, and oozing sores on their skin. They were happy, playful, curious, beautiful children. Four to six per couple. In my opinion, this was clear poverty. Still, in this village, they cleared straw from a shed and built a fire to warm my cold, wet body. (I had just walked alone for eight days across a 16,000-foot snowy pass, and entered their village nearly out of food.) About 30 people crowded into the room; they fed me until I could eat no more, and stayed with me until midnight, laughing and attempting to communicate. They refused any payment. I asked the village leader, who spoke a little English, about the issues of his village. The top two on his list were overpopulation and corporate tea plantations.

My experiences of both grinding poverty and successful simplicity have haunted me ever since my trip to India. My interest has vanished for "sustainability" solutions available only to the world's wealthy — solutions that assume half the world's people will suffer in poverty — and for solutions that assume humanity should continue to dominate nature.

I realize the roots of poverty are complex, and that my treatment here is simplistic; still, the successful wiseacres in Kerala and Zanskar demonstrate that we can live well with much less. I'm not saying we should copy them, but we can allow their example to inspire our experiments — to blow wind into our sails and carry us along as we now take an in-depth look at possible wiseacre lifestyles here in North America.

WISEACRE SCENARIOS

In this section I'll draw on my experience of living on three acres, but also show what could be included in a one-acre and a six-acre lifestyle. I begin with food, go category by category, and discuss ideas for radical reductions. My partner and I have used or experimented with most of these ideas. I can't honestly say it's always been easy, or without discomfort, but we have felt more alive with the challenge. These ideas provide an example; their purpose is to show what is possible and to stimulate your own design process.

Let's begin with a hypothetical footprint distribution among the six categories for each lifestyle goal — one, three, and six acres. See Table D.7: Sample Wiseacre Footprint Distribution in Appendix D.

Three-acre living has been accomplished in North America by five teams of GLP Summer Institute participants (over 75 people) and by the GLP Challenge team. The researchers have reported, on average, a higher life quality at the GLP than at home. This footprint level has become natural for my partner and I in our year-round life; we have gone higher while relocating and lower when we stay put.

In this section you will find tables for each of the categories we've previously tracked (food, stocks, transportation and so on). Specifically, you will see the quantities per month of many of the items on the footprint calculator (Tables A.1 through A.6), that you could consume within each lifestyle scenario. These tables have been created so that you can picture the kind of trade-offs involved in the design process. We are getting down to specifics now; if your math is rusty like mine, trust that it will slowly come back.

You will be rewarded for entering this level of detail. Sticking with these examples will improve your EF fluency, but more importantly, you'll begin to feel, taste, and see your sustainability goal. Create several scenarios for how you might distribute pieces of your wiseacre. Try a bare bones "The nation-state is crumbling, I'm heading for the bush" scenario — if you had to, you could do it. Then design a practical "I know I can do it" version — one that would be a challenge and take some time, but that you know you could pull off. Lastly, design a worst-case scenario, one that contains some contingencies for the "what ifs" of life, such as, "What if I got seriously ill?" Refer to Tables D.1 through D.6 to follow along as we go through the six main categories below.

Wiseacre Food

Table D.1 shows three sample monthly food amounts to suggest how well fed you could be on a 0.4, 1.2, or 1.6 acre food footprint, which correspond to either a one, a three, or a six-acre total EF. Most of us could live quite well on two to three pounds of food a day — that's 60 to 90 pounds a month.

To achieve the 0.4-acre food EF, I've assumed no fossil fuels are used. For the 1.2 and 1.6-acre food EF scenarios, I'm assuming the embodied energy in the food to be one quarter of standard production. This means the food is grown locally, organic, in season, and with a low input level.

In the case of the 0.4-acre food EF, this sample person grows 60 pounds of their monthly veggies, potatoes, and fruit on 256 square yards of fair soil. They had plenty of food, about 2.6 pounds a day, but a slim condiment bar. With all this healthy homegrown food and some grain, beans (pulses), and eggs, this person's energy and dietary needs could be met. If they trimmed from another category, they could have some chicken. They would undoubtedly be healthier than our fellow citizens eating fast foods, supermarket produce, packaged and frozen foods, or school or nursing home food.

For the 1.2-acre food EF, there is now more processed food, bread and enough margarine to coat your toasts. Flour, cereal, grains, and beans all take a significant rise. Half the veggies are home grown and half are purchased locally. Monthly food consumption still totals 2.6 pounds a day, but you have more protein. Fourteen dollars can be dropped each month at the local greasy spoon or juice bar.

A 1.6-acre food footprint includes everything above plus a more complete condiment bar. Small quantities of dairy, juice, wine and beer are included, and $25 a month is spent at restaurants. Less food is home-grown, but purchases are still tightly screened for low production inputs.

Once you've reviewed these samples, consider how you would design a food menu of your liking within your sustainability goal.

In our quest to reduce our food footprint, Rowan and I haven't tried to become food self-reliant; instead, we focus on food that is organic, mostly vegan (aside from the occasional eggs, butter, or roadkill deer), in season, unprocessed and local. We grow some of our food and gather some from the forests. To live on three acres (total EF), we are never deprived of food quantity or quality; we simply select lower footprint foods. To move toward our one-acre goal, we now grow more of our own food.

To our good fortune, Rowan and I recently accepted a lifetime caretaking position for a very productive homestead in East Corinth, Vermont that provided Guy and Laura Waterman with the majority of their food needs for 27 years. After Guy's death, the home and property — including a mature sugar maple forest, gardens, orchards and berry bushes — were donated to the Good Life Center, the organization that maintains Helen and Scott Nearing's homestead in Harborside, Maine. Laura and Guy lived lives dedicated to mountaineering, writing,and music, while literally chopping wood and carrying water. The homestead has no phone or electricity, was built with hand tools, and is accessible only by foot. Our goals feel ever more exciting and possible, especially with the guidance of Laura, who lives only a mile and a half away. She has already helped us create a garden plan, which includes enough for a full root cellars. As this book goes to print, we will be harvesting our first Vermont garden.

Now that we are settling in, we attempt to keep eating out to a weekly bike outing for a soup or a salad, french fries or a muffin, the occasional breakfast special, or a beer and live music. Rarely will we order full meals out; the part about eating out that we enjoy the most is meeting our neighbors.

Reducing Fossil Fuel Inputs in Food

Getting most of the fossil fuel inputs out of your food can be easier than it sounds. Of course you can grow your own garden. You could also sprout seeds. They are tasty, incredibly nutritious, and easy to grow. The shipping footprint is small because the volume of the sprout is so much greater than the volume of the seed. To fully eliminate fuels, you can grow your own seeds. Some sprouts we eat include red and green lentils, mung and garbanzo beans, sunflower, alfalfa, fenugreek and radish seeds, and whole peas. We grow them in wide mouthed mason jars with a square of nylon window screen screwed under the metal ring. They are soaked overnight and rinsed twice a day. They provide live food year round for very little money and need no refrigeration if used when ready. Another option is to locate several local organic growers, or become involved with community supported agriculture (CSA), an up-and-coming movement in which you, the buyer, contract with a grower to purchase a season's worth of produce.

Root Cellar/Dry Storage

A root cellar makes my list of the seven sustainability wonders of the world. Where the temperature is cool enough for winter vegetable storage, this simple hole in the ground made rodent-proof will provide incredible savings of time, footprint, and money. I built one seven years ago and haven't needed a refrigerator since. A root cellar has high humidity and constant cool temperatures, and is perfect for storing all sorts of vegetables and fruits.

The root cellar is the only inexpensive method I know of that is robust enough and easy enough to make bulk purchases of fruits and vegetables possible. This is where the big savings come in. Seven months of vegetables can be bought at harvest time for half to one third the winter price. Purchased out of season, organic produce is expensive and often shipped long distances. And if the cellar works well, a higher quality of produce results compared to store-bought food. Root cellars are silent, use no CFCs, save space in the home, have fewer cracks to clean and don't mind power outages.

Depending on your diet, you may still want a refrigerator, but a small efficient one might do. A small refrigerator can be moved seasonally to keep it in the coolest location, saving energy. If you want to store dairy in the summer, a root cellar may not be cold enough to keep it more than two days; if you eat from your garden in the summer, and are mostly vegan, summertime poses no challenge.

A few other items, such as squash, onions, and garlic can be stored in dry storage — a cool, dry place where they won't freeze. We grow and harvest what we have time for, and buy the rest locally.

Drying and Canning

To supplement our root cellar, we air dry nettles, kale, tea plants, seaweeds, apples, berries, and deer jerky. We use large framed screens fixed close to the ceiling in a warm, airy place in our cabin. The items with more water content, like apricots, plums, or jerky are pierced on a coated wire that is hung above the wood stove. If you live in a humid place, you might need a more elaborate method. We can apples, pears, cherries, raspberries, and tomatoes as time allows. Our indispensable reference book is *Stocking Up*.

Buying Food in Bulk

Many organic grains, sprouting seeds, and pulses can be purchased in 25 and 50 pound sacks. It might take some research to find a local source for these items; however, even if you can't find them locally, the savings in packaging, money, and time shopping still make it worthwhile.

Harvesting Wild or Naturalized Foods

Chances are, there are dozens of useful plants near your home. With wild foods you don't need to water, cultivate, weed, space, protect, manure, or plant — saving time, money, and footprint. However, ethical harvesting is important. Typically, take only a small percentage of the patch, and only when there is obvious abundance, as other animals and neighbors may harvest this area too. Tune into each plant's reproduction cycle and if rare or declining, leave them be. Some plants will grow stronger when harvested, while others can be wiped out quickly. It is worth having several books to cross-reference information about the plants before you start eating them.

Some of the plants I harvest are nettles, violets, aster, bulrushes, watercress, dandelion, clover, ox-eye daisy, cattail, wild rose (petals, leaves, hips), twisted stalk, burdock root, yellow and curly dock, mountain sweet cicely, chickweed, sheep sorrel, wood sorrel, yarrow, goldenrod, fireweed, mint, false Solomon's seal, cleavers, plantain, pineapple weed, horsetail, wild onions, glacier lily, tiger lily, lambs quarters, purslane, chicory, salsify, milkweed, a dozen different berries, seaweeds (dulse, lavar, kelp), and various different mushrooms. The nutritional value of many of these wild plants and weeds are stunningly high when compared to cultivated plants.

Fixing a Lunch for Work

Eating out is an expensive habit. If you go out to lunch four times a week, in one month you could spend $120. On Table A.1, you will find an ff of 55-square yards per dollar spent ($120 x 55 = 6,600 sq. yd. or 1.4 acres) for eating vegetarian food out. You can make a healthy, organic lunch for a fraction of the cost (dollars and footprint) from your inexpensive bulk food stores. If you make extra dinner and pack it at night, you save time as well. To be around people, try the park; if you like cafes, you could eat the lunch you brought from home and then walk or bike someplace for a tea or coffee. Restaurants duplicate your kitchen, rarely use local organic food, and generate a lot of waste.

Wiseacre Housing

According to a 2001 US Census Bureau report, national average housing and heating costs accounted for $12,057 out-of-pocket expenditures in 1999, well ahead of transportation at $7,011. At a real hourly wage of $10 (not what your paycheck says), that's 100 hours of our life energy a month, or 25 hours a week, or five hours a day for 30 years! Is it worth it? Creating a wiseacre scenario for housing can be a rewarding challenge.

Table D.2 demonstrates what a housing EF of 0.3, 1.0, and 1.6 acres might entail. For the 0.3 and 1.0-acre scenarios, I assumed a type of housing construction with one-fourth the EF of standard construction, similar to that of the 390-square-foot strawbale cabin Rowan and I built in British Columbia. Its footprint was five times lower per square foot than standard construction. I assumed it to be super-insulated and heated by either oil or firewood — not both. For sufficient warmth using the small amount of fuel shown, I've assumed excellent passive solar performance — ample southern exposure, indoor, insulated thermal mass and few drafts.

The scenario for the 0.3-acre housing EF allocates 100 square feet of living space per person. Keeping warm might seem tough with only two gallons of fuel oil or thirty pounds of wood a month; however, a friend in upstate New York had the excellent solar performance mentioned above including insulated earth-bermed walls. Even with no fuel, his home never went below 65 degrees Fahrenheit, even in a cold winter.

In this housing scenario, just one gallon of propane per month is used to cook. Conservation, solar cooking and eating raw fruits and vegetables would be a way of life. Three kilowatt hours of electricity per month is enough to run all of the following:

- One 10-watt compact florescent bulb five hours a day (10 W x 5 hr. x 30 days = 1,500 kWh).
- A boom-box at 18 watts for 1.5 hours per day (18 W x 1.5 hr. x 30 days = 810 Wh).
- A laptop computer at 35 watts for 40 minutes a day (35 W x 0.66 hr. x 30 days = 690 Wh).

When one acre is devoted to housing, staying warm in the 150 square foot space is less dependent on solar performance. If you only used the heat during the six coldest months, you'd have 16.6 gallons of fuel oil or 258 pounds of wood per month. If your sweetheart moved in for the winter, you would now have 33 gallons of fuel oil or 516 pounds of wood for the two of you to heat your snuggle hut each month. If you lived in a more conventional house that was shared, cared for, and you were an active conserver, you could possibly keep within the limits of this scenario. With just two gallons of propane for cooking, you might cook on the woodstove whenever possible, conserve, and eat a lot of raw food. With 10 kilowatt hours of electricity each month, you couldn't run a refrigerator or hot water heater, but an electric hot plate, a blender, and occasional power tools are possible.

In the 1.6-acre housing scenario, you could have 150 square feet of standard-construction housing if the life of the house is stretched to 80 years with minimal new paints, roofing and other supplies. It would have to be very well cared for. Although harder to heat, it is similar to what most people currently have. There is enough electricity to run a small refrigerator part of the year. If ice-cold Budweisers are high on your list, you have room to juggle EFs. Cooking fuel is doubled from the previous example and running a gas range is now possible. The larger heating budget might be sufficient for a small but well-insulated conventional house.

With all three housing options, making a simple solar hot water system would be possible. The parts would be accounted for on Table B.5: Monthly Stocks Footprint. For winter use, heating coils can be placed in the fireplace to heat a tank using the thermo-siphon principle. By sharing, caring, and conserving, you might get quite close to your goal without a new home or technology.

Sharing and Community

If one's portion of the house is cut in half or quartered, rents, mortgages and EFs can be halved or even quartered. The time, money and EF associated with cleaning, maintenance, and repairs are all divided. Refrigerators, tools, washers, utilities and kitchens can be shared. With fewer expenses, you can work less, boost savings, or pay off the mortgage. Plus, you will have friends around to share in life's ups and downs.

In San Luis Obispo, I reduced my monthly household expenses by $900 from $1,100 to $200 by renting three of the four rooms in my house. First, I installed a door and an extra kitchen to turn the four-bedroom home into a duplex. Without this downsizing, I wouldn't have had the last 14 years of my life free from paid employment. The $900 a month savings for 14 years, totals $151,120. At a $10 real hourly wage, that is 15,120 hours of life energy.

Caring

By taking good care of your home, you can typically double or triple its life expectancy. There are many simple ways to extend the life of a home.

- Fix roof and plumbing leaks immediately before they do any damage.

- Eliminate any earth-wood contact where termites might enter the building. Learn to recognize their signs. If they're caught early, it is much easier to get rid of them.
- Solve any moisture problems that cause mildew or paint damage. Usually it just means getting the air moving with vents and caulking sinks, tubs and windows.
- Keep paint in decent condition. It protects the wood and prevents infestation. Free paint can be gotten from yard sales, friends or a collection site.
- If you are aching to add on to the house, consider simple improvements to its solar performance and take more walks on the beach.

Conserving

Conserving can be inexpensive, painless, and can save you time over the long run. Once you are a conserver, it is as natural as being wasteful was. Some ideas include:

- Close off rooms not in use.
- Turn off anything not in use.
- Plug up all drafts.
- Weather strip doors and windows.
- Tune up your heater or furnace.
- Set the thermostat lower, put on a sweater, or do occasional exercises.
- Lower the thermostat when you go out and at night.
- Put insulating curtains or quilts over big windows at night.
- Boost your insulation; ceiling insulation is the most important.
- Hot water heaters can be turned on for 30 minutes to an hour before your shower, either manually or with a timer.

Wiseacre Transportation

Limited motor-powered mobility is possible under the scenarios in Table D.3. In addition, the miraculous human body can power a bike, a canoe, or can walk several hundred miles a month on the food amounts outlined in Table D.2.

In the scenario where just a 0.1-acre EF has been allocated to transportation, 52 bus miles within and between cities per month are possible. If the entire 0.1 acre were used to travel by intercity bus (between cities), 122 miles per month are possible. Alternatively, if you traveled with a friend in a car that gets 70 miles per gallon, you could use 0.97 gallons of gas a month (484 sq. yd. / 500 (ff)) and go 136 miles (0.97 g. x 70 mpg x 2 people). To fly the friendly skies, you could stay air-bound for a very brief 5.6 minutes a month. If you fasted from fueled travel for 10 years, you could make one 11-hour round trip flight during that period.

With 0.3 acres allocated to transportation, 52 miles of bus trips and 2.2 gallons of gas are included. A 70-miles-per-gallon car with two people on board could go 308 miles a month, or 77 per week (a 15-mile round-trip, five days a week).

The 1.2-acre scenario includes 0.5 hours of flying per month (or six hours of airtime every year). In addition, 87 miles of bus, 50 miles of train and 4 gallons of gas per month allow significant mobility.

Car-free Living

According to the National Women's Health Resource Center, 60 percent of Americans don't meet basic activity level recommendations and 25 percent are completely sedentary.[2] Human-powered transportation is a great way to give our body the exercise it needs. From coaching bike racers I learned that long-term health improves with seven hours of rigorous exercise a week. An hour a day on a bike could meet most of our motorized mobility needs.

It took me four years to fully adjust to the pace of car-free living. Now I prefer it. In many places, if you want to leave the region there are buses or trains. Carpools can be easily coordinated. Car co-ops are another level of organization, growing in popularity in cities around the country. Some towns are developing bikelane networks, or you can map out your own route on quiet neighborhood streets. If all that can't get you where you want to be, you could still borrow or rent a car, call a taxi, call a friend, hitchhike, or walk — or you could forget the trip and go to your favorite café to relax.

Early on, I felt stranded without a car. But 14 years into a mostly car-free existence, I now feel freer without one. I am free from dealing with insurance companies and motor vehicle departments. Free from the hassles of maintenance and repairs. I am free from supporting environmental and social exploitation by companies like Exxon, Shell, or UNOCAL.

Wiseacre Goods and Services

Table D.4 contains some of the tough trade-offs faced by wiseacres. With sample allocations of 0.1, 0.3 and 0.8 acres, would you think to invest more in education and possibly prevent an illness, or save the money in case you faced a serious illness? As you can see in this table, the allocations are quite small by North American standards. If you were a wiseacre by choice, would you refuse medical treatment beyond a certain point? Would you spend a million dollars worth of resources to recover when this amount could relieve the worst of poverty for 25,000 children? These questions are easy to philosophize about, but when your loved one has cancer or has been in a car wreck, most wouldn't hesitate to use whatever it takes. Still, we can do many things to prevent illness and reduce the EF associated with staying healthy.

With 0.1 acre allocated to goods and services, you might be inspired to take better care of yourself before you got sick. If you avoided medical services until the age of forty, and saved your $4.40 each month, you would have $2,112 to get better. Not much in America, but your worldwide wiseacre friends could relate to your dilemma. If you could get to Mexico or India, your healthcare piggy bank would certainly go farther. This scenario includes $2 of telephone calls per-month, enough to talk for 33 minutes on a friend's telephone with a six-cent-per-minute calling card. With only 0.3 pounds of soaps and hygiene products available per month, you might wash dishes with wood ash as I did at Gandhi's Ashram in India.

The 0.3-acre goods and services scenario offers enough of the basics that an experienced conserver could relax. The $10 a month for education wouldn't pay for basic public education. Saved for 70 years, the $10 per month offers a budget of $8,400. Spread over 12 years, that's $700 a year. You could use libraries or apprentice as a volunteer and still become well-educated. The $10 for medical could repair a cavity ($120), once a year.

With a 0.8-acre goods and services budget, there would still not be sufficient footprint allocation for honest-to-goodness, sitting-in-rows formal education, American style. If you lived to be 75, you could spend $1,930 a year for 14 years. If your education taught you how to live well on smaller footprints, you could allocate an additional 12 acres for six years, then live on 3 fewer acres for the following 24 years, and your 6-acre average would stand. That would give you $17,424 a year for tuition. With $30 a month for medical, you could hurt yourself every 10 years and have $3,600 to recover. With $20 a month for telephone, you could have a home telephone and use it sparingly.

For all these scenarios I excluded paid entertainment, based on the premise that free fun is abundant in the universe.

Wiseacre Stocks

Table D.5 has sample footprint allocations for stocks of 0.1, 0.15, and 0.6 acres. Budgeted amounts of these long-lasting goods can be doubled by doubling their useful life through care. It also helps to buy quality items.

At the level of 0.1 acre budgeted for stocks, a total of 364 pounds of selected possessions is shown. With 40 pounds of gear I have lived outside in all conditions for six months at a time. With 9 backpacks full of stuff (364/40), you might want to make sure you know where your nail clippers are. If half your stuff is shared with a friend, and they shared half their stuff with you, each would have use of 13 backpacks full of stuff. Artfully placed in your 100 square foot space, you could have the basics covered, but no major appliances. Your library would have over 100 books. With 100 pounds of metal, you could have a bike, garden tools, pots and pans, a sink, simple plumbing, and a few outlets and light fixtures.

In the 0.15-acre stocks scenario, a laptop computer, printer and boom box are added to the previous example.

The 0.5-acre example includes higher quantities of most items. Two hundred pounds of appliances could include a small range (103 pounds) and a small refrigerator (77 pounds), and 58 pounds of electronics. The total stocks weigh 1,212 pounds, enough to fill 30 backpacks. In this case, you might be suffering from clutter.

Wiseacre Wastes

In Table D.6, the sample allocations for wastes are 0, 0.05, and 0.2 acres. The rationale for such a small allocation is this: if one had little to begin with, reducing waste would be a first priority.

The one-acre total EF scenario includes no waste. This person would use durable sacks and containers for transporting and storing food items. They would read newspapers at a library. All their bodily and food wastes would be composted. In Kerala, India, I asked a storekeeper where the garbage was. He looked at me puzzled, unsure of what I was asking. Then said, "There is no garbage."

The 0.05-acre waste scenario includes only 1.6 pounds of recyclables a month. If you were living on a three-acre total EF, would you choose to use less of the other five categories for the luxury of throwing more away? Probably not.

The 0.2-acre waste scenario allows for 4.7 pounds of recyclables and 0.2 pounds of garbage a month. This would require reuse of packaging and purchasing from bulk food stores. No more than one or two newspapers a month could be recycled.

A confirmation of the relative accuracy of the footprinting process came about when I developed each scenario for one, three, and six acre footprints, and reflected on the lifestyles of the wiseacres I'd visited. The material abundance of the scenarios reflected what I witnessed. To live on one acre is possible, but would require a much less materially-focused life. Compared to living from a backpack, it's abundance. Motorized travel is possible, but much less frequent; however, human-powered travel can be extensive. Institutional learning would require living on less for decades after your education. To become educated for free, you could use libraries, volunteer and apprentice, ask questions, and spend time in nature. A lot can be learned by simply paying attention.

Healthcare would be a challenge. To completely commit to your wiseacre and not accept government or institutional assistance beyond your chosen EF would put you in the grace of family and community; a wiseacre's best insurance is being a kind and generous person that others would be willing to care for. The second best insurance is to treat the body well — eating healthy, organic food, exercising, reducing stress, being in nature and having a spiritual practice. Knowledge of how to heal common illnesses through working with medicinal plants would be additional insurance. You could investigate a high-deductible catastrophic illness plan for the worst case.

In my experience, a three-acre EF requires little sacrifice. My strongest yearning has been for peace on Earth — not for any material goods I may be "missing." But my progress toward one acre has been slow. Our experiences with the Global Living Project, where participants walk into a lifestyle of drastically reduced consumption (albeit only for a month), is that people seem to adapt quickly, and with little pain. Just like going overseas or moving to a new town, once the culture shock is over, the new life is just the new life. A slow weaning might be more difficult than making a quick, bold change. What would work best for you? From a design standpoint, there is considerable flexibility and cushioning. One can be warm, dry, well-nourished, and have some comforts on a small footprint.

The six-acre option could look like a typical North American lifestyle, just downsized, with less clutter and little waste. With careful choices that reduce our mobility needs and housing size, this option might be a good stepping stone toward your final goal.

Often there are several ways to meet our deeper needs. Some will carry a big EF and some a small one. Just considering the ecological impact of choices in our everyday life moves us toward our wiseacre. If some one asks you how far it is to Kalamazoo, instead of saying "three hours," you could answer "1.4 acres."

ELEVEN

THE ONE-HUNDRED-
YEAR PLAN

In the last chapter, a picture was painted of life on one-, three-, and six-acre footprints. A one-acre lifestyle means a near complete letting go of what are considered basic necessities in this culture. The six-acre lifestyle, by comparison, includes much of what we have today, minus the excess and waste. However, a six-acre average is 0.3 acres higher than the current 5.7-acre average. At this level, humanity consumes the planet's bioproductivity 20 percent faster than it regenerates.

During the winter of 2000, Ivan Ussach, my partner Rowan, and I took on the Global Living Challenge, a six-month attempt to live on one acre each. We faced many of the tough tradeoffs illustrated in the scenarios of the last chapter. Rowan and I were clear on our sustainability goal: one acre. But our food EF was still 1.8 acres, due in part to the amount of fuels used to grow and deliver our organic pulses, grains, and vegetables. Our housing EF was 1.25 acres, including 0.8 acre for heating. Our food would have to be sourced even closer to home and our house would need better solar performance and more thermal mass. In the process we came to more fully appreciate the level of changes necessary to get to a one-acre ecological footprint and maintain it. I had dipped into the one-acre arena for various short-term experiments, but would I be willing to stay with it year after year? The hardest part of sustainability for me is to say no to what is so easy to have. My gut intuition said; "I can live year after year on three acres; with some optimization of our current design, two acres would be possible; and I could achieve one acre if I had to." But given the context of the culture I was born into, I don't think I have the will power to stay with one acre voluntarily. There are just too many consumptive choices that present themselves every day. I could see myself beginning to resent it. The old adage, "You can't expect someone else to do what you are not willing to do yourself" hit home. During those months of footprint shrinking it occurred to me that I needed to look more deeply into the population side of the equation.

When people would say, "Population is the problem, there are just too many of us," it raised my hackles. I'd respond, "Yes, but if we became as skilled at extracting life quality from less land as the people of Kerala, 60 percent of the global bioproductivity could be left wild. Then population wouldn't be such a big deal. The high income countries need to consume less." It seemed unfair for the wealthy to place the burden of change on the poor, given our level of extravagance and waste. What became clear after the Global Living Challenge was that the polarized argument was unnecessary. We need to do both — reduce population *and* consumption.

I took out a piece of scratch paper and ran some numbers to determine how long it would take to reduce the human population to one billion. I was shocked to discover it would take just 100 years if, on average, we had single child families. In 2100, the human population could be only one billion instead of the projected ten billion. Humanity could then average six-acre footprints and still leave 80 percent of the Earth's bioproductive space wild. This was an exciting realization — a solution that doesn't assume humans dominate nature — a solution with no losers.

Globally averaged footprints could actually rise slightly from the current 5.7-acre average, but a dramatic leveling of footprint disparity would be necessary. If Americans kept their 24-acre footprints, four times higher than average, then a group four times the size of America would have to live on four times less than average footprints (6 acres/4 = 1.5 acres). In other words, for America's current 284.5[1] million people to keep their 24-acre average footprints 1,138 million people would each have to live on 1.5-acre footprints to maintain the six-acre average — the current world situation which is not very fair. The wealth and power wielded by industrialized nations allows them to escape many of the downsides of both overconsumption and overpopulation.

The scale of change necessary for Americans to reduce footprints by a factor of four is tremendous, but possible. From the scenarios of the last chapter, we saw that a six-acre lifestyle could still have some comforts and luxuries. The other challenge for Americans would be to reduce their completed family size from its current 2.1-child level to a one-child level. Canadians are a bit closer to the six-acre/one-child averages with an EF of 22 acres and a family size of 1.4 children. Let's now explore some of the encouraging global trends towards smaller families to see if this idea is feasible.

FREELY CHOOSING TO HAVE FEWER CHILDREN

The trend toward smaller families already has a stronghold in Europe and Japan. Even in Catholic Spain and Italy where birth control is discouraged by the church, the average family has just 1.2 children. Europeans have a high level of formal education, which correlates to lower fertility. They choose to delay marriage and have smaller families because they understand the quality of life improvement resulting from that personal choice.

In Kerala, India, family size has reduced from a six-child average to a 1.8-child average over a 40-year period. Both governmental and nongovernmental organizations support women in planning their families. The program works at several levels, the first being a proactive elimination of poverty through land reform and the narrowing of inequity. Countries with the worst poverty have the highest fertility levels. Although another child is another mouth to feed, in the grips of poverty, that child will also offer some security. Second, both men and women are educated in the use of contraception, and various birth control options are available to the entire population.

Once conditions improve, mothers know their children have a high chance of surviving to adulthood. They do not need to have more children to ensure the survival of the family's next generation. Early on in Kerala's program, men had vasectomies, but now it is common for a woman to choose a tubal ligation, often immediately after the birth of their second child. Freely chosen, affordable family planning is a population stabilization method that appears to be a solution that works.

One positive outcome of Kerala's success with population planning is a normal female/male ratio; 104 girls to 100 boys. In most low-income countries, it is skewed in the opposite direction. For example, in Pakistan there are only 92 girls per 100 boys; in China 94 girls, and in India 93 girls.[2] The low number of females is a result of a systemic deprivation of food, health care and education to girls, common in low-income patriarchal societies. Kerala is matriarchal and values women.

THE ONE-HUNDRED-YEAR PLAN

This chapter proposes a realistic path toward a sustainable planet. For the plan to work, it needs to be adopted by rich and poor peoples alike, and the work needs to be done on many levels: governmental, societal, and personal. In keeping with this book's premise, I will focus on the power of the individual to impact global life quality by making different personal choices. In essence, my proposed one-hundred-year plan is a call for individuals worldwide to voluntarily choose:

- Single-child families (on average) until population reaches one billion (about 100 years).
- A personal ecological footprint not to exceed six acres.

After population levels approach one billion, two-child families could resume.

Being one of nine children, I know any solution must be pro-child and pro-family. While honoring the choices people have already made, we must begin the conversation about the reasons smaller families are needed. Couples must remain free to choose their family size. For this plan to succeed, it has to be:

- **Fully voluntary.** No coercion, shame, or guilt; women must have complete control over their fertility, ideally in consultation with their partners.
- **Aimed at alleviating poverty.** There needs to be a radical redistribution of footprints (wealth) so that all have access to the necessities of life. Although redistribution may seem unrealistic, equally unrealistic is achieving world peace when 3.5 billion people live on $520 per year. If the wealthiest continue to put on pounds and buy more toys than they have time to play with as they pursue economic expansion and an increased standard of living, the poorest nations have no example of restraint and less incentive to reduce population.
- **Fully supported by government.** This will ensure that families at any income level have access to their choice of birth control.
- **Locally driven.** The impetus for change must be a grassroots effort, not one imposed by outsiders.
- **Bioregionally focused.** Local communities must have basic food and land security that is independent of global markets. Globalization has systematically undermined local control, exploited workers and the environment, and heavily influenced local politics. Regional self-reliance results in greater stability and less economic disparity.
- **Accomplished through education.** The links between family size and carrying capacity should be made clear.
- **Dynamic.** A dynamic program will better address the issues of increased longevity and an increasingly aging population with fewer young wage earners to support social programs.

WHO ARE HAVING SMALL FAMILIES?

A UNICEF report, *The State of the World's Children 2002*[3] indicates that thirty countries, with a combined population of 750 million, are now having an average family size of 1.5 or less. These low-fertility countries are mostly European, but include Canada, Georgia, and Japan.

They all have a higher quality of life than average for their level of affluence as exhibited by lower infant mortality rates (IMR) and longer life
expectancies. All 30 low-fertility countries report a life expectancy over
70 years, except for three countries at 66, 68, and 69. The average for
developing countries is 62 (the US average is 77).

Of the ten low-fertility countries with incomes below $2,990 per
capita per year (261 million people), all have infant mortality rates
below 15 except for three countries whose rates are 17, 18, and 21. The
average IMR for this income group is 31[4] (the IMR in the US is 7.1).
The ten low-income countries, listed with their total fertility rates are:
Armenia (1.1), Belarus (1.3), Bulgaria (1.2), Georgia (1.2), Latvia (1.2),
Lithuania (1.3), Moldova (1.4), Romania (1.3), Russian Federation
(1.2), and Ukraine (1.1).

The high-income countries with fertility levels below 1.5 include
Austria (1.3), Belgium (1.5), Canada (1.4), Germany (1.3), Greece
(1.3), Italy (1.2), Japan (1.4), Netherlands (1.5), Slovakia (1.3),
Slovenia (1.2), Spain (1.2), Sweden (1.4), and Switzerland (1.5). These
countries all have lower infant mortality rates and longer life expectancies than the average for high-income countries.

Other notable low-income countries that have slightly larger families include:

+ China with 1.2 billion people, TFR = 1.8, IMR = 31, and life
  expectancy = 71.
+ Cuba with an 11.3 million people, TFR = 1.6, IMR = 7, and life
  expectancy = 75.
+ Sri Lanka with 19.5 million people, TFR = 2.1, IMR = 17 and
  life expectancy = 72.
+ Kerala with 30 million people, TFR = 1.8, IMR = 17 and life
  expectancy = 72

The four examples above are all classified as "less developed."
Compared to the averages for all less-developed countries (TFR =
3.2, IMR = 61, and life expectancy = 64) they are doing remarkably
well.

This data supports the assertion that when the conditions of poverty are reduced, as indicated by long lives and low death rates of children, families tend to have fewer children. The most instructive sustainability examples are the low-fertility countries that have dramatically reduced poverty while using a more equitable portion of global wealth and footprint.

Worldwide, 2.5 billion people average two children or less. This group includes those countries already mentioned, as well as the US, France, and several small nations. What might have seemed unlikely is beginning to happen. The *World Population Profile 1998* attributes the dropping fertility levels to factors including increased family planning services, higher standards of living, and higher costs of living in urban areas which encourages smaller families.

MAKING IT PERSONAL — THE OPTIONS

To achieve an average of one child per family would still allow a lot of flexibility in personal choices. In my family, there were nine children and my parents now have eighteen grandchildren, an average of two per offspring. This was a tremendous reduction in family size achieved over a single generation. Two factors that had the greatest impact were the availability of effective birth control methods, and that three of us to remained childless. When we think about family size alternatives, it is important to see the decision as a lifestyle choice with many possibilities:

+ No children, so as to dedicate oneself to a chosen cause.
+ Adopt a child.
+ One child, so as to have time to dedicate to a career or civic work while still having enough time to raise the child ourselves.
+ Two children, knowing that others in the clan have none, by choice or circumstance.

North American cultural perceptions of only-children as spoiled, selfish, or maladjusted also contribute to the cultural bias against small family size. Bill McKibben's book, *Maybe One*, however, details both an environmental and personal argument for single-child families, debunking the myth that only-children are spoiled. In fact, studies report that either there are no differences by number of siblings, or that the differences favor the only child.

SIMPLIFIED POPULATION MODEL

What follows is a simplified demographic model showing the implications of various family sizes. The model assumes an approximate age distribution as it is today, and that all people live to be, on average, 75 years old. The numbers are given in billions of individuals.

One-child Families

If each family on Earth averaged one child, the 2.9 billion current children, once they become adults, would have 1.5 billion children. Figure 12.1 below shows humanity returning to two child families, on average, in 2100, resulting in a stable global population of 600 million in 2150.

Figure 12.1
ONE-CHILD FAMILY POPULATION MODEL

	2000	2025	2050	2075	2100	2125	2150
Grandparents (51 + Years)	1.1	2.1	2.9	1.5	0.8	0.4	0.2
Parents (26-50 Years)	2.1	2.9	1.5	0.8	0.4	0.2	0.2
Children (0-25 Years)	2.9	1.5	0.8	0.4	0.2	0.2	0.2
Total (Billions)	6.1	6.5	5.2	2.7	1.4	0.8	0.6

Two-child Families

With two-child families, the 2.9 billion children, having become parents, would produce another 2.9 billion children. By 2050, each of the three age groups would contain 2.9 billion people and the total population would stabilize at 8.7 billion individuals.

Figure 12.2
TWO-CHILD FAMILY POPULATION MODEL

	2000	2025	2050	2075	2100	2125	2150
Grandparents (51 + Years)	1.1	2.1	2.9	2.9	2.9	2.9	2.9
Parents (26-50 Years)	2.1	2.9	2.9	2.9	2.9	2.9	2.9
Children (0-25 Years)	2.9	2.9	2.9	2.9	2.9	2.9	2.9
Total (Billions)	6.1	7.9	8.7	8.7	8.7	8.7	8.7

Three-child Families

With three-child families, the power of exponential growth is demonstrated. The 2.9 billion children, as adults, will have 4.4 billion offspring. By 2100, the population would reach 30.9 billion humans.

Figure 12.3
THREE-CHILD FAMILY POPULATION MODEL

	2000	2025	2050	2075	2100	2125	2150
Grandparents (51 + Years)	1.1	2.1	2.9	4.4	6.5	9.8	14.6
Parents (26-50 Years)	2.1	2.9	4.4	6.5	9.8	14.6	21.9
Children (0-25 Years)	2.9	4.4	6.5	9.8	14.6	21.9	32.9
Total (Billions)	6.1	9.4	13.8	20.7	30.9	46.3	69.4

I realize this numerical discussion is somewhat dry and abstract; after all, we are talking about children. But the simple math helps clarify the dynamics of family size over time.

FAMILY SIZE VERSUS WILD SPACE

There is a direct tradeoff between average human family size and how much land will be available for other species. Once a child is born, a parent might question this tradeoff, but most certainly will choose to meet his or her child's needs at the expense of nature. With eighty percent of pregnancies in the US being unplanned, it appears that a radical change in cultural norms about communicating reproductive intentions during sexual encounters is definitely needed. Further, the US leads the developed world in teen pregnancy: 59.2 of every 1,000 females between the ages of 15 and 20 become pregnant, compared to 4.2 in the Netherlands.[5] In Europe, contraception goes hand in glove with sex, as evidenced by their negative population growth. In the US, however, it seems taboo to talk about the practical implications of contraception. Deep education on the practical use of birth control needs to be supported by government policies and funds, with access to a wide range of family planning options guaranteed. A real commitment to birth control in the US — and worldwide — would be a huge offering of habitat and freedom to other species.

Sustainability and Family Size

If you recall from the sustainability sweatshop, the sustainability goal you calculated changes dramatically based upon the number of children you have.

If you had no children or one child, you would be contributing toward a world population of one billion by the year 2100. By "contributing," it means that if everyone had your fertility rate for the next 100 years, the population would fall to one billion people. As a population of one billion is approached, society could return to a two-child average and maintain that population indefinitely. Your sustainability goal as part of the 100-year plan could then be set at six acres. Your choices would mean that you have done what you can do with the two factors over which you have direct control — EF and family size — to work toward a goal of having 80 percent of the bioproductive space wild in 100 years.

If you had two children, you would be contributing to a world population of nine billion, tightening your personal sustainability goal from one acre to 0.66 acres. In other words, to keep the same amount of wilderness protected, the percentage of bioproductivity used by people would have to remain constant. If population grows from six to nine billion, a one-acre footprint must drop to 0.66 acres under similar conditions and assumptions. Two-child families, or what is known as replacement fertility, would eventually lead to zero population growth, but only after an initial three-billion person growth spurt. This is due to a disproportionately large group currently in the family-rearing age (2.9 billion people are below the age of 25).

If you had three children, you would be contributing toward a world population of 30.9 billion in the year 2100, bringing your sustainability goal to 0.19 acres. This is the burlap sack scenario, and getting thinner by the day.

If we are to achieve sustainability, the importance of single-child families is on a par with the importance of the wealthy taking less. Even two-child families make the problem nearly impossible — assuming we reject massive suffering from the bag of possible solutions.

A careful look at the three family-size scenarios above shows the crucial importance of having single-child families if we are to leave sufficient habitat for all other species. With the 100-year plan, the full benefits to other species resulting from your smaller family size and lower footprints are realized over the next 100 years. If you are inspired to have your reductions produce more immediate results, you can keep your sustainability goal set lower until the population begins to come down. In this way, you can have both a long-term and a short-term goal.

The 100-year plan offers a clear win-win scenario. If humanity chooses one-child families for the next 100 years, a footprint goal of six acres is achievable without sustainability heroics. The high-income individuals, who now have the most privilege, need to step up to the plate and reduce footprints as an initial gesture of goodwill. Then, after sustained, documentable reductions have been made, they will have the credibility to ask low-income countries to reduce population.

The low-income individuals, those 3.5 billion living on $520 a year,[6] will win as our consumption becomes lower and more bioregional. A sufficient share of their land, now engaged in exports, can then be allocated for local self-reliance. And, with smaller families, their country's overextended land base (currently heavily used for cash-crop exports) will be better able to meet local needs. With smaller populations worldwide, every urgent issue becomes less pressing. Sustainable communities will be much better places to live than an over-extended landscape.

TWELVE

TOWARD A SUSTAINABLE FUTURE

Ow do high-income individuals win by consuming less? Simple: radical simplicity will free up a generous portion of the rest of their lives for what is most important to them. Filmmaker John DeGraff coined the termed "affluenza:" an illness that comes from having too much of what is not fulfilling and not enough of what is.[1] By lowering footprints to six acres or less, you will need to earn much less money, and will free up tens of thousands of hours over a lifetime. Joe Dominguez once said to me, "Consciousness grows faster than inflation." When I first heard this, I believed it on faith, but ten years later, as the personal benefits of radical simplicity continue to expand, his words resonate ever more strongly.

As we deeply align with our own sense of fairness toward all life, everyone benefits. We live in an interconnected world. The cooperative mind, being concerned for the health of the whole, is what will lead us to a world of our dreams: a sustainable, peaceful life on planet Earth.

. . . . .

As Rowan and I paddled toward the mouth of the Koeye River, ribbons of salmon passed beneath our canoe. In a shaded emerald pool, hundreds more waited their turn to head upstream to spawn. We drifted silently, watching a fat bear waddle through the beach grass, gorged with salmon. Rowan pointed to an eagle perched atop a leaning cedar. Heads up, we spotted five more, including two juveniles. A large one dropped from its perch and, several wing strokes later, glided upstream through a towering corridor of old growth trees.

The air was thick with the smell of rotting salmon, spawned out and rapidly being recycled into the land and sea. Away from shore, where the salt and fresh waters mix, whiskered faces of curious otters rose, watched, and then slipped back into the sea. On a sand bar, several dozen gulls picked the fish bones clean, squawking their thanks for nature's plentitude. A large salmon rose to the surface, barely alive, decomposing as it swam, a chunk of flesh missing from its tail section.

The bear caught sight of us drifting nearer the shore, and slowly wandered into the alders. After a while, we beached the canoe and walked through dense brush into the cool, dark forest. The mosses were worn into a network of trails connecting the bears' fishing holes, scattered through the braided delta. Although we had only seen one bear, the heavily trafficked paths indicated that perhaps a half-dozen had been feasting and fattening for hibernation. Near a sandy eddy choked with dozens of still vibrant salmon en-route to spawn, we came across a wolf's track, winding its way upstream. The forest was littered with salmon in various stages of decomposition. Scientist Tom Reimchen states that during a 45-day spawn, a black bear may catch 700 salmon, leaving half of each carcass in the forest. What might appear a wasteful eating habit actually deposits 107 pounds of nitrogen fertilizer per acre onto British Columbia's coastal rainforests.[2] The micro-nutrients of decomposing leaf-litter leave the forests in thousands of tiny streams, feeding aquatic life. The salmon carry the nutrients back up to feed the land in the form of their ready-to-spawn-and-die bodies, then the bears, wolves, eagles and gulls complete the nutrient cycle by broadcasting flesh and scat across the landscape.

In these remote, old-growth watersheds of British Columbia, Rowan and I paddled for weeks, reveling in an exuberance of nature flowing wild and free, a degree of abundance neither of us had ever witnessed.

Two weeks earlier, we had arrived with our bikes by ferry at midnight, prepared to bush camp, when an elder Heiltsuk couple invited us into their home. Helen and Simon are descendants of the original inhabitants of BC's central coast, a region accessible only by water. At one in the morning, Helen put on the teakettle. One of the first things she said was, "stay as long as you want," shortly followed by "you don't need to buy no groceries." Out came the flaked halibut, salmon, dulse and oolichan grease. Helen told us about the potlatch, a lavish feast and gift-giving ceremony. Like the bears, the Heiltsuk understand abundance. They relish their use of nature, but at a rate well below its annual productivity. After 10,000 years, their territory is still prolific, obviously intact and fertile.

There is no reason a lifestyle of radical simplicity can not also have this type of abundance — even as we take on the Wiseacre Challenge. As wild ecosystems recover over the next 100 years in response to our shrinking footprints, nature's exuberance will encircle, inspire, and amaze us. We won't have to go to the end of a continent to find a luxuriantly wild land.

. . . . .

As we get ready to part ways, I want to thank you for joining us on this epic journey. Together we covered some rugged and unique terrain. We set out to achieve what seems impossible: living equitably and harmoniously within the means of nature, or global living. Along the way we laid rest to several cherished "sacred cows," hopefully replaced by many inspiring examples. We worked with some powerful and practical tools capable of carrying you closer to your sustainability goal, not with fancy words, but with measurable results. We even considered a bold and feasible societal plan for living within nature's lovable limits, one that you can start work on tomorrow. As you put the tools to use, the impossible becomes possible. Achieving sustainability is only two steps away:

- Single child families (on average) until population reaches one billion (about 100 years).
- A personal ecological footprint not to exceed six acres.

The more we align with this solution the more we will feel the turning of the tides. As we begin to talk with friends and family about our goals, our conversations will incorporate these new ideas into our culture. We will be taking steps towards a truly sustainable planet. Only in its infancy, this conversation about global sustainability is reaching ever-wider circles.

· · · · ·

You are not alone in your concern for this Earth. If you ever have one of those days where you begin to feel defeated, or feel that what you are doing is inconsequential, take a few deep breaths. Walk into a place in nature that you love. Visualize eighteen football fields' worth of this natural beauty no longer enslaved to meet your individual wants. You are capable of making this happen — reducing your footprint from the 24 acre US average to 6 acres. What a truly worthwhile and consequential feat!

ENDNOTES

Chapter One

1. Pimm, Stuart L. *The World According to Pimm: A Scientist Audits the Earth*. New York: McGraw Hill Professional, 2001.

2. Robbins, John. *Diet for a New America: How Your Food Choices Affect Your Health, Happiness and the Future of Life on Earth*. Tiburon, H.J. Kramer, 1987.

3. Brower, Michael and Warren Leon. *The Consumer's Guide to Effective Environmental Choices: Practical Advice from the Union of Concerned Scientists*. New York: Three Rivers Press, 1999.

4. Merkel, Jim. *The Global Living Handbook*. Winlaw: The Global Living Project, 2000.

5. World Bank. *2000 World Development Indicators CD-ROM*. Washington, DC: World Bank, 2000.

6. Puckett, Jim and Ted Smith (editors). *Exporting Harm: The High-Tech Trashing of Asia*. Seattle: Basal Action Network, 2002. A joint report issued with the Silicon Valley Toxics Coalition.

7. Puckett, Jim and Ted Smith (editors). *Exporting Harm: The High-Tech Trashing of Asia*. Seattle: Basal Action Network, 2002. A joint report issued with the Silicon Valley Toxics Coalition.

8. Mander, Jerry. *In the Absence of the Sacred*. San Francisco: Sierra Club Books, 1991.

9. New Road Map Foundation. *All Consuming Passion: Waking Up from the American Dream*. Seattle: New Road Map Foundation, 1998. In partnership with Northwest Environment Watch.

10. Gatto, John T. *Dumbing Us Down: The Hidden Curricula of Compulsory*

Schooling. Gabriola Island: New Society Publishers, 1991.

11. World Wide Fund for Nature (WWF). *Living Planet Report 2002.* Gland: WWF, 2002.

12. World Bank. *2000 World Development Indicators CD-ROM.* Washington, DC: World Bank, 2000.

13. World Bank. *2000 World Development Indicators CD-ROM.* Washington, DC: World Bank, 2000.

14. Pimm, Stuart L. *The World According to Pimm: A Scientist Audits the Earth.* New York: McGraw Hill Professional, 2001.

15. Vitousek, Peter M., Harold A. Mooney, Jane Lubchenco, and Jerry M. Melillo. "Human Domination of Earth's Ecosystems." *Science* 277 (1997): pp. 494 – 499.

16. McKibben, Bill. *Maybe One: An Environmental and Personal Argument for Single-child Families.* New York: Simon & Schuster, 1998.

17. The Energy Information Administration, Table 8.1. "World Crude Oil and Natural Gas Reserves." *International Energy Annual,* 2001.

18. Ludwig, Art. "U.S. Terrorism?" *Hopedance,* Special Issue, October 2001.

19. Bell, Dick and Michael Renner. "A New Marshall Plan? Advancing Human Security and Controlling Terrorism." World Watch Institute Press Release, October 9, 2001.

20. Castaneda, Carlos. *A Separate Reality.* New York: Washington Square Press, 1991.

21   Piburn, Sydney (editor). *A Policy of Kindness: An Anthology of Writings by and about the Dalai Lama, Winner of the Nobel Peace Prize.* Ithaca: Snow Lion Publications, 1993.

Chapter Two

1. See P. R. Ehrlich and J.P. Holdren, "Impact of Population Growth," *Science* 171 (1971): pp. 1212 – 1217.

2. Meadows, Donella, Dennis Meadows, and Jorgen Randers. *Beyond the Limits: Confronting Global Collapse and Envisioning a Sustainable Future.* Post Mills: Chelsea Green Publishing Company, 1992.

3. World Bank. *2000 World Development Indicators CD-ROM.* Washington, DC: World Bank, 2000.

Chapter Three

1. Gibson, Robert O. *The Chumash.* New York: Chelsea House Publishers, 1991.

2. Dreze, Jean and Amartya Sen. *India: Economic and Social Opportunity.* Oxford: Oxford University Press, 1995.

3. Alexander, Will. *One Problem and Two Solutions.* San Luis Obispo: Self-published paper, 1997.

4. United Nations. *Human Development Report 1997.* Oxford University Press, 1997, pg. 52.

5. Alexander, Will. *Humans Sharing the Bounty of the Earth: Hopeful Lessons from Kerala.* Prepared for the International Congress on Kerala Studies, 1994.

6. Alexander, Will. *Humans Sharing the Bounty of the Earth: Hopeful Lessons from Kerala.* Prepared for the International Congress on Kerala Studies, 1994.

7. Alexander, Will. *Humans Sharing the Bounty of the Earth: Hopeful Lessons from Kerala.* Prepared for the International Congress on Kerala Studies, 1994.

8. Laing, R.D. *The Politics of Experience.* New York: Pantheon Books, 1967.

9. World Wide Fund for Nature (WWF). *Living Planet Report 2002.* Gland: WWF, 2002.

10. Mander, Jerry. *In the Absence of the Sacred.* San Francisco: Sierra Club Books, 1991.

Chapter Four

1. Almedingen, E.M. *St. Francis of Assisi: A Great Life in Brief.* New York: A.A. Knopf, 1967.

2. Report From the Frontier. *The State of the World's Indigenous Peoples.* 1987.

3. See Peter M. Vitousek, Harold A. Mooney, Jane Lubchenco and Jerry M. Melillo, "Human Domination of Earth's Ecosystems" *Science* 277(1997): pp.494-499.

4. Mathis Wackernagel, et al. *Tracking the ecological overshoot of the human economy.*

5. Personal Communication.

6. Pimm, Stuart L. *The World According to Pimm.* New York: McGraw Hill, 2001.

7. Noss, Reed F. "The Wildlands Project: Land Conservation Strategy", *Wild Earth* Special Issue (1993): pp.10-21.

8. Thomas, C.D. "What do real population dynamics tell us about minimum viable population sizes?" *Conservation Biology* 4 (1990): pp. 324-327.

9. Brocke, Rainer H., Kent A. Gustafson and Andrew R. Major, "Restoration on the Lynx in New York: Biopolitical Lessons", From *Transactions of the North American Wildlife and Natural Resources Conference,* 1990.

10. Noss, Reed F. and Allen Cooperrider. *Saving Nature's Legacy: Protecting and*

Restoring Biodiversity. Washington D.C.: Island Press, 1994.

11. Thornton, Russell. *American Indian Holocaust and Survival: A Population History Since 1492.* Norman: University of Oklahoma Press, 1987.

12. Robbins Richard. *Cultural Anthropology: A Problem-Based Approach.* Itasca: F.E. Peacock Publishers, 1997.

13. Zinn, Howard. *A Peoples History of the United States.* New York: Harper Collins Publishers, 1980.

14. United Nations Development Program. *Human Development Report.* New York: Oxford University Press, 1992, 1994.

Purchasing-power parity (PPP) is a method of measuring relative purchasing power of different countries' currencies over similar goods and services. When the World Bank applies this curve to the data, the poor look three times richer, while the rich look slightly poorer. The application of PPP brings several billion people above the $1/day poverty line, an inaccurate reflection of "wealth." Low income countries can not afford to be wasteful and are able to produce cheaper goods and services; high income countries *could* provide far less costly goods and services if incomes were lower and less energy and resources were embodied in their products. The Atlas method (which yields the 250 to 1 disparity) is a comparison of GNP per capita which approximates income (in US dollars). This is how much money you would find in a person's pockets and bank accounts. To reduce errors due to drastically fluctuating currencies, the average exchange rate is taken for that year and the two preceding years.

15. World Bank. *2000 World Development Indicators CD-ROM.* Washington DC: World Bank, 2000.

16. World Bank. *2000 World Development Indicators CD-ROM.* Washington DC: World Bank, 2000.

17. Gray, Charles. *Toward a Nonviolent Economics.* Eugene: Self-published, 1994.

18. New Road Map Foundation. *All Consuming Passion: Waking up from the American Dream.* Seattle: New Road Map Foundation, 1998. In partnership with Northwest Environment Watch.

19. Gray, Charles. *Toward a Nonviolent Economics.* Eugene: Self-published, 1994.

20. World Bank. *2000 World Development Indicators CD-ROM.* Washington DC: World Bank, 2000.

21. McKibben, Bill. *Maybe One: An Environmental and Personal Argument for Single-Child Families.* New York: Simon & Schuster, 1998.

Chapter Six

1.   United Nations, *1996 International Trade Statistics Yearbook*, Vol. I. New York: Department for Economic and Social Information and Policy Analysis, Statistical Division, 1998.

United Nations Conference on Trade and Development (UNCTAD). *UNCTAD Commodity Yearbook 1996*, New York: United Nations, 1996.

Food and Agriculture Organization of the United Nations (FAO). *FAO Yearbook: Production 1997*, Vol. 51. Rome: FAO, 1998.

Food and Agriculture Organization of the United Nations (FAO). *FAO Yearbook: Trade 1996*, Vol. 50. Rome: FAO, 1997.

Food and Agriculture Organization of the United Nations (FAO). *FAO Yearbook: Forest Production 1996*. Rome: FAO, 1998.

United Nations. *1996 Energy Statistics Yearbook*. New York: Department for Economic and Social Information and Policy Analysis, Statistical Division, 1998.

International Energy Agency (IEA). *CO2 Emissions from Fossil Fuel Combustion 1971 – 1996*. Paris: OECD/IEA, 1998.

Food and Agriculture Organization of the United Nations (FAO). *FAOSTAT 98 CD-ROM*. Rome: FAO Statistical Databases, 1999.

United Nations Population Division. *Annual Populations, 1950 – 2050 (The 1998 Revision)*. New York: United Nations, Department of Social and Economic Affairs, 1998.

World Resources Institute. *World Resources 1998 – 1999*. Washington, DC: UNEP, UNDP, World Bank, 1998.

2.   Intergovernmental Panel on Climate Change (IPCC). *Revised 1996 Guidelines for National Greenhouse Gas Inventories: Workbook*, Vol. 2. UK Meteorological Office: IPCC, Organization for Economic Cooperation and Development (OECD) and International Energy Agency (IEA), 1997.

3.   Wackernagel, Mathis and William Rees. *Our Ecological Footprint: Reducing Human Impact on the Earth*. Gabriola Island: New Society Publishers, 1996.

4.   Chambers, Nicky, Craig Simmons, and Mathis Wackernagel. *Sharing Nature's Interest: Ecological Footprints as an Indicator of Sustainability*. London: Earthscan Publications, 2000.

5.   Food and Agriculture Organization of the United Nations (FAO). *FAO Yearbook: Production*, Vol. 43, Rome: FAO, 1990.

6.   Schor, Juliet. *The Overspent American: Downshifting and the New Consumer*. New York: Basic Books, 1998.

7.   United States Census Bureau. *Historical Income Tables — People*. Table P-7.

Washington, DC: Income Surveys Branch, Housing and Household Statistics Division, 2002.

Chapter Seven

1. New Road Map Foundation. *All Consuming Passion: Waking up from the American Dream.* Seattle: New Road Map Foundation, 1998. In partnership with Northwest Environment Watch

Chapter Nine

1. Alvord, Katie. *Divorce your Car!* Gabriola Island: New Society Publishers, 2000.

2. Alvord, Katie. *Divorce your Car!* Gabriola Island: New Society Publishers, 2000.

3. Mollison, Bill. *Introduction to Permaculture.* Tyalgum: Tagari Publications, 1991.

Chapter 10

1. Chambers, Nicky, Craig Simmons and Mathis Wackernagel. *Sharing Nature's Interest: Ecological Footprints as an Indicator of Sustainability.* London: Earthscan Publications Ltd., 2000.

2. National Women's Health Resource Center, "Obesity: Facts to Know", <www.healthywomen.org>.

Chapter 11

1. 2001 World Population Data Sheet (the purple sheet).

2. Alexander, Will. *One Problem and Two Solutions.* San Luis Obispo: Self-published paper, 1997.

3. UNICEF. *State of the World's Children 2002*, New York, UNICEF, 2002.

4. World Bank. *2000 World Development Indicators CD-ROM.* Washington, DC: World Bank, 2000.

5. Center for Disease Control and Prevention, *Vital Statistics Report 49* (2001).

6. World Bank. *2000 World Development Indicators CD-ROM.* Washington, DC: World Bank, 2000.

Chapter 12

1. "Affluenza" is also a one hour television special produced by KCTS in Seattle and Oregon Public Broadcasting. To find out more, visit <www.pbs.org/kcts/affluenza/>

2. Semeniuk, Robert. "Do Bears Fish in the Woods." *The Ecologist*, December 2001.

APPENDIX A:
FOOTPRINT FACTORS

Table A.1: Monthly Food Footprint Factors (ff)

Item	Unit	Average per capita Use in US	STANDARD Foot-print Factor (ff)	Energy Foot-print Factor (eff)	Land or Sea Foot-print Factor (lff)	Unit	METRIC Foot-print Factor (ff)	Energy Foot-print Factor (eff)	Land or Sea Foot-print Factor (lff)
			ff=eff + lff				ff=eff + lff		
Veggies, potatoes & fruit	lb	48.7	33	18	15	kg	63	35	28
Bread and bakery products	lb	7.8	128	47	81	kg	235	86	149
Flour, rice, noodles, cereal	lb	7.8	118	37	81	kg	218	69	149
Maize (corn)	lb	1.1	85	37	48	kg	158	69	89
Beans & other dried pulses	lb	0.7	252	19	233	kg	464	35	429
Milk, cream, yogurt, sour cream	qt	9.1	118	39	79	l	105	35	70
Ice cream, other frozen dairy	qt	1.2	475	78	397	kg	420	69	351
Cheese, butter	lb	2.7	503	122	381	kg	926	225	701
Eggs (number)	#	20	28	5	23	#	23	4	19
Pork	lb	3.8	458	187	271	kg	844	345	499
Chicken, turkey	lb	5.4	335	150	185	kg	616	276	340
Beef	lb	1.2	1180	242	935	kg	2171	449	1722
Fish	lb	5.4	2798	281	2517	kg	5154	518	4635
Sugar	lb	5.5	61	28	33	kg	113	52	61
Vegetable oil (seed and olive)	qt	1.2	1093	94	999	l	966	83	883
Margarine	lb	2.5	655	56	599	l	1208	104	1104
Coffee & tea	lb	0.8	512	122	390	kg	943	225	718
Juice & wine	qt	3	175	98	77	l	153	86	67
Beer	qt	7.3	138	98	40	l	121	86	35
Garden (area used for food)*	sq yd		1 (poor) 2 (avg) 3 (good)			m²	1 (poor) 2 (avg) 3 (good)		
Eating out (meat eater)	$		83	33	50	$	73	28	45
Eating out (vegetarian)	$		55	33	22	$	48	28	20

* If unworked soil is highly productive, use 3, if average, use 2, if below use 1.

Table A.2: Monthly Housing Footprint Factors (ff)

Item	Unit	Average per-capita Use in US	STANDARD Foot-print Factor (ff)	Energy Foot-print Factor (eff)	Land or Sea Foot-print Factor (lff)	Unit	METRIC Foot-print Factor (ff)	Energy Foot-print Factor (eff)	Land or Sea Foot-print Factor (lff)
			ff=eff + lff				ff=eff + lff		
House or Apartment									
Age of home: 40	sq ft	582	12.2	2.2	10	m²	109	19	90
60	sq ft		8	1.4	6.6	m²	73	13	60
80	sq ft		6.1	1.1	5	m²	54	10	44
100	sq ft		4.8	0.8	4	m²	43	8	35
120	sq ft		4	0.7	3.3	m²	36	6	30
Yard or total lot size including building *	sq yd	647	2		2	m²	2		2
Hotels, Motels	$	15	136	90	46	$	115	76	39
Electricity									
From the grid	kWh	323	31	31		kWh	27	27	
Fossil fuel and nuclear	kWh		35	35		kWh	30	30	
Large hydro	kWh		2		2	kWh	2		2
Small hydro	kWh		0.02		0.02	kWh	0.01		0.01
PV solar	kWh		0.3		0.3	kWh	0.3		0.3
Natural gas, city	therms	17.6	232	232		m³	76	76	
Propane	gal	1.2	208	208		l	46	46	
Fuel oil, kerosene	gal	2.4	389	389		l	87	87	
Coal	lb		35	35		l	64	64	
Water, sewer, garbage serv.	$	9	157	152	5	$	133	129	4
Straw	lb		46	7	39	kg	85	13	72
Firewood	lb	240	37		37	kg	69		69

Table A.3: Monthly Transportation Footprint Factors (ff)

Item	Unit	Average per-capita Use in US	Foot-print Factor (ff)	Energy Foot-print Factor (eff)	Land or Sea Foot-print Factor (lff)	Unit	Foot-print Factor (ff)	Energy Foot-print Factor (eff)	Land or Sea Foot-print Factor (lff)
			ff=eff + lff				ff=eff + lff		
Bus, around town	mi	7	17	17		km	9	9	
Bus, inter-city	mi	38	4	4		km	2	2	
Train, light rail	mi	7	11	11		km	6	6	
Train, inter-city	mi	2	17	11	6	km	9	6	3
Taxi/rental/other's car (Divide miles by number in car, exclude taxi driver & kids)	mi		40	37	3	km	21	19	2
Gasoline (Divide fuel by number of people in vehicle; exclude children)	gal	37	500	440	60	l	113	97	16
Parts for repair	lb		663	653	10	kg	1220	1202	18
Airplane	hrs					hrs			
Economy		0.4	5216	5216			4361	4361	
Business		0.4	6040	6040			5050	5050	
First Class		0.4	6864	6864			5739	5739	

Table A.4: Monthly Goods and Services Footprint Factors (ff)

Item	Unit	Average per-capita Use in US	Foot-print Factor (ff)	Energy Foot-print Factor (eff)	Land or Sea Foot-print Factor (lff)	Unit	Foot-print Factor (ff)	Energy Foot-print Factor (eff)	Land or Sea Foot-print Factor (lff)
			STANDARD ff=eff + lff				METRIC ff=eff + lff		
Postal Services									
International	lb	0.2	300	291	9	kg	552	535	17
Domestic	lb	4	60	58	2	kg	110	107	3
Dry cleaning or external laundry services	$		79	77	2	$	66	64	2
Telephone	$	27	13	13		$	11	11	
Medical insurance and serv.	$	47	53	51	2	$	44	43	1
Household insurance	$	27	110	22	88	$	92	18	74
Entertainment	$	24	79	77	2	$	66	64	2
Education	$	20	40	38	2	$	33	32	1
Medicine	lb	2	1325	1305	20	kg	2440	2404	36
Hygiene & cleaning products	lb	2	266	261	5	kg	488	481	7
Cigarettes, tobacco products	lb	0.4	1246	816	430	kg	2295	1503	792

Table A.5: Monthly Stocks Footprint Factors (ff)

Item	Unit	Average per-capita Use in US	STANDARD Foot-print Factor (ff)	Energy Foot-print Factor (eff)	Land or Sea Foot-print Factor (lff)	Unit	METRIC Foot-print Factor (ff)	Energy Foot-print Factor (eff)	Land or Sea Foot-print Factor (lff)
			ff=eff + lff				ff=eff + lff		
Construction, wood	lb		254	7	247	kg	467	12	455
Wooden furniture	lb		483	32	451	kg	890	60	830
Plastic & metal furniture	lb		397	391	6	kg	732	721	11
Major appliances	lb		994	980	14	kg	1830	1803	27
Small appliances	lb		663	653	10	kg	1220	1202	18
Clothes & Textiles (if used, count at 1/3 of weight)									
Cotton	lb	1.3	1342	131	1211	kg	2474	240	2234
Wool	lb	0.1	1886	130	1756	kg	3472	240	3234
Synthetic	lb	0.5	133	130	3	kg	244	240	4
Durable paper (e.g. books, magazines, files, non-rcyclable, e.g., toilet paper, paper towels, etc.)	lb	3	569	228	341	kg	1049	421	628
Metal items & tools	lb	8	397	391	6	kg	732	721	11
Leather	lb	0.5	2119	130	1989	kg	3904	240	3664
Plastic products & photos	lb	10	331	327	4	kg	610	601	9
Computer & electronic equip.	lb		1325	1305	20	kg	2440	2404	36
Glass & porcelain	lb	3	99	98	1	kg	183	180	3

Table A.6: Monthly Waste Footprint Factors (ff)

Item	Unit	Average per-capita Use in US	STANDARD Foot-Print Factor (ff)	Energy Foot-print Factor (eff)	Land or Sea Foot-print Factor (lff)	Unit	METRIC Foot-print Factor (ff)	Energy Foot-print Factor (eff)	Land or Sea Foot-print Factor (lff)
			ff=eff + lff				ff=eff + lff		
Assume everything compostable is composted									
Household recyclables									
Paper and cardboard	lb	21	194	124	70	kg	359	231	128
Aluminum	lb	1	83	81	2	kg	153	150	3
Other metal	lb	2	335	330	5	kg	622	613	9
Glass	lb	5	69	68	1	kg	128	126	2
Plastic	lb	5	98	97	1	kg	183	180	3
Garbage (all you discard)	lb		481	271	210	kg	897	505	392

Table A.7: Common Conversion Factors

Conversion Table	
1 hectare	10,000 square meters 107,639 square feet
1 acre	0.4 hectares 4,840 square yards
1 mile	1.6 kilometers 1,609 meters 1,760 yards
1 yard	3 feet 0.9 meters
1 square yard	9 square feet 0.8 square meters
1 square meter	10.7 square feet
1 cubic meter	35.3 cubic feet
1 pound	0.45 kilograms
1 gallon	4.5 liters
1 liter	1 quart
1 ton	2,000 pounds 0.9 metric tonnes
1 Gigawatt Hour	1,000,000 kilowatt hours 3,600 gigajoules 34,120 therms 3.4 billion Btu's 8.5 trillion calories

APPENDIX B: FOOTPRINTING WORKSHEETS

Table B.1: Monthly Food Footprint

Item	Amount Used per Month	Units Standard	Units Metric	Standard Footprint Factor	Metric Footprint Factor	Footprint (EF) (in sq yd or m²
		QTY X ff = EF in sq yd or m²				
Veggies, potatoes & fruit		lb	kg	33	63	
Bread and bakery products		lb	kg	128	235	
Flour, rice, noodles, cereal prod.	3 0	lb	kg	118	218	
Maize (corn)		lb	kg	85	158	
Beans & other dried pulses	1,	lb	kg	252	464	
Milk, cream, yogurt, sour cream		qt	l	118	105	
Ice cream, other frozen dairy		qt	l	475	420	
Cheese, butter		lb	kg	503	926	
Eggs (number)		#	#	28	23	
Pork		lb	kg	458	844	
Chicken, turkey		lb	kg	335	616	
Beef		lb	kg	1180	2171	
Fish		lb	kg	2798	5154	
Sugar		lb	kg	61	113	
Vegetable oil (seed and olive)		qt	l	1093	966	
Margarine		lb	kg	655	1208	
Coffee & tea		lb	kg	512	943	
Juice & wine		qt	l	175	153	
Beer		qt	l	138	121	
Garden (area used for food)*		sq yd	m²	1 (poor) 2 (avg) 3 (good)	1 (poor) 2 (avg) 3 (good)	
Eating out (meat eater)		$	$	83	73	
Eating out (vegetarian)		$	$	55	48	
SUBTOTAL						

* If unworked soil is highly productive, use 3, if average, use 2, if below use 1.

Table B.2: Monthly Housing Footprint

Item	Amount Used per Month	Units Standard	Metric	Standard Foot-print Factor	Metric Foot-print Factor	Footprint (EF) (in sq yd or m²
		QTY X	ff	= EF in sq yd or m²		
*House or Apartment (living area per person)**						
Age of home: 40		sq ft	m²	12.2	109	
60	/	sq ft	m²	8	73	
80		sq ft	m²	6.1	54	
100		sq ft	m²	4.8	43	
120		sq ft	m²	4	36	
Yard or total lot size including building **		sq yd	m²	2	2	
Hotels, Motels		$	$	136	115	
Electricity						
From the grid		kWh	kWh	31	27	
Fossil fuel and nuclear		kWh	kWh	35	30	
Large hydro		kWh	kWh	2	2	
Small hydro		kWh	kWh	0.02	0.01	
PV solar		kWh	kWh	0.3	0.3	
Natural gas, city		therms	m³	232	76	
Propane		gal	l	208	46	
Fuel oil, kerosene		gal	l	389	87	
Coal		lb	l	35	64	
Water, sewer, garbage serv.		$	$	157	133	
Straw		lb	kg	46	85	
Firewood***		lb	kg	37	69	
SUBTOTAL						

*Divide the total square footage of the house by the number of people sharing it for a per-person number. If there are rooms that only some people use, you need to account for this in your calculation. The system is calibrated to understand that the total area is entered each month.

**If you include garden area on Table B.1, do not count this area again as yard. Do not count land that is kept natural such as wildlife habitat.

***A cord of wood is 128 ft³ (4 x 4 x 8 ft) and contains roughly 3,500 pounds of wood.

Table B.3: Monthly Transportation Footprint

Item	Amount Used per Month	Units Standard	Units Metric	Standard Footprint Factor	Metric Footprint Factor	Footprint (EF) (in sq yd or m^2
		QTY	X	ff	= EF in sq yd or m^2	
Bus, around town		mi	km	17	9	
Bus, inter-city		mi	km	4	2	
Train, light rail		mi	km	11	6	
Train, inter-city		mi	km	17	9	
Taxi/rental/other's car (Divide miles by number in car, exclude taxi driver & kids)		mi	km	40	21	
Gasoline (Divide fuel by number of people in vehicle; exclude children)		gal	l	500	113	
Parts for repair		lb	kg	663	1220	
Airplane						
Economy		hrs	hrs	5216	4361	
Business		hrs	hrs	6040	5050	
First class		hrs	hrs	6864	5739	
SUBTOTAL						

Table B.4: Monthly Goods and Services Footprint

	Amount Used per Month	Units		Standard Footprint Factor	Metric Footprint Factor	Footprint (EF) (in sq yd or m²
		Standard	Metric			
Item	QTY X ff = EF in sq yd or m²					
Postal Services						
International		lb	kg	300	552	
Domestic		lb	kg	60	110	
Dry cleaning or external laundry services		$	$	79	66	
Telephone		$	$	13	11	
Medical insurance and serv.		$	$	53	44	
Household insurance		$	$	110	92	
Entertainment		$	$	79	66	
Education		$	$	40	33	
Medicine		lb	kg	1325	2440	
Hygiene & cleaning products		lb	kg	266	488	
Cigarettes, tobacco products		lb	kg	1246	2295	
SUBTOTAL						

Table B.5: Monthly Stocks Footprint

Item	Amount Used per Month	Units		Standard Footprint Factor	Metric Footprint Factor	Footprint (EF) (in sq yd or m²
		Standard	Metric			
	QTY X ff = EF in sq yd or m²					
Construction, wood		lb	kg	254	467	
Wooden furniture		lb	kg	483	890	
Plastic & metal furniture		lb	kg	397	732	
Major appliances		lb	kg	994	1830	
Small appliances		lb	kg	663	1220	
Clothes & Textiles (if used, count at 1/3 of weight)						
Cotton		lb	kg	1342	2474	
Wool		lb	kg	1886	3474	
Synthetic		lb	kg	. 133	244	
Durable paper (e.g. books, magazines, files, non-rcyclable, e.g., toilet paper, paper towels, etc.)		lb	kg	569	1049	
Metal items & tools		lb	kg	397	732	
Leather		lb	kg	2119	3904	
Plastic products & photos		lb	kg	331	610	
Computer & electronic equip.		lb	kg	1325	2440	
Glass & porcelain		lb	kg	99	183	
SUBTOTAL						

Table B.6: Monthly Waste Footprint

	Amount Used per Month	Units		Standard Foot-print Factor	Metric Foot-print Factor	Footprint (EF) (in sq yd or m^2
		Standard	Metric			
Item	QTY X ff = EF in sq yd or m^2					
Assume everything compostable is composted						
Household recyclables						
Paper and cardboard		lb	kg	194	359	
Aluminum		lb	kg	83	153	
Other metal		lb	kg	335	622	
Glass		lb	kg	69	128	
Plastic		lb	kg	98	183	
Garbage (all you discard)		lb	kg	481	897	
SUBTOTAL						

Table B.7: Worksheet 1 – Monthly Flows

Name: _____ From: _____ To: _____
(date)   (date)

Item	Description	Measurement per Person	Cost	Income

Table B.8: Worksheet 2 – Monthly Stocks

Name: _____ From: _____ To: _____

(date)   (date)

Item	Description	Weight	# of Users	Life Exp. (Months)	Weight/ Month	Cost or Value	Clutter, yes, no some?

Table B.9: Monthly Totals

Name: _____ From: _____ To: _____
                                         (date)   (date)

Categories	Footprint		Dollars Spent	Income
	sq yd	m²		
1. Food				
2. Housing				
3. Transportation				
4. Goods & Services				
5. Stocks				
6. Waste				
TOTAL				

Divide square yards by 4,840 to get _____ acres.

Divide square meters by 10,000 to get _____ hectares.

Table B.10: Footprint Summary

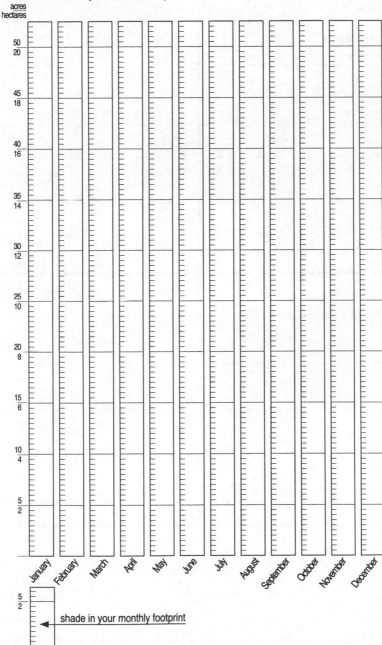

shade in your monthly footprint

Table B.11: Big-Ticket Items and Low-hanging Fruits

Big-ticket Item	Low-hanging Fruit
1. _____	1. _____
2. _____	2. _____
3. _____	3. _____
4. _____	4. _____
5. _____	5. _____

Big-ticket Item	Low-hanging Fruit
1. _____	1. _____
2. _____	2. _____
3. _____	3. _____
4. _____	4. _____
5. _____	5. _____

APPENDIX C:
YMOYL WORKSHEETS

Table C.1: Monthly Food – Money, Life Energy & Values

Item	Real Hourly Wage: $				
	Dollars Spent per Month	Hours of Life Energy	Fulfillment Mark +, -, or 0	Alignment Mark +, -, or 0	After FI Mark +, -, or 0
Veggies, potatoes & fruit					
Bread and bakery products					
Flour, rice, noodles, cereal prod.					
Maize (corn)					
Beans & other dried pulses					
Milk, cream, yogurt, sour cream					
Ice cream, other frozen dairy					
Cheese, butter					
Eggs (approx. 50 g each)					
Pork					
Chicken, turkey					
Beef					
Fish					
Sugar					
Vegetable oil (seed and olive)					
Margarine					
Coffee & tea					
Juice & wine					
Beer					
Garden (area used for food)					
Eating out (meat eater)					
Eating out (vegetarian)					
SUBTOTAL					

Table C.2: Monthly Housing – Real Hourly Wage Versus Fulfillment

Item	Real Hourly Wage: $				
	Dollars Spent per Month	Hours of Life Energy	Fulfillment Mark +, -, or 0	Alignment Mark +, -, or 0	After FI Mark +, -, or 0
House or Apartment					
Age of home: 40					
60					
80					
100					
120					
Yard or total lot size including building					
Hotels, motels					
Electricity					
From the grid					
Fossil fuel and nuclear					
Large hydro					
Small hydro					
PV solar					
Natural gas, city					
Propane					
Fuel oil, kerosene					
Coal					
Water, sewer, garbage service					
Straw					
Firewood					
SUBTOTAL					

Table C.3: Monthly Transportation – Real Hourly Wage Versus Fulfillment

Item	Real Hourly Wage: $				
	Dollars Spent per Month	Hours of Life Energy	Fulfillment Mark +, -, or 0	Alignment Mark +, -, or 0	After FI Mark +, -, or 0
Bus, around town					
Bus, inter-city					
Train, light rail					
Train, inter-city					
Taxi/rental/other's car (Divide miles by number in car; exclude taxi driver & kids)					
Gasoline (Divide fuel by number of people in vehicle; exclude children)					
Parts for repair					
Airplane					
Economy					
Business					
First Class					
SUBTOTAL					

Table C.4: Monthly Goods and Services – Real Hourly Wage Versus Fulfillment

Item	Real Hourly Wage: $				
	Dollars Spent per Month	Hours of Life Energy	Fulfillment Mark +, -, or 0	Alignment Mark +, -, or 0	After FI Mark +, -, or 0
Postal Services					
International					
Domestic					
Dry cleaning or external laundry services					
Telephone					
Medical insurance and services					
Household insurance					
Entertainment					
Education					
Medicine					
Hygiene & cleaning products					
Cigarettes, tobacco products					
SUBTOTAL					

Table C.5: Monthly Stocks – Real Hourly Wage Versus Fulfillment

Item	Real Hourly Wage: $				
	Dollars Spent per Month	Hours of Life Energy	Fulfillment Mark +, -, or 0	Alignment Mark +, -, or 0	After FI Mark +, -, or 0
Construction, wood					
Wooden furniture					
Plastic & metal furniture					
Major appliances					
Small appliances					
Clothes & Textiles (if used, count at 1/3 of weight)					
Cotton					
Wool					
Synthetic					
Durable paper (e.g. books, magazines, files, non-rcyclable, e.g., toilet paper, paper towels, etc.)					
Metal items & tools					
Leather					
Plastic products & photos					
Computer & electronic equip.					
Glass & porcelain					
SUBTOTAL					

Table C.6: Monthly Wastes – Real Hourly Wage Versus Fulfillment

| Item | Real Hourly Wage: $ | | | | |
	Dollars Spent per Month	Hours of Life Energy	Fulfillment Mark +, -, or 0	Alignment Mark +, -, or 0	After FI Mark +, -, or 0
(Assume everything compostable is composted) *Household recyclables*					
Paper and cardboard					
Aluminum					
Other metal					
Glass					
Plastic					
Garbage (all you discard)					
SUBTOTAL					

Table C.7: Net Worth Worksheet

Life Earnings	$ _____
Liquid Assets	$ _____
Fixed Assets +	$ _____
Subtotal =	$ _____
Liabilities (subtract) -	$ _____
Net Worth =	$ _____

Table C.8: Hourly Wage Versus Real Hourly Wage (RHW)

Hourly Wage – Your salary (after taxes) per week divided by the hours you work.

Basic Salary (after taxes)	Dollars/week	Divided by	Hours/week	=	Dollars/hour (Hourly Wage)
	$ _____		_____ hrs.		$ _____

Real Hourly Wage – Your salary (after taxes) per week adjusted by the extra job-related expenses and the unpaid time associated with your job.

Job-related Expenses and Lost Time	Dollars/Week	Hours/Week
Commuting:		
Wear and tear	$	hrs
Gas and oil	$	hrs
Public transit	$	hrs
Parking and tolls	$	hrs
Walking or bicycling	$	hrs
Costuming:		
Clothes for work	$	hrs
Makeup for work	$	hrs
Briefcase and such	$	hrs
Shoes for work	$	hrs
Shaving for work	$	hrs
Child Care:		
Educational programs	$	hrs
Tutor	$	hrs
Babysitters	$	hrs
Driving kids around	$	hrs
Meals:		
Coffee breaks, vending machines	$	hrs
Lunches	$	hrs
Entertaining for work	$	hrs
Food rewards for unpleasant job	$	hrs
Convenience food	$	hrs

con't...

Decompression:		
Unwind time	$	hrs
Recreational substances	$	hrs
Time processing	$	hrs
Work politics	$	hrs
Time until you can be productive on your own project	$	hrs
Escape Entertainment:		
Movies, cable TV	$	hrs
Bars	$	hrs
Weekend retreats	$	hrs
Vacation, Expensive Toys:		
Vacation to _____	$	hrs
Exercise and sports equipment	$	hrs
Boat, summer home	$	hrs
Country club dues	$	hrs
Job-related Illness:		
Colds, flu, rashes, stress, etc.	$	hrs
Back problems	$	hrs
Hazardous materials, eye damage	$	hrs
Hospitalization	$	hrs
Other Job-related Expenses:		
Conferences	$	hrs
Trade magazines	$	hrs
Professional licenses	$	hrs
Union dues	$	hrs
Home computer	$	hrs
Hired Help to:		
Clean house	$	hrs
Mow lawn	$	hrs
Fix car	$	hrs
Wash and iron clothes, dry cleaning	$	hrs
Other:	$	hrs
Money and Time Spent Maintaining (Total Adjustments)	$	hrs

con't...

Step A- Add together all your unpaid expenses and unpaid hours and write the totals in the table.

Step B- Subtract the total dollars of unpaid expenses from your weekly salary and place the results below in (A).

Step C- Add the total of your unpaid job-related hours to your time on the job each week and place the result below in (B).

Step D- Divide (A) by (B) to get your real hourly wage.

Salary, with Adjustments (actual totals)	Dollars/Week $ _____ (A)	divided by	Hours/Week _____ hrs. (B)	=	Dollars/Hour (RHW) $ _____

I trade my life energy for $ _____ per hour (RWH).
Record RHW at the top of Tables C.1 - C.6 under Real Hourly Wage: $

Divide the 60 minutes that make up an hour by your real hourly wage to determine how many minutes it takes you to earn each dollar.

60 divided by _____ (RWH) = _____ minutes to earn a dollar.

APPENDIX D: WISEACRE WORKSHEETS

Table D.1: Wiseacre Food

Item	Units	One Acre Total EF 0.4 acres for Food (assume no fossil fuels) Amount Used per Month	Three Acre Total EF 1.2 acres for Food (assume 1/4 average fossil fuel) Amount Used per Month	Six Acre Total EF 1.6 acres for Food (assume 1/4 average fossil fuel) Amount Used per Month
Veggies, potatoes & fruit (store-bought)	lb	10	25	30
Garden (area used for food)*				
Good soil	sq yd		110 (25 lb)	85 (20 lb)
Fair soil	sq yd	256 (60 lb)		
Poor soil	sq yd			
Bread and bakery products	lb		3	4
Grain, flour, noodles, cereal products	lb	5	15	20
Beans & other dried pulses	lb	2	4	5
Milk, cream, yogurt, sour cream	qt			1
Ice cream, other frozen dairy	qt			0.25
Cheese, butter	lb			0.4
Eggs (approx. 50 g each)	#	8	13	12
Sugar	lb	0.5	1	2
Vegetable oil (seed and olive)	qt	0.05	0.5	0.5
Margarine	lb	0.12	1	1
Coffee & tea	lb	0.20	1	1
Juice & wine	qt			1
Beer	qt			1
Eating out (vegetarian)	$		13	23
Approximate lbs/month	lb	78	78	90

* The amount given in parentheses is the average yield of vegetables you could expect from a garden of the given size. This amount of vegetables is supplemental to the amount bought at the store.

Table D.2: Wiseacre Housing

Item	Units	One Acre Total EF 0.3 acres for Housing — Amount Used per Month	Three Acre Total EF 1 acres for Housing — Amount Used per Month	Six Acre Total EF 1.6 acres for Housing — Amount Used per Month
House (living area per person) *				
Standard Construction (80 yrs) **	sq ft			150
Simple Strawbale	sq ft	100	150	
Electricity				
From the grid	kWh	3	10	20
Bottled gas (e.g., propane)	gal	1	2	4
Water, sewer, garbage	$		1	1.5
Heating (choose one)				
Fuel oil or	gal	2	8.3	13
Firewood	lb	21	87	139
Total EF	sq yd			

* Divide the total square footage of the house by the number of people sharing it for a per-person number. If there are rooms that only some people use, you need to account for this in your calculation. The system is calibrated to understand that the total area is entered each month.

** In this example, we assume the home is well cared for and lasts 80 years.

Table D.3: Wiseacre Transportation

Item	Units	One Acre Total EF 0.1 acres for Transportation Amount Used per Month	Three Acre Total EF 0.3 acres for Transportation Amount Used per Month	Six Acre Total EF 1.2 acres for Transportation Amount Used per Month
Bus				
Around town	mi	10	10	
Inter-city	mi	42	42	87
Train				
Around town	mi			
Inter-city	mi			50
Taxi, rental, other car (divide miles by # in car, exclude taxi driver and kids)	mi	6		
Car (your own)	gal		2.2	4
Airplane (economy class)	ml			0.5
Total EF				

Table D.4: Wiseacre Goods and Services

Item	Units	One Acre Total EF 0.1 acres for Goods and Services Amount Used per Month	Three Acre Total EF 0.3 acres for Goods and Services Amount Used per Month	Six Acre Total EF 0.8 acres for Goods and Services Amount Used per Month
Postal Services				
Domestic	lb	0.2	0.4	1
Telephone	$	2	10	20
Medical insurance and services	$	4.4	10	30
Education	$		10	30
Medicine	lb	0.1	0.2	0.4
Hygiene and cleaning products	lb	0.3	0.5	0.7
Total EF	sq yd			

Table D.5: Wiseacre Stocks

Item	Units	One Acre Total EF 0.1 acres for Stocks		Three Acre Total EF 0.15 acres for Stocks		Six Acre Total EF 0.6 acres for Stocks	
		Amount	Longevity Years	Amount	Longevity Years	Amount	Longevity Years
Construction, wood & furniture	lb	120	50	120	50	300	50
Major appliances	lb					192	20
Small appliances	lb	14	20	14	20	20	20
Clothing/textiles							
Cotton	lb	12	10	12	10	24	10
Wool	lb	14	40	14	40	19	40
Fossil based	lb	10	20	10	20	20	20
Durable paper products	lb	72	60	72	60	150	60
Metal items, tools	lb	100	50	100	50	300	50
Leather	lb	2	10	2	10	4	10
Plastic	lb	10	10	10	10	25	10
Computer & electronics	lb			14	6	58	6
Glass and Porcelain	lb	10	20	20	20	100	20
Total EF	sq yd	364		388		1,212	

Table D.6: Wiseacre Wastes

Item	Units	One Acre Total EF 0 acres for Wastes Amount Used per Month	Three Acre Total EF 0.05 acres for Wastes Amount Used per Month	Six Acre Total EF 0.2 acres for Wastes Amount Used per Month
Paper **	lb	0	0.3	1.5
Other metal	lb	0	0.3	1.2
Glass	lb	0	0.5	1
Plastic	lb	0	0.5	1
Garbage	lb			0.2
Total EF	sq yd			

* Assume everything compostable is composted.

** Paper includes all you recycle (e.g., newspaper, free papers, junk mail and office paper). If it isn't recycled, it's included in the
   garbage category. Unrecycleable paper such as toilet paper and paper towels go on chart 5 under durable paper.

Table D.7: Sample Wiseacre Footprint Distribution

Consumption Category	Sustainability Goal					
	One Acre		Three Acre		Six Acre	
	sq yd	acres	sq yd	acres	sq yd	acres
Food	1,936	0.4	5,808	1.2	7,744	1.6
Housing	1,452	0.3	4,480	1	7,744	1.6
Transportation	484	0.1	1,452	0.3	5,808	1.2
Goods and Services	484	0.1	1,452	0.3	3,872	0.8
Stocks	484	0.1	1,452	0.3	2,904	0.6
Wastes		0.0	242	0.05	968	0.2
Total	4,840	1	14,520	3	29,040	6

INDEX

Figures are indicated by an "f" following the page number.

ABOUT THE AUTHOR

Originally a military engineer and arms trader, Jim Merkel changed his life at the time of the Exxon Valdez disaster, quitting his job and devoting himself to environmental service and world peace. He downsized his life and 14 years later continues to volunteer and live on $5,000 a year.

Jim founded the Alternative Transportation Task Force in San Luis Obispo, California, and held an elected Sierra Club position while honing urban simple living skills. He has lobbied in Washington for wilderness, peace, and Native American rights. In 1994, he received a fellowship to research sustainability in Kerala, India. The following year he founded the Global Living Project (GLP) and initiated the GLP Summer Institute to discover what "fair share" of Earth each individual might be entitled to. At the GLP, with plenty of help from friends and his partner Rowan Sherwood, a permaculture home and demonstration site were designed and built. The GLP is still going strong.

Jim also instigated a "Cycling for a Sustainable Future" speaking tour that has logged over 10,000 miles and delivered hundreds workshops on sustainable living. Cycling continues to be his primary transportation both around town and for adventures — to Mexico, across Canada twice, and through Europe and India.

His passions include wild edible plants, wilderness, and making homestead improvements from items salvaged from dumps. Rowan and Jim recently relocated to a homestead in Vermont to be near their families.

The Global Living Project
Jim Merkel and Rowan Sherwood
P.O. Box 261, East Corinth, VT 05040 USA
(802)439-6158
www.globallivingproject.org / glp@globallivingproject.org

If you have enjoyed *Radical Simplicity*,
you might also enjoy other

BOOKS TO BUILD A NEW SOCIETY

Our books provide positive solutions for people who want to
make a difference. We specialize in:

Sustainable Living ✦ Ecological Design and Planning

Natural Building & Appropriate Technology ✦ New Forestry

Environment and Justice ✦ Conscientious Commerce

Progressive Leadership ✦ Resistance and Community ✦ Nonviolence

Educational and Parenting Resources

New Society Publishers

ENVIRONMENTAL BENEFITS STATEMENT

New Society Publishers has chosen to produce this book on New Leaf EcoBook 100, recycled
paper made with 100% post consumer waste, processed chlorine free, and old growth free.
For every 5,000 books printed, New Society saves the following resources:[1]

39	Trees
3,533	Pounds of Solid Waste
3,887	Gallons of Water
5,070	Kilowatt Hours of Electricity
6,422	Pounds of Greenhouse Gases
28	Pounds of HAPs, VOCs, and AOX Combined
10	Cubic Yards of Landfill Space

[1]Environmental benefits are calculated based on research done by the Environmental Defense Fund and
other members of the Paper Task Force who study the environmental impacts of the paper industry.

For more information on this environmental benefits statement, or to inquire about environmentally
friendly papers, please contact New Leaf Paper – info@newleafpaper.com Tel: 888 • 989 • 5323.

For a full list of NSP's titles, please call **1-800-567-6772** *or check out our web site at:*

www.newsociety.com

NEW SOCIETY PUBLISHERS